Global Borderlands

Also in the series:

Indigenous Autonomy at La Junta de los Rios: Traders, Allies, and Migrants on New Spain's Northern Frontier, by Robert Wright

Mexican Americans in West Texas: The Borderlands of the Edwards Plateau and the Trans-Pecos, by Arnoldo De León

DRAMA UNDER THE SKIN

BAROQUE CATHOLIC RITUAL IN NORTHERN NEW SPAIN

JUANA MORIEL-PAYNE

TEXAS TECH UNIVERSITY PRESS

This book is typeset in Adobe Caslon Pro. The paper used in this book meets the minimum requirements of ANSI/NISO Z39.48-1992 (R1997). ⊗

Designed by Hannah Gaskamp
Cover design by Hannah Gaskamp

Library of Congress Cataloging-in-Publication Data

Names: Moriel-Payne, Juana, author. Title: Drama Under the Skin: Baroque Catholic Ritual in Northern New Spain / Juana Moriel-Payne. Description: Lubbock: Texas Tech University Press, [2024] | Series: Global Borderlands | Includes bibliographical references and index. | Summary: "Uses Catholic ritual to examine race and identity formation of both free and enslaved people of African descent and Indigenous groups in Northern New Spain"—Provided by publisher.
Identifiers: LCCN 2024003862 (print) | LCCN 2024003863 (ebook) |
ISBN 978-1-68283-215-8 (hardcover) | ISBN 978-1-68283-216-5 (ebook)
Subjects: LCSH: Catholic Church—Mexico—Hidalgo del Parral—History—17th century. | Catholic Church—New Spain—History. | Catholic Church—Customs and practices. | Black people—Religious life—Mexico—Hidalgo del Parral. | Indigenous people—Religious life—Mexico—Hidalgo del Parral. | Hidalgo del Parral (Mexico)—Religious life and customs. | New Spain—Religious life and customs. | Mexico—History—Spanish colony, 1540–1810.
Classification: LCC BX1431.P39 M67 2024 (print) | LCC BX1431.P39 (ebook) |
DDC 282.72/16—dc23/eng/20240808

LC record available at https://lccn.loc.gov/2024003862
LC ebook record available at https://lccn.loc.gov/2024003863

Texas Tech University Press
Box 41037
Lubbock, Texas 79409-1037 USA
800.832.4042
ttup@ttu.edu

www.ttupress.org

Para Johnny
for knowing
la différence
between
History
and a Story

CONTENTS

CONTENTS

ACKNOWLEDGMENTS

I am grateful to many people who contributed to making this book: Roberto Baca Ornelas, director of the Archivo Municipal de Hidalgo del Parral, for his patience and diligence in locating and sending archival materials. My gratitude to the University of Texas at El Paso (UTEP) Library's beautiful people Juanita Rivas, Media and Microfilm director, and her student team who assisted me in locating guides and files, and to Claudia Rivers, head of Special Collections, and Abbie Weiser, assistant head of Special Collections, for their support and encouragement.

I give special thanks to a special person, Dr. Samuel Brunk, a historian and intellectual I respect and admire who has believed in me more than I do in myself and who has constantly encouraged me to do and be the best I can.

DRAMA
UNDER
THE SKIN

FORTUNES AND MISFORTUNES OF A MINING TOWN

It was a cold day in January 1748 when the society of the mining town San Joseph del Parral, which still went by its Hebrew name, gradually appeared on the scene. The faithful Christians, men and women of various calidades (social quality), passed by the main square and gathered in the Parish of San Joseph to celebrate the misa rezada (prayed Mass), that day dedicated to a notable deceased Spanish woman, Doña Catalina de Olarte. Her compadre (her son's godfather), who was also the patrón (overseer) of the capellanía de misas rezadas (investment funds for prayed Masses) that she designated in the testamentary clause, had already lit the lamp that she donated to the church as part of a pious work, thanks to the profits her late husband made in the business of mining and agriculture. With the donation they received from the rental properties of Doña Catalina's capellanía, the members of the confraternity Nuestra Señora del Rayo (previously La Cofradía de Nuestra Señora de La Candelaria de Los Naturales and composed mainly of Native individuals who arrived from Central and South Mexico), had strategically placed lilies offered to the Virgin for whom their brotherhood was named.

After the prayed Mass, members of La Cofradía de La Purísima Inmaculada Concepción de Los Pardos—constituting African descendants, mestizos, Indigenous, and more mixed individuals—began the fiesta they dedicated each year to their Marian devotion in la plaza mayor (main square). Corridas de toros (bullfights), theater, comedy, satire, card games, fireworks, processions, food stalls, and other amusements competed for the crowd's attention. Los gachupines (born in the Spanish peninsula) and individuals who presumed to be Spanish were seen everywhere wearing their best clothes. They seemed to want to show off their black corduroy capes, which some of them could afford because of their economic success in agriculture, mining, and other business. More than anything, they gave the impression of wanting to highlight their service to His Majesty as God intended. They oversaw order and stipulated good manners that "people without reason" did not have. Above all, they monitored the behavior of Indigenous, mulatos, mestizos, and mixed people, including the Pardo brothers who, according to gachupines, were naturally inclined to drink and scandal.

But that day the Pardo brothers made a pleasant impression with an excellent theatrical representation of the Battle between Moors and Christians. With the few resources available, they tried to emulate the drama of this crusade that took place in the Spain of the Reconquest many years before and was still taking place in the peninsula and throughout New Spain. With a few planks, the Pardo brothers formed fortresses and swords and, with some rags, they made costumes to represent the Great Turk and the Captains. Among the crowd, more than two commented that the Pardos had acted naturally, mainly due to their skin color, similar to the Moors' complexion. However, harmony and order were disrupted with a few card fights and bets that some Pardo brothers, mestizo, Indigenous, and more mixed people—not counting the entry that a tribe of enemy Indians undertook—carried out, putting the entire mining town on its heels.

The next day, following Sunday Mass, word spread after the town crier gave the news: the priest and the alcalde mayor (city mayor) had agreed that no more fiesta permits would be granted to the Pardos since, again, they had provoked and participated in shameful riots. But that remained to be seen because, as all people believed, those Pardos were fierce and did not give up so easily; they would continue to turn that baroque world upside down before, during, and after religious festivals for many more years.

The narrative above is a pliego suelto, a theatrical broadsheet in which historical actors who lived in silence in the archives talk and act, representing themselves in the historical scene in a place now called Hidalgo del Parral, in the state of Chihuahua, Mexico.[1] That is how the participants introduce this book's focus: the Northern New Spain mining town of San Joseph del Parral's religious and cultural life between 1632 and the end of the 1800s. The town's name appears as "San Joseph" in the archival documents for most of the seventeenth century. "Joseph" is a Hebrew name, and its pronunciation is Yoséf. Eighteenth-century archival documents featured both José and Joseph. This book will employ the name Joseph throughout the analysis. The research began after noticing how the municipal and parochial archival documents contain documents about two Catholic religious brotherhoods organizing festivities for their Marian devotions whose official names referred to their members' race: La Cofradía de La Purísima Inmaculada Concepción de Los Pardos and La Cofradía de Nuestra Señora de La Candelaria de Los Naturales.[2] The Pardo brothers included individuals of African descent, Indigenous, and mixed individuals. The Naturales brothers incorporated persons that belonged to a foreign Indigenous group, Mexicanos, also called Mexicaneros, from South and Central New Spain.

Moreover, the primary documentation also discloses how Spanish women actively funded capellanías de misas rezadas for when they and family members would die. This data provoked some initial questions: How did Northern New Spain include individuals of African descent and foreign Indigenous groups? How could they participate in cultural manifestations in a mining town historically portrayed mainly in two extremes: rich in silver and inhabited by rebellious Indigenous groups? Was there a connection between the Moors of the Reconquest and the dark-lighted skin of Pardo brothers performing as Gran Turco in the theatrical representation of Moor and Christians? How and why did women's involvement in capellanías occur in a highly patriarchal society? Was this participation possible due to silver richness in a town far away from the viceroyalty's centers of power? This last question's affirmative answer is the start of this investigation. It builds on Lisa Voigt's *Spectacular Wealth* when expressing that in Potosi and Minas Gerais mining communities, "distance and heterogeneity allowed the varied and conflicting agendas of those partaking in festivals to come into focus more sharply than in those planned and performed at centers of power (Mexico City, Lima, and Salvador de la Bahia)."[3]

This research considers that geographical location and the time of European arrival in Northern New Spain's territory of La Nueva Vizcaya (from 1620 to 1786, approximately, comprised the states of Durango, Chihuahua, and part of Coahuila) were pivotal for creating a peculiar society that allowed all segments of the society to participate in the religious institutions and festivities that took place in San Joseph del Parral and the entire Provincia de Santa Bárbara to which it, and other agricultural and mining localities, belonged.[4] Its remote location marked a physical and perhaps a mental distance from Mexico City, the center of power. This distance was reflected in the late arrival of goods, people, and news, as well as religious institutions and royal ordinances, which shaped unique political, social, economic, and cultural practices. Nonetheless, there were other elements that played a role in the mining town's distinctive sociocultural development. As Cheryl E. Martin informs in her research about governance and society of the city of Chihuahua during the eighteenth century, San Joseph del Parral did not have a cabildo (municipal council); therefore, authority fell to the alcalde mayor, who often belonged to the oligarchy or the mining elite.[5] Aware of the economic importance the Spanish Crown placed on the production of silver, Chantal Cramaussel's demographic history study reveals that those power entities interfered in various social and religious-cultural aspects of the town, trying to control, economically and politically, their success in the place.[6]

The location also affected the conformation of a diverse workforce in mining and agricultural enclaves, as Robert West, pioneer researcher on the mining workforce and production in San Joseph del Parral, exposes in his book.[7] Furthermore, in her ethnohistory work, Susan Deeds indicates that the Chichimeca Indigenous group (as Spaniards from central and south New Spain called the Natives in the north) was in fact composed of various and different factions and dispersed throughout La Nueva Vizcaya. Deeds notes how some of them were rebellious, and most did not readily submit to integration into Franciscan and Jesuit missions, nor responded favorably to labor in encomiendas and repartimientos.[8] Those characteristics indicate that mining areas of Northern New Spain did not include long-established local Indigenous elites. Faced with the scarcity of the Indigenous workforce, Spaniards resorted to Reconquest practices: the transfer of docile-conquered groups and slavery. Thus, they brought, by will or by force, Indigenous people from North, Central, South, and other parts of Mexico, and African and African-descent people from Africa, the Caribbean, and other portions of New Spain to ensure labor in the mines and on the farms, yielding in this way a diverse society.

The location also interfered with the implementation of religious festivities in mining areas. The scarcity of people, the absence of homogenous and sedentary Native communities, and the insufficient resources in the provincia did not allow the inclusion of splendid festivals such as those in larger cities of New Spain that Juan Pedro Viqueira Albán and Linda Ann Curcio-Nagy analyze; of Peru, as Carolyn Dean studies; or of both Peru and Brazil, as Lisa Voigt investigates.[9] Nonetheless, archival documentation exposes that in San Joseph del Parral, Catholic institutions did open spaces for the involvement of diverse groups and individuals, from the absent figure of the king and the Spanish elite to Africans and African descendants, local and foreign Indigenous individuals and groups, mestizos, and other mixed people from the area. This participation is highly relevant, since New Spain society intended to separate the various social groups rigidly.[10] However, the Catholic Church and the Spanish Crown sought to regulate diverse society involvement in public affairs throughout New Spain. The Habsburg and later the Bourbon House tried to limit their vassals' immersion in celebrations to control the viceroyalty's public life.[11] Therefore, cultural diversity and rule became issues of primary importance for public policy.[12] In Mexico City in the seventeenth century, council members tried to follow the royal and ecclesiastical ordinances for public celebrations: fulfillment of civic duty, maintenance of Spanish customs, strengthening the legitimacy of the government, and the demonstration of personal prestige and wealth. However, these council members also wanted to create and establish a local identity.[13]

San Joseph del Parral's primary documentation also divulges a complex religious apparatus, where the sacred, secular, and even profane elements manifested in fiestas, cofradías, and capellanías. Usually, cofrades (confraternity brothers) organized festivities for their Marian advocations, participated in celebrations held to honor members of the Spanish Crown, and pursued earthly and spiritual well-being for members. The capellanía was the maximum expression of those latter two distinct benefits in a very complex way. From approximately 1600 to 1800, Catholicism centered on the idea of purgatory and the possibility of saving the human soul through capellanías. This Catholic institution funded itself with valuable assets, including real estate, mines, and enslaved people. After the founders died, the rental of those estates produced capital that would pay for eternal prayed Masses for them and their family members, so that they could secure a place in Heaven.[14]

In this manner, capellanías came to embrace fiestas and cofradías.

They were vehicles with which to cover the expenses of festivities and Masses, convey pious works, and acquire valuable objects, such as lamps and other relics. Often, capellanías' founders named cofrades as patrones to supervise assets and organize prayed Masses, always including a monetary recompense. With it, the brotherhoods could assist their members' earthly and spiritual well-being and organize fiestas for their Marian advocations. In this way, they could close and open a cycle made up of different yet interrelated Catholic rituals. How did those three forces—the religious, governance, and faithful partakers—come together? What was the sequence that led them to build this complicated apparatus? This book believes that the thread that brought those three entities together was the Spanish Baroque, a shared ideology centered on living a good Catholic life to have a better afterlife.[15]

As a historical concept, the Spanish Baroque goes beyond aesthetics and style. It manifested from approximately 1600 to 1680 in European areas such as France, Northern Italy and Rome, Spain and Portugal, among others.[16] It was an artistic-intellectual movement. In art, the baroque thought contains the idea of an ephemeral nature of life, which simultaneously goes hand in hand with spiritual eternity, only achieved after death. Hence, baroque painting highlights particular objects that are "illuminated by God," whereas baroque writing does so through language that makes objects and characters visible.[17] From 1550 to 1650, the Italian Baroque brought European culture to the most public or popular spheres.[18] Eventually, the division between mundane-earthly life and the grace of eternal life was appreciated in festivals and pilgrimages. Religious objects and symbols starred in these events in an ostentatious way, while the mortal faithful occupied a modest place, but at the same time, indispensable: the place of adoration and veneration that corresponded to them.[19]

In Spain, the baroque has a reformist origin that more clearly explains the fusion between the civic, the urban, the religious, the individual, and the public. Around 1530, the Catholic Church suffered a severe blow with the rise of Protestantism. The latter established that the human being was unworthy, that God was incomprehensible, and that mortals could find salvation only in the faith that one had in the merits of Christ. This ideology stripped the Catholic Church of its intermediary role between the faithful and God. Consequently, this religious institution created a Counter-Reformation, through which a legal doctrine was built based on the Theological Summa of Saint Thomas Aquinas. That dogma gave the Catholic Church the spiritual power to exercise dominance in the civil realm. Thus, it spread the idea that human beings, unable to curb their low passions, needed authority to guide them in life and ensure them a place in Heaven after death. Hence, the pious works, cofradías, capellanías, and all the Catholic rituals encouraged the Christian faithful to participate. The rite (especially that of the Holy Mass) was mainly oriented to obtain divine indulgences (or favors) to help the faithful departed undergo their transit through purgatory with less anguish.[20] Ultimately, the Spanish Baroque mentality and the Catholic Church encompassed the idea of living a devoted Catholic life to achieve Divine Grace at the time of death.[21]

In fact, since the Spanish Crown was consolidated as such, it used public acts, religious festivals, and royal ceremonies to create, communicate, and establish order, and to consolidate power. In the period of its rise, the Catholic Baroque ideology employed rhetorical strategies of both the crown and the Catholic Church in all artistic visual aspects. That is, these media, such as painting, sculpture, and architecture, functioned as "the voice" by which the government and the Church convinced, persuaded, praised, and/or condemned the masses. Among the largely illiterate lower classes, the most effective visual medium they used to raise the voice of their power was public events.[22]

The pious visual speech among the faithful had such an impact that with it, the Catholic Church consecrated its image as the universal promoter of civilization.[23] The Catholic Church's universality also derived from Philip II's claim: the Monarchy of Spain, along with the Catholic Church, was the Fifth Universal Monarchy that would last forever, and it consolidated such an image when Pope Alexander VI recognized Spain's claims over North and South America with the Treaty of Tordesillas.[24] Because the Church controlled much of the wealth in Spain, it emerged as the principal patron of art outside the court. Artistic talent flourished in provinces, marking the line to follow regarding the preponderant religious motifs and themes of the Spanish Baroque in all branches of culture.[25] The Spanish Catholic Baroque's religious painting, for example, inspired the religious theater of the Catholic Reformation.[26]

All this gave the Catholic Church universality and an excellent position for Spain.[27] From Spain, the baroque propagated in America, giving relevance to culture in the construction of social reality. Visual acts of veneration of the Heavenly promoted it, and its main interest was integrating people into the modern state and creating a hegemonic culture.[28] Religious festivals such as Corpus Christi, for example, were the ideal occasions to merge the crown with the Divine, and hence the interest of American cities organizing and participating in large fiestas. Those occasions allowed the integration of new vassals but at the same time left the door open to tolerance, syncretism, and local cultural diversity.[29] It is important to note that no matter where the baroque manifested, "in the baroque city, churches were constructed, fiestas were organized, and theater locales staged representations."[30]

The archival evidence underlying the premises of this book reveals how San Joseph del Parral's Catholicism intended to satisfy a civic obligation, preserve Spanish customs, and reinforce the legitimacy of the crown. At the same time, the universal Catholic Church acted as an intermediary between the individual and God, consolidating a hegemonic culture. Moreover, from the first third of the seventeenth century to the end of the eighteenth, the primary documents reveal how Catholic institutions, rituals, and participants were intrinsically related through Spanish Baroque thought in public and private religious theatrical representations. How the diverse population in San Joseph del Parral engaged with Catholic rituals, negotiated their place in society through that engagement, and built community and culture are the central questions posed here.

To answer those questions, this research uses the religious ritual as a lens through which to study the participation of those actors in acts of veneration.[31] As a social phenomenon, the religious ritual involves pragmatic or spiritual participation in a symbolic, meaningful, and communicative way. Although the formality of the religious ritual has been seen as repetitive, performative, stylistic, rigid, standardized, and invariant, this investigation aligns with a scholarship that goes beyond the execution of a ritual.[32] In San Joseph del Parral, the participation, symbols, and meaning in religious rituals transformed over time; therefore, this book is interested in examining ritual's change outside its formality. Indeed, this research approaches rituals as acts of representation that expose the construction of meaning through signs and concepts. That is, rituals are opportunities to change how participants think and feel about themselves and the world in which they live, "creating or recreating new logos and language, new cultural memories and identities, and new social customs, reflecting a new local character of belonging."[33] As this book is concerned with "the symbolic and its representation" and studies "the process of symbolic mediations through which human beings make sense of their world," it is a work of cultural history.[34]

By exploring these issues, this book argues that people of African descent, Indigenous people, and Spanish elite women took advantage of Catholic institutions and rituals that, immersed in Spanish Baroque ideology, provided them with occasions to engage in religious rituals, negotiate their place in society through that engagement, and build community and culture. In representing themselves as devoted Catholics in religious fiestas, cofradías, and capellanías, they transformed the rituals of the universal Catholic Church according to their local reality. This transformation created a collective cultural memory and identity they intended to preserve for future generations. The analysis of this participation focuses on exploring the use of language in various forms, including the representation and expression of ideas in archival documents supported by various methods and theories.

Methodology and Theory

This book primarily consulted the Archivo Municipal de Hidalgo del Parral (AMHP-UTEP) and the Archivo Parroquial de San Joseph del Parral (APSJP-UTEP).[35] The municipal and parochial documentation has certain limitations.[36] Although they feature a guide and are well organized according to time, many of the files contain damaged, mixed, or incomplete papers. The parochial archive offers a more complex time organization since it includes documents with different years in one roll or file. One of the main challenges was the scarcity of information about specific occurrences, such as carnivals and other cultural-religious practices. The lack of sufficient or precise information about the marginalized individuals and groups, mainly African, of African descent, and Indigenous, supplied another obstacle. In most primary documentation, the subjects do not have a Christian first or last name. If they do, a racial adjective follows—for example, Diego mulato or Miguel Indio Mexicanero. As a result, tracking them through the archives was impossible.

To tackle those obstacles, this investigation approached the archival documents as an intellectual task, developing and applying research methods to illuminate the individuals' and groups' participation in cultural affairs that governmental and historic repositories have obscured due to subjects' calidad, class, or gender. This research adopted an "against the grain" analysis by taking subtext and silences into consideration and weaving layers of complex information to go beyond the formality of the colonial text.[37] In performing this task, this book adheres to post-structuralist critiques of colonialism and its language (colonial discourse) as a vehicle of communication and applies it to the archives to underscore the Polysemy of the Symbolic Form (the lexical ambiguity of words) that those texts could have.[38] That is, words, sentences, and phrases in a manuscript can have more than one meaning and more than one interpretation simultaneously, always depending on the historical context.[39] Furthermore, it is through the contextualization process that a single document or set of manuscripts could contain various sociohistorical languages with a unique meaning, an occurrence theorist Mikhail Bakhtin identifies as heteroglossia.[40] Additionally, this book proposes that a post-structuralist analysis of colonial language informs about the transmission, influence, creation, recreation, and application of ideas. The overall intention of this methodological approach (the underscoring of the Polysemy of the Symbolic Form and the contextualization and texts' content heteroglossia) is to scrutinize how, through language, Spaniards understood themselves and tried to govern their subjects and how the latter appropriated and transformed that language in Northern New Spain.[41]

This multifaceted task required historical imagination to "speculate on what might have happened; to think outside the box to develop plausible explanations of case materials and historical events, and the ability to draw abductive inferences by walking the fine line between objectivity and subjectivity."[42] Although for a historian the writing and reading of history has always required a level of imagination and speculation because the "filtering process is affected by time, place, and individual," the reconstruction of absent or obscured historical actors in the archive and history, in general, incite the historian's imagination, speculation, and interpretation.[43] In researching the Atlantic slave trade, cultural historian Saidiya Hartman observes how the archive could make "visible the production of disposable lives" and how a repository could be "a mortuary, a tomb, an inventory of property of those that were not meant to appear other than objects; the nameless, the forgotten, the resistant object."[44] The scholar uses critical speculation to face those archives' challenges. She created "critical fabulation," a research method that derives from fábula (fable), a narrative of events caused and experienced by actors/agents of action, to reconstruct/fill the gaps of the resistant object/the agent of action's history, speculating and imagining what might have been and writing about it applying fiction narrative techniques.

Derived from Hartman's research method, this book uses theatrical narratives at the beginning of each chapter to offset the archival challenges: Afro-descendants and Indigenous people's lack of Christian first and last names and the absence of chronicles that could narrate festivals or rituals in Northern New Spain, to mention just two archival nuisances. Those theatrical narratives are inspired by pliego suelto: popular comedies, street ballads, or romances that were delivered orally but were written and often published during Spain's Baroque epoch.[45] No chroniclers indeed ventured into this remote area to record the town's festive life as many did in Europe, including Spain and the principal cities of the viceroyalty in America, but primary documentation and secondary sources support the image of Joseph del Parral with baroque churches, fiestas with fireworks, and theatrical locales, such as the one the Pardo brothers organized in the pliego suelto that opens this book. Then, performing historical imagination/speculation through pliegos sueltos attempts to liberate or revive historical actors from the archives so they can perform and represent themselves in the historical scenario they crafted and in which they participated, and that reflected the theatrical rituals of the Catholic Baroque ideology.[46] In a way, pliegos sueltos are chronicles that rerecord a more inclusive history where the marginalized are part of the human endeavor of "making history."[47]

Furthermore, to underscore one of the many ways Indigenous, African-descent, and mixed people were dispossessed and to represent them with the human dignity they deserve in the historical "scenario," this book capitalizes their racial adjectives as they appear in primary documentation: for example, Diego "Mulato" and Miguel "Indio Mexicanero."

This research includes social and cultural theories that facilitated the comprehension of the contextual significations of archival documents, the individuals' and groups' representations in the public sphere, the opposite forces struggling to dominate the scene, and how the sacred and the profane coexisted in Catholic institutions and rituals. Mikhail Bakhtin's theory of the carnival contributed to understanding how two dissident groups, the Spanish/mining elite and the Catholic Church "against" the Afro-descendants and Indigenous groups, struggled to create and establish hegemony in the mining town of Joseph del Parral. Juan Villegas's social theatricality helped study those people's behavior and system of codes in religious rituals and related legal cases where "the social sectors codified their perception of the world and the way of representing themselves on the social scene."[48] Finally, as the Catholic rituals and institutions on most of the occasions included both the sacred and the profane, Kathryn Burns's spiritual economy helped the investigation to understand how in the religious sphere, "the spiritual and economic/the material and sacred, merge and cannot be disassociated," helping to uncover how fiestas, cofradías, and capellanías were interrelated in cyclical performances.[49] Through pliegos sueltos and sociocultural theories, this cultural history book underscores the role some ideologies played in the development of the Northern Frontier. In particular, it exposes how the Spanish Baroque embraced the entire San Joseph del Parral community across the Catholic rituals. Thus, this book challenges the idea of Spanish supremacy and New Spain's vision of a distant mundo bárbaro (barbarian world), offering instead a picture of people rich in silver but also in culture.[50]

Book Contribution and Chapter Descriptions

In the study of some adjacent places to La Nueva Vizcaya and the Chihuahua frontier's mining and diverse population, this book is profoundly appreciative of the research works of Robert C. West, D. A. Brading, P. J. Bakewell, and Oscar Alatriste about the mining industry in Northern New Spain and its economic impact through silver exports, as well as the socioeconomic effect on mine workers in San Joseph del Parral, Zacatecas, Guanajuato, Pachuca, and Sonora, during the time of both the Habsburg Crown and the Bourbon reforms. Also highly valued was Susan Deeds' ethnohistory on the Indigenous groups in Eastern Sinaloa, Northern Durango, and Southern Chihuahua, Mexico, concerning resistance and adaptation after the Spanish Mission system from the sixteenth century to the middle of the seventeenth. The demographic history work of Chantal Cramaussel in La Provincia de Santa Bárbara is pivotal in this research, as the historian provided the basis to reconstruct most of the provincia's *modus vivendi*. Finally, through Cheryl E. Martin's social history in colonial Chihuahua, this book confirmed the importance of time and place regarding towns and cities' foundation. In 1632, for example, San Joseph del Parral lacked what Chihuahua's establishment had in the eighteenth century: authorities that planned, organized, and supervised its creation.[51] As we will see, this distinction had a variety of repercussions, among them the lack of formal records of Indigenous and Afro-descendant people in the seventeenth century as an obstacle to identifying those individuals and reconstructing their lives.

With this book, I decided to focus on the cultural history of a mining town since scholars have yet to fully explore and research the cultural contributions of individuals of African descent, Indigenous, and Spanish women in Northern New Spain history. Understanding their involvement in Catholic rituals and institutions is essential to fully knowing those peoples' participation strategies. In performing this effort, this book appreciates Ignacio Martínez's book, *The*

Intimate Frontier. This cultural/intellectual history work analyzes the idea and language of "friendship" in bringing together and regulating Spaniards and Indigenous people's relations in colonial Sonora.[52] Furthermore, with this analysis, Martínez contributes to the current endeavor to appreciate frontiers and borderlands histories within a local-global framework.[53] *Drama Under the Skin* joins this local-global basis and builds on borderlands and frontiers to reveal that the historical actors' lives went beyond violent experiences constructing the culture of their regions.[54]

Furthermore, by applying ritual as a lens on the Catholic life of people of African descent, this book contributes to African diaspora history and studies by exploring the possibility of African cultural prevalence up to Northern New Spain. This interest results from scholar James Sweet's provocative statement that in some regions of the Caribbean, African enslaved people could maintain an African Thought while "recreating" their culture. Following Sweet's assertion, this book engaged with more literature about Africa's diaspora and culture. Thanks to John K. Thornton, this book's author understood the importance of Central African people's involvement with Christianity and European culture in previous forced migrations to the Atlantic and Americas, as individuals were able to use that knowledge to survive and prevail. In studying the creolization phenomenon, Walter Hawthorne's view of various African diasporas helped in the comprehension of "the failure to identify multiple and overlapping boundaries of African cultures and cultural identities." Frank T. Proctor III's approach served as an inspiration to "explore slavery from the perspective of slaves" in New Spain, placing special attention to their culture in transforming their experiences "within the confines of power structures."[55] This book devotes particular attention to the demographic history of African and African descendants' experiences in San Joseph del Parral made by Vincent V. Mayer Jr. and Florence Barkin.[56] Last, this research includes historian Nicole von Germeten's book

Black Brotherhoods, in which she devotes a chapter to San Joseph del Parral's Cofradía de La Purísima Inmaculada Concepción de Los Pardos and concludes this brotherhood lacked the success other religious units had in more developed urban areas in New Spain. That assertion is challenged here.[57]

This book joins the historiographical efforts in contesting the idea of a homogeneous Northern society in New Spain during the seventeenth and eighteenth centuries. It is the first that analyzes the cultural-religious history, paying particular attention to marginalized groups and individuals to unveil how their life experiences went beyond mining and agriculture work. The book also questions local chroniclers' manuscripts that have perpetuated the idea of Spaniards' superiority, diminishing the presence and culture of non-Spanish groups and individuals.

Chapter 1, "La Nueva Vizcaya: A Medieval Mask," gives temporal, geographical, and ideological context to the provincia and the town's formation. It starts with a pliego suelto that theatricalizes the fusion of two sets of religious beliefs, those of mission pueblo Indigenous people and those of Franciscan friars. The scene opens the discussion of how distance from the center of power, natural resources richness, and non-sedentary Indigenous groups who resisted Spanish entrance invited various historical voices or beliefs that sometimes collided, fused, transformed, recreated, or created a new but ambiguous historical voice. The adelantados, Spanish men who first entered Northern New Spain, had to put the Spanish Crown's modern ideas aside, wear their medieval Christian knights' garments, and recur to beliefs and practices that were still fresh in their minds, such as the Reconquest experience, to solve the difficulties they encountered trying to fulfill their utopian vision of the New Spain frontier. The medieval mind of adelantados opened the door to a Spanish oligarchy that revived some Reconquest practices such as La Guerra Justa (Just War) to enslave Native people and create mission pueblos, encomiendas and repartimientos systems, the spread of the African slave trade, and the transfer of different Indigenous groups from Central, South, and Northeast New Spain, making the frontier zone a highly ethnic and ideologically diverse zone.

Chapter 2, "The African Diaspora: A Borderlands Labyrinth," takes some people of African descent out of archival darkness and places them as historical actors in a pliego suelto that recreates the presence of African enslaved people in San Joseph del Parral. The chapter offers a summary of the African diaspora, from Africa and Iberia to Hispaniola, and from there to America and New Spain up to La Nueva Vizcaya and San Joseph del Parral, in an attempt to follow the diasporic voyage of the historical actors and to highlight the relevance of Hispaniola in conveying the message and perhaps a pattern of African and Indigenous people resisting enslavement. It also introduces the intricate African diaspora experience, including as it does Moors and Muslims from both Africa and Iberia in the Portuguese slave trade and the impact of this variety of "diasporas" in America at the time of the Christianization of the African enslaved population. As such, this chapter prepares the terrain to better understand the challenges the Pardos' cofradía faced from the mid-seventeenth to the eighteenth century.

Chapter 3, "New Spain's Frontier: A Diverse Cauldron," opens with a pliego suelto that represents the diverse population of San Joseph del Parral attending a public ritual of death. It serves as an antechamber to reveal the mining town's true face: diverse in many modes. The European population reflected medieval ideologies and practices, with their involvement in the enslavement of Indigenous and African-descent people, social divisions, paterfamilias (the male of the house), the just war, encomiendas and repartimientos, and creating a highly mixed population and, consequently, many scandals. At the same time, this chapter underscores how African-descent, Indigenous, and mixed people lived both their public and not-so-private lives when they escaped, denouncing physical abuse, or claiming freedom. Along with the previous two chapters, this section brings together the necessary sociocultural elements to continue analyzing the ritual life of San Joseph del Parral.

Chapter 4, "Carnival: A Mining Town Upside Down," examines the 1649 alcalde's discourse about how mine workers and the population in general should behave during the carnestolendas/carnival days. Reading it as a "colonial text" and "against the grain," this chapter discloses the alcalde's ambiguity of words, phrases, and ideas when placing it in historical context, revealing at the same time the coexistence of various sociohistorical languages (heteroglossia). Furthermore, Bakhtín's sociocultural theory of the carnival unveils how the oldest documented festivity in the town was a place and occasion for the struggle between two opposite forces: Christian and pagan, spiritual and pragmatic, and civilized and vicious. In his discourse, the alcalde presented the town's cultural memory as rooted in medieval beliefs and practices, whereas the mining town's workforce was immoral but necessary. That is how this chapter builds the idea of the Spanish oligarchy, further noting that the Catholic Church opened the door for workers to start giving the town a local character. This notion can be appreciated in the pliego suelto, which starts the chapter with a scene in which the inhabitants participate in a gracious Corpus Christi parade celebrated in a humble but enthusiastic mining town.

Chapter 5, "Naturales´and Pardo´s Cofradías: A Local Taste of the Universal Church," opens with a pliego suelto that depicts the precise moment the Naturales' confraternity transforms itself after a local-environmental event. Initially, the chapter gives the background of confraternities as religious institutions, from their formation in the Middle Ages to the mid-seventeenth century, highlighting their baroque element in America. Divided into two parts, the section first analyzes La Cofradía de Nuestra Señora de La Candelaria de Los Naturales, a brotherhood formed of Mexicanos Indigenous people. The chapter detects primary sources' heteroglossia with the coexistence of two sociohistorical languages that underscores a Northern cultural memory that still praised European culture. The second section exposes La Cofradía de Los Pardos' struggle to conform and formalize its congregation due to the mining elite's control, an element that historian Germeten uses to label this confraternity as "unsuccessful." Nonetheless, the chapter demonstrates how the Pardo brothers challenged Spanish hegemony with tenacity and their notions about the value of cultural memory that could signal the creation or recreation of African culture in Northern New Spain.

Chapter 6, "Naturales´and Pardos´Cofradías: A Rota Fortunae at the Turn of the Eighteenth Century," analyzes the different ways in which the Bourbon reforms impacted how La Cofradía de Los Naturales and La Cofradía de Los Pardos participated in the Catholic ritual. Those reforms tried to eradicate the ignorance and superstitious atmosphere that the Spanish Baroque imposed and perpetuated. Instead, the Bourbons praised reason and wanted it reflected in the mining town, although the Catholic Church's role was ambiguous. However, the study of primary sources as "colonial texts," underscoring their ambiguous meanings when placed in historical contexts, establishes the Naturales and Pardo brothers as being people of reason since they adapted themselves to the enlightened reforms' changes and challenges. That is precisely what the pliego suelto that initiates the section communicates, taking the Pardo brothers out of the archives. As historical actors, in this scene, they show their sagacity in auctioning their corridas de toros, unveiling the authorities' contradictions at the same time: allowing the Pardo brothers to include entertainments that Bourbon reforms considered harmful to the common good.

Chapter 7, "A Town in Quicksand: Between Baroque Fervor and Enlightened Reason," opens with a pliego suelto where historical actors represent Bourbon reforms' effect over the town's most popular form of entertainment: card games. This section is informative rather than analytical, presenting a period of global and local change. It addresses how the Bourbon reforms contributed to forming a new powerful actor in San Joseph del Parral: the mining guild, which performed as the creator and guardian of the new industrious mining worker. The Catholic Church and the Bourbon House supported and encouraged this guild to instruct and control the workers when the Spanish Crown was trying to survive diverse challenges.

Chapter 8, "Pardos' Fiestas: A Carousel in a Diasporic Frontier," opens with a pliego suelto where the Pardo brothers perform what seemed to be their favorite theatrical event: the Battle between Moors and Christians. The scene introduces one of the Pardos' negotiation skills they used throughout the eighteenth century when Enlightenment thought encouraged the Spanish Crown to renovate socially, culturally, economically, and politically. However, despite those intents, La Cofradía de Los Pardos managed to create or recreate various negotiation tools that refer to a "social theatricality," an acculturated discourse, and "ancestry," an African culture element they knew how to use in their favor to prevail until the end of the eighteenth century, proving in this way that rather than being a failure they were a confraternity of success.

Chapter 9, "Capellanías: Spiritualized Lives in a Silver House of Mirrors," uses spiritual economy to show how some elite Spanish women took advantage of their economic position and the pious-baroque discourse to express their desires and claim profane and spiritual benefits. Documents show their active involvement in holy works or capellanías and attest to their role as mediators between Catholic institutions and the Indigenous and mixed population, as well as their predominant role in creating a local culture through the universal-Catholic ritual, as all show a complex, unique system of codes, beliefs, and values. The chapter also examines the intricacy of those religious institutions in handling the "spiritual economy" of both Christians' souls and their valuable assets. Furthermore, it communicates how capellanías closed and reopened the Catholic Baroque ritual circle in the pliego suelto that opens the section: a scene that portrays how crucial a pious object and baroque light were during a prayed Mass for a soul to pass through purgatory with fewer adversities.

Lastly, "Drama's Dénouement" concludes the book, offering a glimpse of a current cultural memoir about Hidalgo del Parral that continues evoking and praising Northern New Spain's "Spanish-honorable" legacy through certain privileged surnames. Then, the dénouement proceeds with a summary that reminds us how the hands, minds, and souls of men and women that live in the archives' darkness, with or without last names, also crafted the history of this remote area. As this is a "drama dénouement," it closes with a dramatic but genuine inquiry.

CHAPTER I

LA NUEVA VIZCAYA

A MEDIEVAL MASK

It was midday during harvest season at El Valle de San Bartolomé, a blessed town that graciously has celebrated the miracles of Mother Earth. A good-sized group made up mainly of Indigenous Conchos, Tepehuanes, and Tobosos that had not yet left the pueblo—only the Christian God knows why—made way for their leader. He was Gregorio Francisco Indio Mexicano. They chose him some weeks before due to his age and upstanding reputation to start the first of the dances dedicated to their almighty gods (the ones that, according to many people, lived hidden since the Europeans arrived), who procure food from the earth's heart to the hands of those who, willingly or not, have settled, occupying a piece of land they work daily (only that it does not belong to them, except for some lucky Indigenous Mexicanos, like Gregorio Francisco).

Adorning their bodies with what has remained of those good ancient times, they appeared in the center of the farmland at high noon before the tired gazes of the Franciscan priests, now stripped of their dreams of attending the souls of mortals living in a civilized, ordered, sophisticated renaissance city. Three participants—Nicolás Concho Indio, Miguel Franco Indio, and Juan Francisco Indio—played the drums. The rest followed them, making a tinkling noise with the rattles that they had attached to their feet and moving with grace and elegance.

They advanced towards the Florido River, followed by dogs and chickens, and by the clouds: those clouds, all loaded with divine water, promising a good downpour. With the pinch of humanism that remained in the holed pockets of their pants, the Franciscans tried to dissuade those barbarians (as they called the Indigenous peoples). How? By replicating the Catholic, Apostolic, and Roman Church bells that called for them to wash their sins in Holy Mass.

But nothing stopped those free-spirited souls. They seemed to be the true adelantados that arrived years ago in this area that do not embrace, that do not trap, that do not ask for anything more than a few drops of rain to wash and refresh the path and the spirit of the wanderers of the north.

Not to be left behind, or rather to impose their will, the poor Franciscans took the holy image of the Virgen de la Candelaria and Apostle Santiago out of the church and, in a sad and shameful procession, carried the divine figures to the Florido River. With a song they could barely sing, but with great reverence, they lowered and placed the Virgin and the Apostle in the middle of the circle that the Natives had formed on one side of the river. The Indigenous stopped playing the little drums and moving their feet; even the dogs stopped barking. Everyone looked at each other. The eyes of women, children, and older men eventually agreed: let Doña Candelaria and Don Santiago in; after all, parents are not to blame for the sins of their children.

I n this pliego suelto, Gregorio Francisco Indio Mexicano, Nicolás Concho Indio, Miguel Franco Indio, and Juan Francisco Indio depict the ideological clash between the Old and the New World.[1] Of New Spain's frontier, the Spaniards' view could be summed up in a single word: "barbaric," an adjective they applied to the Chichimecas, the rebellious Indigenous group that inhabited an unknown area that was too far away from Mexico City for their comfort. Parts of that frontier zone were later El Reino de La Nueva Galicia, formed by the states of Jalisco, Nayarit,

Guanajuato, Aguascalientes, and Zacatecas—and, beyond it, El Reino de La Nueva Vizcaya and its Provincia de Santa Bárbara. Europeans had great expectations about the richness and prosperity of this part of the New World. However, perhaps due to distance, extreme climate, Spanish ways, lack of sedentary Indigenous groups, and instability of mining zones, La Nueva Vizcaya and its provincia had difficulties attracting new settlers during its formative years and throughout different stages of the Spanish presence in mining and farming areas. To La Nueva Vizcaya belonged, among other places, the mining and agricultural town of Santa Bárbara, Durango, and the farm town of El Valle de San Bartolomé; San Joseph del Parral would join them later.[2]

This chapter explores how Northern New Spain's location and its Native population could have awakened Spanish's recent memory: the Reconquest experience, as many of the Spaniards' responses to the frontier challenges reflected medieval ideas and practices. In their desire to expand their territorial dominance to this part of the viceroyalty, the Spanish faced two obstacles: to enter and to populate a vast area they viewed as La Frontera Bárbara. In performing the task, the newcomers demonstrated one of the Spanish Crown's contradictions: the arrival of an adventurous Spanish modern force filled with an ideology and practices anchored in the Reconquest. This paradox reverberated in all aspects of La Nueva Vizcaya life as the transmission, recreation, and application of that medieval experience molded a vision that privileged and continues to privilege, as chapter 5 will indicate, European cultural memory.

The Spanish Reconquest Spirit

Spain was not always Spain. For many centuries it was a territory made up of several "Españas," peoples who shared a lifestyle and economy but who were actually very far from forming a union since they differed in culture, language, and religion. Dominated by the Romans from the second century BC until the early fifth century AD, it was known as Hispania. Neighboring enclaves such as Greece looked at Hispania territory as divided into regions, each with a name. If described as a unit, it would be that of a territory called Iberia. During the Middle Ages (476–1500, approximately), the territory was spoken of as a mosaic of kingdoms. However, in the tenth century, it was also called Al-Andalus, when much of the Iberian Peninsula was under Muslim rule. In the Modern Age (fifteenth to eighteenth century), foreigners (mostly chroniclers) generally/globally identified this territory as Spain. In reality, it was not until the 1800s that one could speak of Spain as a political entity.[3] Throughout all this time, apart from the name, Spain experienced several transformations due to specific events and ideological currents, although the most effective transformation that led it to consolidate as an empire consisted of the fusion of the kingdom and the Church.

Since the late 700s, the Catholic Church found itself in need of reform, due not only to the presence of Islam but also to the rise of Christianity initiated by Charlemagne, plus the series of violent invasions that occurred in different parts of Europe. Following the Augustinian-medieval image of a chosen people launching into a war against evil, the Catholic Church turned to its warrior peoples to defend itself. These Christian enclaves followed the monastic reform of the Benedictine order of Cluny, which among other objectives intended to resume the Roman Rite and end the Mozarabic Rite.[4]

In Spanish Iberia, the warrior spirit consolidated the image and myth of the Apostle Santiago El Mayor (James the Great). The legend says that he was one of the favorite disciples of Jesus Christ and a witness to the Glory of the Son of God. On this basis, he imposed on Santiago the task of going to the Al-Andalus territory to announce, teach, and preach the Gospel.[5] In the ninth century, after the apostle supposedly had traveled from Palestine to the Al-Andalus area, Galician Christians discovered his body and erected a shrine. From then on, ecclesiastical members and the faithful promoted the saint to the category of "Patron of the Fight Against Muslims." This discovery cemented the Iberian warrior spirit. Under the rule of Alfonso VI (1072–1109), son of Fernando I, the Reign of Castile established itself as the leader of the Christian cause: the "Reconquista" (Reconquest), the struggle to recover a territory that supposedly belonged to Hispanic Christians by right. During this long period, distinguished soldiers on the battlefield demanded rewards such as land grants and even noble titles, plus the right to receive tribute and forced labor from the subjugated Muslim population.[6]

From the twelfth century on, the Church involved itself in the chivalry of the lay nobility and a campaign to Christianize it, which was the new ideal of the Christian knight. In this we must consider the influence of the reform of the Church made by Pope Innocent III in the last years of the twelfth century: moral renewal through the fulfillment of the commandments of the Church was at the heart of this reform.[7] The fusion of religion and the army occurred when at the end of the twelfth century, three monastic military orders of Christian knights formed in Castile: the Orders of Calatrava, of Alcántara, and Santiago, which had the mission of defending the border with Muslim territory.[8]

Around the twelfth century, Spain envisioned a unity that would leave a scattered territory behind to open the doors to what would become imperial Spain. Although different reigns, regions, and peoples that underwent constant reorganization constituted Iberia during the Middle Ages, the situation began to change when Ferdinand III (1217–1252) assumed the Crown of Castile and became monarch of León. It was when the union of both kingdoms, Castile and León, concluded.[9] Then, the unification promoted expansion to the Mediterranean as Ferdinand III extended freedom of trade to foreign merchants. He also facilitated commerce among traders of various nations and Hispanic society gradually entered the trade, among which chief exports were mercury, leather, wool, and wine.[10] Finally, Spain achieved its strength after the Aragon and Castile kingdoms united, with the expulsion of the Jewish community in 1492, and eventually of the Muslim population between 1609 and 1614.[11]

At the beginning of the fifteenth century, Castilla showed signs of a united system of government: it had cortes (courts), prosecution, a currency system, foreign trade, and an army, in addition to having been awarded Italy and Flanders. Late in the fifteenth century, of all the European nations, Castile was the one in the best condition to carry the Augustinian spirit due to its historical situation: years of struggle with Islam, which led to a messianic ideology with the figures of the Virgin of the Immaculate and the Apostle Santiago de Matamoros, already converted into a heavenly warrior.[12] Late medieval years observed this warrior spirit in many towns and villages, where representations of the Battle between Moors and Christians had been taking place during festivals; local people dressed variously as Moors and Christians fought, and the latter always won.[13] The creation of an Augustinian lifeforce symbolized by the Virgin of the Immaculate and Apostle Santiago was the center of a new Spanish cultural memory and identity that, at the same time, was opening the doors to new ideologies that required Spain to modernize.

Although Italy had a society and culture distinct from the rest of Europe during the fourteenth and fifteenth centuries, it was linked to it by religion, politics, economy, people, books, and ideas. While large portions of central and eastern Europe (notably Germany) lacked effective centralizing institutions, and the northern societies lacked the large, populated cities, self-governing communes, and wealthy merchants that could provide the social basis for a humanistic culture, French, English, and Spanish royal courts adopted a humanistic culture.[14] The emergence of the Renaissance (fifteenth–sixteenth centuries) in European urban centers meant a rebirth of the medieval city. It was a symbol and resource of a social and

cosmic order with an urban-civic ideology that developed a collective identity. At the same time, it gave way to a social organization
and the perception that the city boasted superior morals and cultural
values. These characteristics linked spiritual conceptions, hence the
exaltation of the city as a privileged space inhabited by Order and
Grace, where the divine and the mundane coexisted.[15] Likewise, the
political (humanist) discourse placed the city as the entity to forge
governmental decisions regarding power and political authority.
The birth of urban descriptions or civil chronicles placed the city
as the ideal space to lead a civilized life, in contrast to rural areas
that experienced rudimentary life.[16]

From the fifteenth to the sixteenth century, the intellectual
movement known as humanism set its anchor in much of Europe,
revolutionizing the conception of the "self" concerning time and
space. Also, the development of the printing press made possible
the dissemination of travel literature that valued and encouraged
learning other languages and cultures. The diffusion of these texts
opened the eyes of Europeans to travel to different places as part
of a personal improvement that would satisfy scientific curios-
ity and a cultural search.[17] This literature went beyond offering
images of novel localities since it also led to the emergence of a
utopian-medieval feeling: that of the wild man, l'homme sauvage
(the savage man), or what was more, le bon sauvage (the good savage
man). The "good wild man" was perceived as a creation of nature:
happy and virtuous. This type of literature and these images and
perceptions of "the natural man" had a heyday during the sixteenth
century, although the concept continued to develop and expand
more rapidly in the seventeenth and eighteenth centuries.[18]

Spain manifested interest in Italian Renaissance literature at the
beginning of the sixteenth century. Although Spain was a much
more tightly controlled society in the sixteenth century than France,
it followed a parallel development in education. In fact, like France,
Spain experienced the emergence of humanistic education toward

social advancement.[19] Spain insisted on establishing its language and literature to gain a sense of cultural unification. For this outcome, getting the same language at home was essential as the instrument that would promote the communication of "Spanish" ideas and the distribution of humanistic wisdom to a broader audience.[20] Once Spain unified its language, it disseminated outstanding humanistic texts. Then, it created and spread its literature in the form of a "humanistic brotherhood" with epistolary literature, whose themes emphasized friendship, dignity, strength, and knowledge, among others.[21] The participation of historians, on the other hand, comprised the recreation of Spanish history with a glorious and noble past, highlighting the exploits of the most outstanding knights and warriors in different battles and the feat of the Reconquest.[22]

Spain achieved a peak of literary greatness in the later Renaissance, an age conventionally known to Spanish literary historians as the Golden Age, coming directly from Italy.[23] Humanist ideas were present in Spain, gradually becoming a Spanish humanism focused on achieving an ideological union and launching the "discovery" of other territories.[24] The first chronicles of America, for example, created an image of expectation and the possibility of traveling to and writing about remote places of the American land.[25] In America, the office of adelantado retained the same duties and privileges it had in medieval Spain: spiritual and economic objectives to conquer land in the hands of Indigenous peoples and, in northern areas, approval to widen the frontiers for Christianity.[26] Thus, the Spaniards who advanced to Northern New Spain carried a Reconquest spirit that was reflected in how those men tried to solve two main obstacles in advancing north: arriving in and occupying a vast territory they perhaps considered "new" but that was not.

Advance to the North: A Land of "Barbarous Warriors"

From the time Christopher Columbus arrived in the Caribbean in 1492 and the Spanish people came to New Spain in 1519, only twenty-seven years had passed, and from this time to when they headed to the northern frontier, only ten years had elapsed. It is not surprising, then, that Spanish adelantados sent to Northern New Spain brought with them the warrior spirit of the Apostle Santiago, demanding land grants and the right to receive tribute and forced labor. The word adelantado means "advance man," but the contextual origin of the word within the medieval Spanish ideology is rooted in the Reconquest. Adelantados were men who "advanced" and entered to recover territories the Moors occupied in the name of the monarchy. Usually, they had economic means and were from aristocratic families. The monarchy granted a charter to conquer a specific area, commanded private armies, and recruited their soldiers.[27]

After almost three centuries of the Spanish empire's presence in New Spain, the frontier attracted the Spanish conquerors, inevitably even before they arrived. And why not? The Renaissance set the stage for European men to travel, discover, improve themselves, and seek out, imbued with a Reconquest spirit and the image of l'homme sauvage. The expeditions of Nuño de Guzmán to Sinaloa in 1529 and other areas in 1531 that later constituted the kingdom of La Nueva Vizcaya, or that of Francisco de Coronado in 1540 headed to the north in search of the fantastic cities of Cíbola and Quivira, perhaps conceived as Renaissance cities: rich, superior, privileged. These incursions began a long, complex, and permanent advancement process towards the north that functioned as a chain. At first, peninsulares, who enjoyed legal and political support from the crown, promoted the endeavor. Still, over time development was only possible with the economic and human resources of the northern enclaves themselves.[28] In the seventeenth century, the kingdoms of Mexico formed, and those adelantados advanced to the realms of Nueva Galicia, Nueva Vizcaya, and then Nuevo León and New Mexico. New Spain added Coahuila, followed by Sonora and Sinaloa from the sixteenth to the seventeenth century.

During the seventeenth and eighteenth centuries, Texas and Baja California emerged, and during the eighteenth, Tamaulipas and Alta California appeared.[29]

Thus, for all that time, the Spanish could have seen the northern frontier as a promising space. But there was an obstacle: no longer the Moors but the Chichimecas, the Indigenous groups that Franciscan missionaries saw as homogeneous and identified as "the monsters of nature," since for the priests, "chichimeca" meant "man who drinks blood," or "dog." Over time, the term came to mean "bandits, destroyers of civilization, or demons."[30] They created that image for those Indigenous groups probably because they ignored their history. Defined on the West by the highlands of the Western Sierra Madre and the Tepehuan, Tarahumara, and Joya pueblos; on the East by deserts of the Bolsón de Mapimí; on the Northeast by Chihuahua and Coahuila; and on the South by Zacatecas, La Nueva Vizcaya had a long occupation history. In fact, it goes back to the third or fourth century AD, when an Indigenous group, the Chalchihuites, arrived at what is now the borderline between Durango and Zacatecas states. This community was politically organized, had sophisticated technology, and developed a culture that consisted of large ceremonial centers and the manufacture of elaborate ceramics, baskets, and handled vessels. In the subsequent centuries, Chalchihuites spread northward, between the Sierra Madre Occidental and the desert, into northern Durango, possibly already occupied by the Loma people, with whom the newcomers interacted.[31] However, the Chalchihuites entity ended around or after AD 1350. The Loma people reemerged and lasted longer. Between the eleventh and fourteenth centuries, the Indigenous people who lived at the foot of the Sierra Madre Occidental Mountains, between Zacatecas and the Río Conchos, had a cultural unity called the Loma de San Gabriel Chalchihuites. These groups engaged in terraced agriculture, hunting, and gathering, had ceremonial centers, and created pottery.[32]

Another element regarding the Chichimeca community that those priests and adelantados probably ignored was that it was composed of various Indigenous tribes that occupied the Northern zone: Otomí, Pames, Guamares, Guachichiles, Tecuexes, and Cazcanes. But facing them as one entity, the Spaniards—perhaps as their ancestors had struggled to recover a territory they believed belonged to Hispanic Christians during the Reconquest—were going north, little by little penetrating the "Chichimeca" territory, cultivating land or raising cattle.[33] Their early Spanish settlement occurred in 1530, in a town they named Santa Bárbara, on the central river valley region surrounded by the lower drainages of the Conchos, Florido, San Pedro, and Chuvíscar Rivers.[34] There, Spaniards developed small mining and ranching districts. They devoted the ranches to stock-raising and farming. Timber, salt, saltpeter, and other resources supported mining.[35] But periods of production were constantly interrupted by violent confrontations between Spanish and Indigenous groups. The first encounter between the Spaniards and the Indigenous Otomí, Pames, Guamares, Guachichiles, Tecuexes, and Cazcanes arose in the Mixtón War, or Jalisco War (1541–1542). Augustinian and Franciscan friars arrived at the end of this battle, and evangelization of Natives began.[36] A rich mining city eventually developed in the kingdom of La Nueva Galicia, in the city of Zacatecas, along with the city of Durango and two farming towns that were crucial to supplying food to the mining areas in La Nueva Vizcaya's provincia: Santa Bárbara and El Valle de San Bartolomé, the old neighbors of San Joseph del Parral.

The Kingdom of La Nueva Vizcaya

Several silver mine sites were discovered around 1546 in Zacatecas, part of the Nueva Galicia kingdom. These were in San Martín, Sombrerete, Avino, and Guanaceví.[37] Eventually, more mining spots, Indian villages, towns, cities, farms, ranches, and roads began to appear amid wars, captures, and diplomatic strategies. In any case, the inhabitants had to protect the streets since the travelers, especially those porting loads of silver, were subject to the assaults and attacks that supposedly some Indigenous tribes carried out. The authorities thus established defense presidios against those "bellicose" Indians, just as Peninsular Spain had in North Africa during the sixteenth century in the face of Muslim attacks. In fact, it was precisely in 1550 when the Chichimeca War occurred, where the Spanish fought against the Guamares, Pames, Zacatecos, and Guachichiles Indigenous groups. This combat extended and covered the second half of the sixteenth century. It was a prolonged war that lasted from1550 to1600.[38]

The most protected and most important road during almost the entire viceroyalty period, which eventually reached as far as New Mexico, was the Camino Real de Tierra Adentro. Around 1550, it linked Mexico City with Zacatecas.[39] Zacatecas's new mining sites had ethnic and cultural diversity, as Spaniards, people of African descent, Indigenous people from the north and south, mestizos, and more mixed people inhabited it. The mining city was founded in 1564. Initially, it had a society divided between workers and mine owners (almost always Spanish), who had to solve the food supply issue in an area not conducive to agriculture. The mining wealth, however, reached the hands of the mining workers, who had various remunerations. Apart from clothing and food, the mine owners allowed them, after meeting their quota, pepenar el metal (to pick and choose the metal) to mine it, sell it, and keep the profits. Often, the pepena system yielded more to the workers than their salaries.[40] Apart from the pepena, historians point out, a good number of mining workers received wages high enough to allow them some extravagance and even overindulgence, hence the increased sales and success of the merchants who had stores around the mines.[41]

However, the economic success came with misfortunes associated with mining work that included accidents; it was not unusual for pit roofs to collapse, crushing workers to death. The laborers also contracted throat conditions, often due to carbon monoxide poisoning from toxic air and fumes from candles and campfires. Pneumonia was likewise a common disease among mining workers. While the most common illness in the mining region was silicosis, contracted while laboring in fine dust from ore mills, one of the most feared diseases was mercury poisoning; although it was the mules that trampled the amalgam on the patio floors, the personnel had to walk through the muddy mineral to collect and wash it.[42]

Mining illnesses did not impede the town's economic good fortune, which the authorities exhibited during public fiestas. During those events, the local government and inhabitants spent large amounts of pesos on "the rejoicing and exaltation for the birth of the kings of Spain." One of those celebrations occurred in 1708 and was "a splendid celebration for the birth of Don Luis I." However, people had the same enthusiasm for religious festivities.[43] It is unsurprising that this mining community, with all its success, could have been compared to a Renaissance city. Its mining wealth was such that fluctuations in silver production were reflected in transatlantic trade, affecting European economic conditions. Around 1630, the place started a decline in metal production. After exhausting the veins and having served as a starting point for future exploration further north, in 1635, for example, Zacatecas decreased its silver production, affecting the value of the metal internationally.[44] That was when it opened the way to other nearby mining areas such as Santa Bárbara, San Joseph del Parral, and Chihuahua, among others, thus initiating a pattern of settlement and abandonment that would persist for the rest of the century and the next.[45] This phenomenon was not part of the utopian vision of the Renaissance man, who praised stable and well-maintained urban spaces and civilized societies, only to witness towns and cities of Northern New Spain, in many cases, vanish like magic.

In 1563, Francisco de Ibarra entered his new kingdom, which he named La Nueva Vizcaya, and where that same year he founded the city of Durango and claimed the entire region in the name of the Spanish Crown. However, the Indigenous Tepehuanes and their ancestors had lived there for centuries. Reference to this Native group is scarce. According to some anthropologists, it had a relationship with the prehistoric Chalchihuites-Loma people. Tepehuan was a community with a considerable number of inhabitants. As such, the area and group were attractive to Spaniards; they latter could use the former as a labor force. After the Spanish arrival, Tepehuanes were friendly, but after approximately four decades, in 1616, they organized a rebellion to expel the Spanish invaders but were unsuccessful, subsequently withdrawing into inaccessible parts of the Sierra Madre.[46]

Ibarra continued looking for favorable zones in the vast territory of La Nueva Vizcaya. In 1567 he discovered more metal in Santa Bárbara (the location established in 1530), where he started the first mining town of the several that later made up the provincia. He did not arrive alone but was accompanied by Christian soldiers that received lasting political power, like those of the Calatrava army in Castile who demanded rewards, noble titles, and land during the Reconquest. They oversaw appointing the first local authorities: mayors and justices. Later, these commanders came to depend on mayors, whom the governor of Nueva Vizcaya appointed. Contrary to what happened in the rest of New Spain, in the north, the alcaldes mayores could be vecinos (residents) of the jurisdiction assigned to them.[47] For the same motive, it is unsurprising that newly arrived rulers or local oligarchs initially controlled various parts of this frontier zone, which was more agricultural. Mining developed later, once those powerful men had to some degree addressed the lack of a workforce.

Once installed in Santa Bárbara, by 1570, the agricultural town of El Valle de San Bartolomé was functioning but not as the Spaniards wished. The inhabitants of the Tepehuan country vanished quickly under the Spaniards' demands for labor, and soon the Europeans were trying to solve the problem.[48] They had to look farther north for the labor force, and thus, along San Pedro and Concho Rivers, they found the Indigenous Conchos community. There they relied on another medieval custom Christian warriors practiced in Castile during the Reconquest in the eleventh and twelfth centuries: the transferring of groups of people to other communities to inhabit towns that had been vacated (in that instance by the Muslims) when Spaniards recovered them.[49]

The Concho community seemed to comprise many people. However, no count or estimate of their population is available. Their social and cultural past is little known, except that they lived in small settlements, practiced agriculture, and probably were sedentary. Some Spanish accounts suggest that Concho was a vast area with a single language that included more than one linguistic group. People from that community joined the Spanish, working for them and fighting for the Spanish Empire when necessary. Indian leaders or caciques provided military forces and workers. This cooperation developed the larger political Conchos' administration unit with an Indian leader appointed, along with the governor's office. At the same time, the "conchería" population grew as other tribal groups joined, such as Salineros and Tobosos. The relationship between Conchos and Spaniards was not always pacific, with the Indigenous directing two major revolts in 1644 and 1684 against Spaniards.[50] More Indigenous people continued arriving in the provincia from neighboring areas, not of their own will but as captives slated for forced labor in encomiendas and repartimientos or as enslaved people. The viceroyalty abolished this compulsory work without remuneration in 1551 as part of a law that, as this book will show, was generally neglected.[51]

The Just War and Slave Trade: A Viable Medieval Resource

A Spanish Reconquest version of slavery manifested in the provincia. By the seventeenth century, in some cities of Spain and especially in the Mediterranean area, the primary sources that provided enslaved people were La Guerra Justa (penal labor), and commercial activity. These two channels took on a particular significance with Muslims. The Christian mistrust of the Mudéjar, Muslims that remained in Spanish Kingdoms after the Reconquest, and free Muslims, led Christian institutions to control and subjugate them in ways other than their capture in war. For example, authorities apprehended any Mudéjar who left the kingdom without a royal license. This type of capture was considered a justified tactic of a "good war." Thus, these Mudéjar became enslaved criminals of the crown. Convicted of capital offenses, the captives were offered an alternative to being stoned or whipped to death: the king granted them life in perpetual slavery.[52] Moreover, especially in Seville, it was common for the elite to have enslaved Africans in domestic service, in factory workshops, or as workers in other companies.[53]

In the middle of the sixteenth century, Spanish legislation prohibited the slavery of Native Americans due to their exacerbated reduction after the epidemics brought from Europe. This law applied to the center and south of New Spain but not the north. The justification for this discrepancy was the need for labor in the northern mines, but above all, because the "war Indians" inhabited this vast area: a perfect opportunity to recur to La Guerra Justa and, by this means, to make enslaved people of those captive Natives.[54] Two large missionary zones—one Jesuit located in Sonora and another Franciscan situated in New Mexico—provided enslaved captives as labor to meet the demands of the agricultural, ranch, and mining production of the towns of the provincia.[55] The clergy opposed the capture of Indigenous people through La Guerra Justa due to the cruelty the soldiers showed in the hunting of these groups. Nevertheless, the viceroyalty government and society justified almost any war policy in the North. It was frequent, for example, that the Spaniards, the Just Warriors, deprived these communities of some goods to provoke resistance or rebellion and to turn them into "indomitable Indians of war," whom they could legally make captives.[56]

Other arbitrariness arose when the Natives defended themselves from Spanish abuse, escaped, or failed to pay tribute, as the governing authority considered all these actions as uprising. Thus, with the permission of the governor, or even on his initiative, the Spanish inhabitants of the provincia launched La Guerra Justa against the Indigenous rebels throughout the seventeenth and early eighteenth centuries.[57] By the time of the establishment of Santa Bárbara, for example, authorities had already distributed lands and Indigenous people among the settlers.[58] In fact, around 1581, people knew that the town of Santa Bárbara was a "slave market." Owners used these enslaved people for personal or hacienda service.[59] And it was the encomienda or repartimiento system that distributed forced Indigenous workers.[60]

The repartimiento system, commonly known as encomienda, had its roots in medieval Spain. During the Reconquest period, the Spanish used the land and people they took from the Moors. They acted on their presumed right and jurisdiction to regard them as a workforce (feudal service). This system took on a different character in the Americas. The Spanish no longer had land rights over the Indigenous territories, but they did over the inhabitants under tribute. During the Spanish expansion, the system frequently took the form of labor obligations.[61] The first estancias (small farms) of grain established around 1570 throughout El Valle de San Bartolomé employed the encomienda and repartimiento systems, although here and throughout the provincia, those two systems existed separately and had different meanings. The differences were few, especially after 1582, when Indigenous labor was seasonal. The encomienda reserved Indigenous peoples for the Spaniards, who requested these workers each season to secure a permanent workforce. Repartimiento did not commit the labor force for anyone. Spanish individuals could requisition them according to their labor needs each season.[62] However, captive Indians were not a reliable workforce in the provincia, as some fled, taking refuge in the enclaves of the Sierra Madre. Others perished due to the epidemics that struck the area in the sixteenth century, reducing these groups considerably.[63]

To face that inconvenience, Spaniards had to rely, again, on the medieval custom of transferring groups to reconquered places. To El Valle de San Bartolomé, they transferred Mexicano Indigenous groups of "paz" (peace) to serve as an example of proper behavior to the Conchos. The transfer comprised a few dozen families from the central highlands who spoke Nahuatl but were not Tlaxclatecas. Although it is true that in 1590 the famous transfer of Tlaxcala Indians to Saltillo took place to settle in San Esteban de la Nueva Tlaxcala, no document affirms that the provincia's newcomers were part of the Tlaxcala group. Still, the arrival of Indigenous Mexicanos at El Valle de San Bartolomé was probably part of that massive, forced migration.[64]

Those Indigenous people settled in places called naboríos or laboríos. The word "naborío" is the equivalent of "yanacona," a word of Quechua origin that Spaniards used in South America to distinguish "helpful" Indigenous people.[65] New Spain used the word naborío. Over time, the north identified them as mine workers living in "labor," and from there the term "laborío" surged.[66] Creating a Jesuit mission in El Valle de San Bartolomé was another medieval effort to transfer Indigenous groups in 1602. That year, around 500 Tepehuanes from the central north settled.[67] After the loss of the Indigenous population in the central highlands, there were no more transfers of Indigenous of "peace." At the end of a century, as we will see, the Mexicanos Indians of El Valle de San Bartolomé disappeared, joined the laborío estates, mixed, fled, or died.[68] In fact, conditions in the area were not favorable to create the Jesuit mission because of the increase of Indigenous rebellions.[69] The Acaxees, for example, rebelled in 1601 and 1603.[70] By 1604, the inhabitants of the town of Santa Bárbara forgot about mining and turned instead to agriculture. Around 1607, though, new metal deposits were discovered in the village of Minas Nuevas. This event caused a good number of inhabitants of the provincia to emigrate to this mining town, including some residents of Santa Bárbara.[71] Eventually, the efforts to create a prosperous community in El Valle de San Bartolomé slipped away since the Indigenous rebellions continued. The Xiximes fought in 1610 and 1611, for example, with the largest Indigenous revolt in the Nueva Vizcaya being that of the Tepehuanes in 1616.[72]

Franciscan Missions

In the provincia, mission work was supposed to solve at least two crucial issues for Spaniards: facilitating and organizing agricultural labor and Christianizing those workers. However, those goals were simply unfulfilled ambitions. The religious orders' endeavors in the area started around 1590. While Jesuits concentrated in the Sierra Madre's Indigenous communities, Franciscan missionaries started administering the Conchos Indigenous people and eventually established convent missions in the towns of Santa Bárbara, El Valle de San Bartolomé, and other towns.[73] In 1598, Franciscans founded Parras Mission and in 1604, San Francisco de Conchos Mission, where they transferred Conchos Indigenous people to work on the haciendas.[74] The priests' endeavor continued in a northern area called Jesucristo Northern mission field where in 1608 they founded Tepehuanes Mission; in 1611, San Pablo Balleza Mission; and in 1680, the Upper Tarahumara Mission. There are no useful records left of the missionary Franciscan work. Those that exist are incomplete or fragmented and do not inform about the tribal affiliation of Indigenous inhabitants because the priests did not keep a record of that information, at least not until 1657. Some scholars judge those priests as ignorant of Indian ethnic affiliation. Nonetheless, some documents mention the Franciscan Convent in

El Valle de San Bartolomé, which began around 1663. The data reveal that since the beginning, Spaniards brought all or almost all the Natives from elsewhere to work on the farms and ranches and placed those workers in haciendas. The Franciscan mission in El Valle de San Bartolomé and Santa Bárbara was an illusion because the priests could never reduce local or foreign Indigenous people to a town or pueblo. In 1622, for example, the provincia had 1,003 Indians as inhabitants. The number grew to 1,125 in 1630, of which 1,075 lived outside the area.[75]

In San Joseph del Parral, as early as 1632, some of them belonged to foundry crews that Juan de Inurso and Juan de Paz supervised and were also found on lists of Indigenous debtors, as some of them owned money to Capitán Rodrigo Aldana Beltrán.[76] By the second half of the seventeenth century, some Indigenous people worked as assistants to muleteers and carters, or were part of the staff of the Nuestra Señora de la Candelaria, an Indian hospital in the Yaqui neighborhood.[77] In rare cases, Indigenous men—most of them among the Mexicanos who were transferred from Central and South Mexico during the sixteenth century—managed to acquire land, and some even made wills. One land title was registered in 1632 to Gregorio Francisco Indio Mexicano. In 1634, Juan Francisco Indio Naborío listed his foundry farm and ranch in his testament. In 1665, Miguel Franco and Juan Francisco, and in 1673 Juan Diego Indio, left testaments that indicated they owned lands as well.[78] This information invites us to inquire if belonging to a foreign Indigenous group included having certain privileges such as owning property. It is an aspect to be explored in the coming chapters. However, outside the work environment, there were occasions when Indigenous men were the protagonists of some disorders in the town. In 1633, Nicolás de la Nación Concho was accused of "serious and heinous crimes that he has committed in the company of others . . . raiding the fields, slaughtering cows, and stealing married women from their husbands."[79]

By the second half of the seventeenth century, of the approximately 8,500 San Joseph del Parral inhabitants, 5,500 were Indigenous people, local or foreign. In the late sixteenth century and early seventeenth, Indigenous men primarily engaged in agricultural or mining work.[80] In 1700, only eight to ten Natives lived there. Actually, by the first decades of the 1700s, many of the Indigenous groups had become assimilated and acculturated, and by the end of the century, Indigenous people were a minority.[81] Nonetheless, we can assume that the Franciscans' methods contributed to the reduction of Indigenous people in the missions. In 1715, the Bishop of Durango conducted an inspection tour of Nueva Vizacaya's Jesuits and Franciscan missions. The Jesuits' holdings required no remedy, but the Franciscans' revealed the opposite. Among items on the long to-do list were rectifying the meager conditions of churches: e.g., the absence of religious adornments/ornaments and a repository for the Holy Sacrament. Furthermore, the Indigenous people were poorly instructed in the Spanish language and Catholicism. The report detailed how those individuals lived in poverty, learned no skill or trade, did not know how to read or write, and did not even have church music. The truth was that the Franciscan friars did not learn the Native tongues, except Mexican or Nahuatl. The statement also reflected the Indigenous people's dissatisfaction with missionaries, and the reasons were varied: they had to pay the fathers with a certain amount of goods when they did not assist with corn crops, were used as messengers and sent to distant places, were not allowed to elect an Indian town governor, and were little assisted to maintain separate ethnic groups at the missions.[82]

Santa Bárbara's mining venture did not last. By 1626, as the industry declined, the population gradually dispersed to the point that the place became a ghost town.[83] Formed around 1620, the agricultural town of San Francisco de Conchos survived longer. People built houses behind the Church of San Pedro and opened new irrigation canals to cultivate gardens using labor from the missions. Muleteers, cart drivers, humble merchants, and adventurers came from different parts. Inhabitants sowed vegetables and fruits. Nevertheless, once again, the town was rapidly depopulated.[84] This phenomenon characterized most mining sites of Northern New Spain, at least until the provincia began a renaissance with an increase in population.

During the middle of the seventeenth century, the need for regular and specialized labor in the provincia led the landowners and miners of the area to resort again to transferring free Indigenous workers from the center and south, from the northwest of New Spain, or adjacent places. Relevantly, the Sonora and Sinaloa Indians and the Mexicanos and Tarascos had experience in mining and metallurgy. They were also necessary for planting wheat, extracting metals, and populating towns lacking enough inhabitants. Even so, these foreign Natives, together with the few Spaniards and other ethnic groups that occupied the area, never represented a significant number of people to provide sufficient and constant labor.[85]

During this renaissance period, the settled Spanish population grew with those who preferred to stay and not emigrate to New Mexico. Other Spaniards also arrived hoping to benefit from the encomienda or repartimiento of Indigenous people to start mining and hacienda production. In addition, the Spanish hunting of captive Indians in the area decreased, mainly due to the arrival of Indians newly detached from the missions and the repartimiento system. This situation allowed agriculture and livestock development in the provincia, so that it became a vital settlement place. In 1619 it was considered the most productive agricultural area of Nueva Vizcaya, after Saltillo. In the same way, the settlers took advantage of the local Tepehuanes and Tarahumaras workforce, which had increased because of the launch of more missions in the area that continued to group and grant Indigenous people in encomienda.[86]

In 1624, the missions of the Society of Jesus appeared: Santa Cruz del Río Nazas, with 400 Indigenous Tepehuanes and Xiximes; Santa María del Cerro Gordo, with Indigenous people from the plains; San Miguel de las Bocas, with Tarahumaras; and San Felipe.[87] The last instituted were the missions of San Jerónimo de Huejotitán in 1633 and, six years later, San Felipe del Río Conchos, with Jesuits administering both.[88] Among the Indigenous groups that provided labor on the haciendas, the Tarahumaras distinguished themselves by being a source of free and temporary work. They generally belonged to Jesuit missions and were never subjected to forced labor, in part because they were somewhat rebellious.[89]

Population growth during the first three decades of the seventeenth century was resulted from a good number of deserters from the town of Indé and El Valle de San Bartolomé removing to villages of the provincia. In addition, the Franciscan priests returned to the town of Santa Bárbara, where they located Indigenous of "paz" in their convent. Likewise, between 1631 and 1634, the inhabitants of the town adjacent to the parish of San Pedro in El Valle de San Bartolomé went to try their luck with the newly established mines: San Diego de Minas and San Joseph del Parral.[90] By 1632, the provincia consisted mainly of the towns of San Miguel de las Bocas, San Buenaventura de Atotonilco, San Diego de Minas Nuevas (mining town), San Francisco del Oro (mining town), Valle de San Bartolomé, Todos los Santos, Río la Ciénega, San Francisco de Conchos, Santa Bárbara, Indé, and San Joseph del Parral (mining town).[91]

San Joseph del Parral emerged between 1631 and 1632 and soon would face situations it was not able to solve and that affected its population in different periods. In 1640 and 1642, the town experienced droughts. In 1643, famine and plague beleaguered the provincia. From 1644 to 1645, the Indigenous Conchos war occurred, while in 1647, the plague reappeared. The epidemics continued until 1649, and in 1651 the plague reappeared once again. A Tarahumara uprising occurred between 1655 and 1657, and in 1668 another famine, followed by an influenza epidemic.[92] Nonetheless, the mining town became one of the most prosperous in Northern New Spain. The *provincia* showed population and mining stability until around 1730, with the founding of San Felipe El Real de Chihuahua, a town rich in silver and inhabitants.

End of the Account of the Conquest of La Frontera Bárbara

The idea the Spanish men had about Northern New Spain vanished; the utopia was far from reach. The *adelantados*, with the support of the crown and the Catholic Church's messianic ideas and Augustinian spirit, managed to enter the vast frontier territory and ventured beyond Nueva Galicia. Perhaps as medieval-like warriors, they were ready to face the northern Indigenous groups as the Apostle Santiago had the Moors during the Reconquest. Only they never found the prosperous Renaissance American cities described in various chronicles or spread by word of mouth throughout Spanish cities.

In their ignorance, they did not know that Northern New Spain had a past, too. The Chalchihuites and Loma peoples' culture was the predecessor of different Indigenous groups such as the Tepehuanes, Conchos, Tecuexes, Cazcanes, Acaxees, Xiximes, and others that the *adelantados* viewed as Chichimecas, or demons. As most of those native communities resisted being reduced under mission pueblos, the Spaniards forgot about the civilized-modern cities they were supposed to create to solve real issues: the lack of agricultural and mining labor in the *provincia* led them to impose practices from Reconquest time that seemed to be still fresh in their minds. As Gregorio Francisco Indio Mexicano, Miguel Franco Indio, Juan Francisco Indio Naborío, Nicolás Concho Indio, and the rest of the Conchos, Tepehuanes, and Tobosos Indigenous people portray in the *pliego suelto* that opens this chapter, the Spanish memory of the medieval infidel, barbarian and warlike, found fertile soil in Northern New Spain to serve God and the king as any good Christian warrior had previously done. They revived previous practices such as the transfer of Indigenous people from the center and south of New Spain, the repartimiento system, La Guerra Justa, the slave trade, and the control of Indigenous people through permits to be removed from their territories, among other. Nonetheless, they faced the harsh reality of the northern mining zones: instability, illnesses and accidents, the sudden depletion of mineral veins, and the necessity of the migration of mining communities to survive. The impossibility of retaining workers impeded the mining venture, as Indigenous people escaped and took refuge in the complex geography of the Sierra Madre. As more Indigenous groups and enslaved people of African descent arrived from different parts of New Spain, the zone experienced transformations, although the medieval thought had already prearranged the role each actor would play in a historical scenario that required modern ideas and practices.

THE
AFRICAN DIASPORA

A BORDERLANDS LABYRINTH

In San Joseph del Parral, like in the principal cities in the Viceroyalty of New Spain, people are very devoted to religious fiestas. But Beatriz Negra Criolla, as do most of the inhabitants, prefers the Corpus Christi festivity because of its religious significance and its grandiosity. She arrived at the mining town in 1642 from the Taxco mines, located near Mexico City. On that midday, she walked around the plaza mayor with the rest of the individuals of different calidades who could be seen every year during this festive occasion. Among them were gachupines, Spanish women, men from different parts of New Spain, local and foreign Indians, and enslaved Africans, such as Diego Criollo Esclavo and Domingo Criollo Esclavo, who arrived at the town in the same decade as Beatriz. Suddenly, there was Ángela Esclava de la Nación Angola and Pedro Esclavo running through the bustle to catch up with Beatriz, Diego, and Domingo. All of them walked confidently, as if only for one day the town was theirs, except for María de Tierra de Angola and her three children, who were recently sold in the middle of the plaza. Perhaps that was why she walked as if looking for someone or something. Soon, María and her children joined Beatriz, Ángela, Diego, Domingo, and Pedro. Gossiping and laughing together, all joined the procession that was about to start.

But in the town, there are also free Africans, as well as pardos and mestizos with many different skin tones, like those called chinos, moriscos, coyotes, lobos, and others of mixed blood. Daily, these persons dedicate themselves to their trades or jobs as merchants, miners, housewives, landowners, servants, tenateros (metal carriers), tailors, muleteers, or shoemakers. That day, many of them were also part of the festivity.

For the Corpus Christi celebration, all the faithful joined the procession that went through the streets laid out in 1635, the few urbanized blocks with plenty of vacant lots in that town in a valley squeezed between hills. The parade passed between houses, offices, and businesses in a cloud of dust. In a short time, everyone arrived at La Cruz Street, parallel to the Camino Real, and then to the main square, located in front of the San José Church, between El Camino Real y la Calle Veracruz that ran parallel to the river.

From there, some of the faithful looked at the houses located in the upper part of Calle de La Cruz, although these, like the rest of the town's dwellings, were modest, one-story buildings and "were not worthy of drawing attention," as Governor Diego de Guajardo declared in 1649.

It is true that in the great Mexico City, during Corpus Christi celebrations, the actors wear make-up and dress in the streets while rehearsing librettos for the plays they will present later, with which they stage the lives of various sanctified characters. There, people dressed as demons or giants lead the processions and stop to pray in front of the altars that the inhabitants build along the streets dedicated to the parade.

But the fascinating element in San Joseph del Parral is that, on the day of Corpus Christi's Mass, the religious institutions do their best to show off the Parish of San José. The faithful clean up the church, place the priest's throne, and decorate the enclosure with candles. During Holy Mass, the inhabitants, most of them repentant for their sins, delight themselves with the melodies from the harp, guitar, and organ the musicians play. There is no doubt that Beatriz, Ángela, Diego, Domingo, and María and her three children enjoyed every part of the festivity, as their faces looked pleased when they returned to their owners' houses.

T here is a long and complicated history behind this pliego suelto. The religious celebration it describes required a stable and organized society, and it was difficult for San Joseph del Parral to arrive at this point. Perhaps it was not until the influx of a variety of people, not only from different regions in New Spain but also from as far as Africa, that this mining town could organize a Corpus Christi celebration as pictured in the opening scene, thanks to the Catholic religious calendar that included those memorable days, when enslaved people could act as devoted Christians.[1]

This chapter introduces the African community in Northern New Spain—a subject that, as mentioned, has not received the attention it deserves in the historiography of La Nueva Vizcaya. The historical actors appearing in this pliego suelto have been living deadened lives, remaining silenced and hidden, manifest in the lack of surnames that, in fact, reflect the human dispossession they suffered when leaving their regions to be treated as merchandise. This chapter attempts to summarize the development of the slave trade since before the Spanish set foot in America, from Africa to the Canary Islands to Hispaniola, then to New Spain and its northern frontier, including San Joseph del Parral. Although no account can capture the degradation African people suffered during that shameful period in history, this section aspires to understand how people like Beatriz, Ángela, Domingo, Diego, Pedro, and María and her three children arrived in San Joseph del Parral. It also intends to show how people of African origin claimed their freedom long before arriving in America and how their demand continued up to the northern frontier. This chapter intends to reconstruct the historical setting for people of African descent to better comprehend their active involvement in religious rituals that reveals their capacity for both adaptation and continuation of cultural beliefs. Overall, this section wants to communicate how because of the insidious slave trade the Old World and New World were no longer the same; a different language was forged from modern and medieval ideologies and practices to justify cruelty.

From Africa and Iberia to the Atlantic

If it is true that Africans were strangers in the New World, they were not unknown for those who came from the Old World. Slavery had been part of Iberia's experience since the Roman occupation. However, it did not play a significant role in society until the fifteenth century, when the Portuguese started the slave trade between Africa and Europe.[2] Africa resisted early Portuguese attempts at raiding their coasts from 1482 until 1579, when due to wars and treaties the latter occupied Angola and initiated the slave trade.[3] Since the early fifteenth century, then, Africa experienced widespread religious conversions, starting with the Kongolese elite and eventually spreading to the rest of the population. How deep their understanding of Catholicism went is unclear, but scholars believe that they practiced a distinctly African form of Catholicism.[4]

It is also unknown whether Africans' exposure to Catholicism during those years contributed to the gradual increase of the African presence in Lisbon and Seville, the leading centers for African slavery by the turn of the sixteenth century. Although there are no accurate numbers of enslaved Africans in Spain, the census reflected that in 1565, 6,327 of the total population of 85,538 were enslaved individuals who mainly were Africans but included Moors and Moriscos as well, all concentrated in the cities of Seville, Cádiz, Málaga, Cartagena, and Granada. Those enslaved peoples were primarily used as household workers or as nursemaids and were active in Spanish cultural and religious life, as they could be members of cofradías, for example. They received the sacraments and could even be eligible to be buried in the parish cemeteries.[5] Nonetheless, the history of the African presence in Spain complicates even more with the coming of Muslims from Africa. The arrival was possible due to Arabs' control over coastal North Africa, among the Berber tribes since the middle of the seventh century. The process of Islamization of Africans was long and complex. Diverse elements intervened in its progression: for instance, men of religion communicating with local rulers, Arabs helping Africans to overcome droughts, and the need for conversion if Africans wished to join commercial networks.[6]

During the fifteenth century, Europe's development in navigation opened the maritime route toward the Atlantic, and its exploration was an expensive international operation. English, French, Polish, and Italian people, ships, and capital joined Iberians to reach areas that had no previous contact with the outside world. The Canary Islands were the first profitable places in the Atlantic, with sugar and wine production as well as cattle and slave markets. Eventually, French and Spanish-Castilla colonized the islands, and this experience propelled a more adventurous dream in 1492: to reach India. Its dreamer was Christopher Columbus, who received Spanish funding only to arrive, by mistake, in Hispaniola.[7]

Before 1503, the first African people in Hispaniola arrived illegally, and Taíno Indians were the first to face and succumb after the violent arrival of Spaniards, but not without resistance. Today's Hispaniola, comprising Puerto Rico, Dominican Republic, and Haiti, first received the African enslaved men and women from the Iberian kingdoms. Nevertheless, between 1504 and 1518, about 2,000 of them arrived directly from Africa, those that survived the horrors of the Middle Passage to serve as personal servants or to labor in mines and construction. By 1520, the demand increased due to the growth in the sugar industry and the reduction of the Indigenous population after the European spread of diseases. Perhaps because of those circumstances and the fact that Indians still outnumbered Africans, in 1519, the cacique Enriquillo started a rebellion among Taíno Indians and officially declare war in 1523. Furthermore, on Christmas Day of 1521, African people rebelled. The result of these uprisings reverberated among the Indigenous and African people.[8]

In 1526, the Ordenanzas of Granada were instituted to prevent Indigenous revolts and to protect the Indians from enslavement and exploitation in parts of America. By 1537, Pope Paul III declared all Indians free, and the New Laws of 1542 surged to regulate the encomienda system. As for the African people, in its attempt to prevent those individuals' insurrections, the crown issued an order that included the Catholic Church's recommendation: Africans would be more content if allowed to marry and to work for wages so they could eventually buy their freedom. But this order was only one side of the coin; the other side stated the order was issued in hopes that the Africans refrain from rebellions and fleeing to the mountains.[9]

For the history of America, the importance of Hispaniola resided in the formation and spread of relation patterns between enslavers and enslaved individuals, including rebellions.[10] However, those were not the only extended patterns transferred to America. Since their presence and occupation of Hispaniola, Ferdinand and Isabella showed their intentions to protect their Christianized Indians. Therefore, they prohibited the transfer to America of Moors, Jews, heretics, and new converts, except if they were enslaved Black people.[11] However, academics who have studied Santiago de la Paz's documentation propose that Blacks brought directly from Africa in the early sixteenth century could have come from the Cape Verde Islands, and previously from West African Upper Guinea. Among those Africans were Muslims, as their last names that were part of an inventory list from 1547 revealed.[12] As we will see, this pattern was transferred to America: from Hispaniola to Cuba to Central Mexico and from there out to the future provinces, from Florida to Honduras, but not before passing by New Spain provinces. Among them was La Provincia de Santa Bárbara and its town San Joseph del Parral where, as the pliego suelto that opens this chapter describes, Beatríz Negra Criolla, Diego Criollo Esclavo, Domingo Criollo Esclavo, Pedro Esclavo, Ángela Esclava de la Nación Angola, and

María de Tierra de Angola and her three children had much fun one day at the Corpus Christi celebration. Now we would like to know their diasporic experience; how did they arrive in that corner of the world?

To New Spain up to Nueva Vizcaya

African people, directly from Africa or from Iberia, had accompanied the Spaniards since they first set foot on the American lands they hoped to conquer, most often as enslaved individuals but also as explorers and, on occasion, as conquistadores.[13] However, the direct and massive importation of enslaved African men and women to America occurred until the end of the sixteenth century, with the decline of the Indigenous population due to the epidemics brought from Europe. That situation created a need for labor. The Spanish Crown solved this problem by granting the monopoly of African trafficking to Portuguese merchants from 1595 to 1640. In New Spain, the most significant remittances for domestic trade occurred between 1595 and 1622. During this time, authorized landings totaled approximately 50,000 enslaved Africans or "bozales" (from Africa) in the port of Veracruz, usually obtained employing smuggling or as captives.[14] It is important to emphasize that numbers are approximate. Before 1650, for example, the illegal entrance of African enslaved people was common. Furthermore, New Spain's domestic trade had no formal structure. Usually, local vendors unconnected with external trade sold the enslaved people, including "criollos" (born in Mexico/New World), directly to their masters. Consequently, documents do not inform about a particular pattern for the internal distribution of enslaved people in early New Spain except for Veracruz, Puebla, and Mexico City.[15]

During the first half of the sixteenth century, nearly 500 Africans arrived annually in New Spain. However, the numbers for the years between 1521 to 1639 grew to 900 Africans per year.[16] From 1545 to 1556, of 196 bozales, only 80.1 percent were from the Senegambia

and Guinea regions, and 12.3 percent from other parts of West
Africa.[17] The census of 1570 noted the presence of 8,000 enslaved
individuals that came from Guinea and Cape Verde and 1,000
mulatos (mixed African and European), all living in Mexico City.
Nonetheless, the height of the slave trade in New Spain was from
1580 to 1640. As the numbers grew, the origin of Africans brought
to Spanish America changed. By 1595, for example, most were
identified as Angolans. By 1640, the number of enslaved people
coming from Africa reached 110,000. The 1646 census indicated
that the total number of people of African descent in New Spain
was 151,618, with 62,814 located in the archdiocese of Mexico,
23,840 in the dioceses of Michoacán and Tlaxcala, and 42,409 in
the dioceses of Nueva Galicia, Yucatán, and Chiapas. Furthermore,
of 151,618 individuals, 116,529 were largely free mulatos, while
35,089 were still enslaved.[18] The ethnic composition of African-born
individuals in the seventeenth century was Angola-Luanda (the
majority) and Kongo-Bakongo peoples. This change was a consequence of English, Dutch, and French challenges to the Portuguese
monopoly on the Guinea coast; the latter then moved southwards to
find cheaper enslaved individuals, but the ethnic variation was also
due to the aggressive entrance of Portuguese to the Angola region.[19]

With those numbers, New Spain became the second-largest
enslaved population and the most extensive group of free people
of African descent in the New World.[20] Nonetheless, the ethnic
composition of people of African descent experienced an expected
change: criollos' numbers eventually grew in the second half of
the sixteenth century and in the initial decades of the seventeenth.
Between 1570 and 1646, the criollo population grew from 2,437 to
116,529. Furthermore, by 1670, the number of free mulatos and persons of African-Indigenous heritage (pardos) increased. Generally,
African descendants physically blended only to become absorbed
by the mestizo population to the point that, by 1810, of the total
population of 624,000, only 10 percent were considered people of

African descent.[21] Before we arrive at those late years in New Spain, however, we enter into the lives of people of African descent who, perhaps miraculously, arrived at the northern frontier to be an active part of its unique cultural development.

The first requests for African enslaved people to perform mining work in Northern New Spain started around 1580 when Viceroy Martín Enríquez asked the Spanish Crown for 2,000 to 3,000 enslaved individuals. Epidemics had devastated the Indigenous workforce and, consequently, the mining industry causing the closure of various mines in Zacatecas. It is unknown how many of those individuals were sent to Zacatecas, but after 1576 some traders acquired licenses to deliver enslaved people in the area. However, records indicate that the numbers were insufficient to solve the labor problem in the mines because from 1582 to 1584, Viceroy Lorenzo Suárez de Mendoza continued to make those requests. Then, in 1586, Viceroy Marqués de Villamanrique complained that the Indians had to perform hazardous work at the mines and needed to be relieved with 3,000 to 4,000 African enslaved workers. In 1590, he sent a letter again but with a different request: besides the 3,000 African enslaved workers, at least 8,000 free and mulatos in New Spain should be forced to work in the mines. The crown rejected his "idea." Lastly, Viceroy Don Luis Velasco continued with the task of writing letters to the crown to request African enslaved labor for Zacatecas mines in 1593, 1954, and 1596.[22]

The shortage of mine workers continued in 1601, including for the mines in Nueva Vizcaya. On this occasion, a letter asked again for 3,000 to 4,000 African enslaved individuals over the course of two or three years. The letter also requested Chinese, Japanese, and Javanese people from the Philippines since, according to the letter, those individuals were "more domesticated" than enslaved African people. The crown, in its attempt to solve the mining problem, in 1602 issued an order: free mulatos and negros (bozales) convicted of criminal offenses would be condemned to mining work. Although there are no exact numbers for the arrival of African enslaved people during all those years, scholars estimate that the first three decades of the seventeenth century were years when the slave trade increased in the mining zones.[23] In 1605, for example, the city of Zacatecas had about 800 enslaved people, bozales and mulatos, destined for the mines.[24] However, the mine crisis resurged again as the slave trade diminished by mid-1630. Then, authorities sent a series of petition letters in 1636, 1637, 1644, and 1645 asking for enslaved people for the Nueva Galicia and Nueva Vizcaya mines.[25]

African People in San Joseph del Parral

Usually, the enslaved African people who came to San Joseph del Parral were young, between 10 and 30 years old. Of the purchases made between 1632 and 1657, San Joseph del Parral residents acquired 80 percent.[26] There are about 800 records of sales of enslaved negro/bozal and mulato individuals. These transactions occurred between 1631 and 1675, even when Spain, after 1640, redirected slave imports to South America.[27] Another source indicates that this mining town had 1,100 enslaved African people in 1650. Twenty years before, the cost of enslaved African men under 45 was 900 pesos, more expensive than in central New Spain. However, the massive arrival of Indigenous people from other parts of the viceroyalty eventually reduced the price.[28] These enslaved individuals came mainly from Central and Eastern Africa, especially Angola, Mozambique, and Congo lands the Portuguese had colonized. Fewer enslaved people came from Manor than Biafra, Calabar, and Guinea. However, as noted, not all enslaved people were bozales in San Joseph del Parral; there were also criollo enslaved people.[29] These individuals generally came from Puerto Rico, Cuba, and Guatemala. In addition, other enslaved people called chinos arrived in the area, usually brought from India or the Portuguese Philippines (although the caste that arose from a mixture of Moorish-Spanish was also called chinos).[30] Furthermore, in the mining town there were individuals identified as mulatos.[31]

Taking into consideration the information provided in this chapter to follow the traces of Beatriz Negra Criolla, Domingo Esclavo Criollo, Diego Esclavo Criollo, Pedro Esclavo, Ángela de la Nación Angola, and María de la Tierra Angola and her three children—all of them inhabitants of San Joseph del Parral from 1640 to 1658—we can conclude that they were around 10 to 30 years old. However, there is no information about the children's ages. Most of those dates reflect the petition letters sent to the crown asking for enslaved Africans for La Nueva Vizcaya mines in 1637, 1644, and 1645. Furthermore, all of them were enslaved individuals, which agrees with the data about the number of free mulatos in New Spain increasing until 1670. However, this situation would apply only to Pedro Esclavo, since the rest were criollos or bozales, although the number of criollos grew during the first decades of the seventeenth century in New Spain.

According to primary sources, African criollos came from Puerto Rico, Cuba, and Guatemala to San Joseph del Parral. Nevertheless, due to the irregularities in recording the arrival of people of African descent and their illegal entrance, we should consider that those criollos could have arrived from La Nueva Galicia, Yucatán, or Chiapas. However, at those sites most of the people of African ancestry were free. Therefore, we could ask why Beatriz, Domingo, and Diego were not free during the first decades of the seventeenth century. Weren't they able to buy their freedom even though they were criollos and not "recently" arrived enslaved individuals?

Another possible explanation for the lack of freedom of those individuals is that they may have been free but were resold back into slavery. There is information that allows this assumption. A property title issued in 1642 identifies Alferéz Antonio de Robles as the seller of Beatriz Negra Criolla, who came from Taxco mines, to Fernando de Valdez, but that Captain Matías previously acquired her under the authorization of Juana Laures de Casaziego, a resident of Mexico City.[32] Even though Beatriz came from Taxco mines, she could have arrived there from Puerto Rico, Cuba, or Guatemala. Additionally, a claim issued by Juan Martínez de Yrigoyen and María Rodríguez against Sebastián de Montenegro for failure to comply with the contract for the sale of Diego Negro Criollo in 1640 could indicate that he arrived from the potential places as had Beatriz, which implies the possibility that he was resold.[33]

As for Ángela Esclava de la Nación Angola and María de Tierra de Angola and her three children, who arrived in the town in 1644 and 1658, respectively, their presence concurs with the information about more African people arriving from Angola in the first decades of the seventeenth century. Furthermore, identifying them through African places in official documentation could indicate they came directly from Africa but perhaps passed through different places in Mexico before they arrived at San Joseph del Parral, where Ángela Esclava de la Nación Angola was sold for 260 pesos, and Governor and Captain General del Reino de La Nueva Vizcaya y Caballero de la Orden de Santiago, Enrique Dávila y Pacheco bought María de Tierra de Angola and her three children around 1658.[34] All the data supplied in this chapter is important because it gives detailed information about the arrival of people of African descent to the mining town, material that will be helpful in the coming chapters that address the cultural contribution of the African community in New Spain and La Nueva Vizcaya.

Closing the African Diasporic Labyrinth

This summary about the Atlantic slave trade reveals thoughts and practices shared by imperial powers of the Old World that turned a blind eye to the dignity of people in favor of Western prosperity. Since the European exploration of the Canary Islands, Europeans realized how "unused" lands could be profitable to satisfy one of the new European demands: sugar. Their productivity was possible only with cheap Indigenous and African labor. Hispaniola's value was transferring slavery ideas and practices, including rebellions. This element indicates that the horrible Middle Passage was not passive. Since then, Africans have shown their survival struggle, interest in, and need to preserve their culture. As mentioned in the introduction, here we want to explore the possible transmission, creation, or recreation of African culture in San Joseph del Parral with Pardo's cofradía.

The early religious conversions among Congo people and their understanding of Catholicism, the increase of African individuals in Spanish cities probably due to exposure to Catholicism, the presence of Moors and Moriscos and Muslims from Africa, and all those people's active participation in cofradías are inciting details that complicate even further the African diaspora and the survival of African ideas and practices. This book will retake this theme in chapters 5 and 8 as it is necessary to first appreciate how the society of San Joseph del Parral functioned. In the coming chapter we will see how a northern culture developed as more diverse people arrived from different parts of Africa, Europe, Spain, and New Spain. The European culture praised the paterfamilias archetype, valued the social category of vecino, and normalized the use of Indigenous and African-descent people as forced labor, a custom that required the Spanish to look back, again, to their medieval Reconquest ideas and practices at a time in which they pretended to be modern.

CHAPTER 3

NEW SPAIN'S FRONTIER

A DIVERSE CAULDRON

It was early in 1646, on a winter morning, when even the clouds seemed to be grieving at the sad news. Just as the drops from the sky were falling, the inhabitants of San Joseph del Parral left their houses dressed in black to attend the funeral. Only God could contemplate the less fortunate from the heights as ants in rows coming out of the peripheral neighborhoods of San Nicolás, San Francisco, La Candelaria, Los Barrios Altos, and San Juan de Dios. Despite the weather and the sad occasion, criollas and mulatas, and even coyotas and lobas (coyote and wolf women, as other mixed individuals were called) carried their children. They seemed somewhat relieved, perhaps because the impeding event interrupted the hard work at their homes. And yes, Beatriz Esclava Criolla and Ángela Esclava de la Nación Angola could be seen among them carrying a child in each arm and another two among the long skirts. María de Tierra Angola, who was already a grandmother, also attended.

Everyone was heading to the plaza mayor, where the procession would leave. By the time more mixed-blood people from the peripheries arrived, the gachupines and others of their lineage had already reached it a long while before, since almost all lived in the central area where the principal events took place. As always, those Spanish men and women did not miss the opportunity to show off their clothes that morning, all clad in black. Some gachupines, who belonged to religious-military orders called Los

Caballeros de la Orden de Santiago and Los Caballeros de la Orden de Calatrava, helped to organize the pilgrimage and to ensure order and composure for those mining and service people who distinguished themselves by the lack of lights on their heads.

It was extremely necessary, even required, that these poor people and the rest of the faithful listen carefully to the baroque sermons that would remind them that life is transitory, that death is constantly stalking, and that none know when it would appear to wake mortals from their dreams and lead them, if they were good Christians, to the true and eternal life in Heaven. A couple of Franciscan priests prepared the sermons, accompanied by El Señor General Don Enrique Dávila y Pacheco, who at one time was Governor and Captain General of the Kingdom of Nueva Vizcaya, continued to be a Caballero de la Orden de Santiago (a knight of the Order of Santiago), and was the owner of María Esclava de la Nación Angola and her three children, whom he bought several years before.

After the sermons and other formalities, the procession began, which slowly, between religious songs, sobs, and the screams of children and some drunk individuals, went around the square to culminate in front of the church's cemetery, where they would bury the deceased. Two other Caballeros de Santiago carried a coffin, which was empty of the body but full of the soul of the departed one: Elizabeth of France, the wife of King of Spain Felipe IV. She had died more than two years before, but due to the distance, the news had just arrived, and it took time to get the money and organize the event. Thanks to the town crier's gossip, people quickly learned and talked about the details of poor Elizabeth's life and death. "She died at 41. She was young. No, she was old. She was sick. What kind of sickness? She died of bearing so many children, living and dead (and the abortions the poor woman had). She died of anger due to the infidelities of her husband. No—if that were the case, we would all have died by now." The laughter of the women closed the ceremony.

Some Spanish people then went to the plaza mayor to see the new merchandise, on that cold morning mostly Indian boys and girls captured during guerras justas a sangre y fuego ("just" wars of blood and fire) that

Andrés García Mulato and Sebastián Muñoz had brought from New Mexico. Some commented that those merchants did not have authorization to sell captive Indians as the Indigenous enslaved people seller Juan Manso did, but perhaps because of that the market was cheaper and sold fast. Still, as sometimes cheap retail is expensive, on occasion the stock was already sold.

Because of the intense cold and lack of money, the mixed people went to their jacales and, although the mine owners demanded that their workers return to labor after the funeral rite, none did.

This pliego suelto portrays a common day in the life of San Joseph del Parral society around 1640. It reminds us of the long distance between this area and Mexico City, and between the latter and the Iberian Peninsula, as significant news arrived very late. But it also reveals how a relatively young mining town had already formed as a diverse society walked through buildings and streets, joining the ritual. That did not mean they all were equals, though. Class and calidad divisions were clearly expressed through neighborhoods, clothing, the role each one played in the event, and racial categories that put everyone in their exact, "deserved" place. Spanish individuals with means, for example, could have both African and Indigenous enslaved people at their homes, thanks to some Reconquest practices still in vogue. The pliego suelto further introduces the chapter's main points: the town's notions and practices of class and calidad, where Spanish and people of European descent occupied the highest rank; the society's collaboration in the capture and trade of Indigenous people; the personal life of people of African descent; and the perplexity that existed with racial categorizations. Nonetheless, before covering the details of the diverse and complex society of San Joseph del Parral, this chapter summarizes the town's formation and conformation immediately after the finding of metal in what would be the place's precious jewel: Mina La Negrita.

Around 1632, the discovery of La Negrita mine opened the way to the establishment of San Joseph del Parral. From the time of the mine's discovery, almost all surrounding neighborhoods arose with around 300 residents and 400 mining estates. Mine owners and workers built houses, haciendas, and structures for civil and religious offices, merchants' businesses, barbershops, medical offices, carpenters' shops, tailors' houses, and butchers' shops, among other industries. Typically, the wealthy Spaniards established their homes in the center of town, near the Church of San José and the plaza mayor. Most houses were generally modest constructions, usually with a garden and a corral, and were attached. But the humble scope of the town did not prevent the governor of Nueva Vizcaya from establishing his residence there from the second half of the seventeenth century to the first half of the eighteenth.[1] By the middle of the seventeenth century, all those buildings surrounded La Iglesia de San José, the miners' santo patrón (patron saint), with la plaza mayor in front of it. While at this time the place had laid out the streets, some lots remained empty, but not for long since by 1640 the population increased.[2]

Data reflecting the number of inhabitants in the mining town are irregular. Historians estimate that in 1633 there were 1,200 to 1,300 individuals, of whom 400–500 were Spanish and 800 were servants. In 1635, the number increased to 5,000, with about 1,000 Spanish and 400 workers. However, the 5,000 inhabitants did not include repartimiento and foreign Indians since they were supposed to return to their places of origin. Those individuals arrived in large numbers from Sonora, Sinaloa, and New Mexico—between 1,300 and 3,500 of them during those years—as they replaced the workforce that escaped or died. Enslaved Indians were not part of the population censuses either since they were supposed to be sold and perhaps leave the town. There were approximately 1,000 of those during the second half of the seventeenth century. Therefore, if registers included foreign, repartimento, and enslaved Indians, by

1640, San Joseph del Parral could have had approximately 8,500 inhabitants, with 5,500 Indians: 2,000 permanent, 1,500 in repartimiento, 1,500 in nearby missions, and 500 enslaved.[3]

Most of those individuals lived in the peripheral areas, in the neighborhoods of San Nicolás, San Francisco, La Candelaria (later called Nuestra Señora del Rayo, and Barrio Yaqui), Los Barrios Altos, the Maese de Campo, San Juan de Dios, and Guanajuato. Each had a church or a chapel and boasted at least one bakery. In the second half of the seventeenth century, a direct stretch of the Camino Real, Camino de Carril de la Línea de Presidios, opened, linking the mining city of Zacatecas with San Joseph del Parral. That route had three presidios (garrisons): San Miguel del Cerro Gordo in 1646, El Pasaje in 1685, and San Pedro del Gallo in 1687. The route facilitated communication and the transfer of people and merchandise. This panorama constituted the northern mining area until the eighteenth century.[4]

Another factor that contributed to the lack of accuracy in population counts or censuses was that the number of vecinos does not precisely correspond to the number of inhabitants. When authorities established a mining town, they usually granted the title of vecino to all the men who requested it to secure a settlement. A vecino represented not an individual but a head of a family with a populated house, children, women, relatives, servants, or farm workers. In fact, individuals recently arrived in the new Hispanic towns were estantes (temporal inhabitants). They became vecinos only when they acquired a house, and almost all the men who came to a mining town aspired to have access to land, Indigenous people, and positions in local governments.[5]

This desire implied meeting the requirement of forming a paterfamilias unit: a family based on the Western European model that was patriarch-headed. It was expected to exercise firm yet benevolent and divinely granted authority over wife, children, and servants. This type of family was simultaneously a metaphor for a civil-urban society, the renaissance city ideal, which the Spanish elite mainly followed. For the man, marriage was a sign of stability and respect, especially if he wanted some public office in the government. Hence, Spanish men already in Northern New Spain were pressured to bring their wives and children in, if they had them, from Spain or wherever they were. Should the men lack such family ties, society expected them to get a wife and form a paterfamilias establishment.[6]

This situation does not necessarily imply that women did not benefit from belonging to a family as well. For them, marriage also provided security, of an economic nature especially among the elites, and was a sign of respect in general. Thus, through a paterfamilias position, they could acquire the designation of vecina, as indicated in several testamentary documents used in this investigation, where the name of the husband, living or deceased, precedes their name. Thus, indirectly, women could achieve the recognition given to the husband, in many cases employing an auto de vecindad, an official document in which the authority included the name of the new vecino in the cabildo book. Settlers with greater economic means could even be vecinos of several towns. For the less fortunate individuals, on the other hand, acquiring the status of vecino consisted of residing permanently, without the economic means necessary to maintain a paterfamilias model. Still, regardless of their being patriarchs or not in the full sense of the word, all these types of neighbors swore not to leave the place without the corresponding authorization, as well as to defend the town "in the name of the king."[7]

Class, Casta, and Calidad

The caste system originated in the Middle Ages when the mixtures of Christians, Jews, and Muslims occurred (the "Mozárabe/Mozarabic," for example, resulted from these blends). The phenomenon emerged in New Spain in the second half of the sixteenth century when the mixed population grew. Individuals identified as mestizos or mulatos began appearing in official administrative documents. During the eighteenth century, the caste system spread, including such classifications by authorities as coyote, mestizo-coyote, and mulato-coyote. These categories varied according to region or period.[8] However, in New Spain, access to bureaucratic or honorary positions, admission to regular convents, the reception of holy orders, obtaining ecclesiastical benefits, and access to the university required blood purity. Since the end of the seventeenth century, it could be requisite in case of opposition from relatives to marry into noble families. But everyday life did not rigorously demand pureza de sangre (purity of blood)—or rather, as will be seen, individuals transgressed that protocol without reservation. In many cases, caste separation did not have rigid formulas during the sixteenth century, and the subsequent century was inconsistent in its practice. In the eighteenth century, though, there was indeed more concern about distinguishing mixtures between individuals due to the high percentage of miscegenation. During the permanence of the viceroyalty, it was the concept of calidad, rather than pureza de sangre, that was more closely observed.[9]

Ordinarily, in New Spain's society, calidad was expressed in racial terms: Spanish, Indian, mestizo, mulato. At times, it reflected the individual's reputation, skin color, occupation, degree of economic resources, and even the purity of the blood, honor, integrity, and place of origin. Class, on the other hand, was understood in the classical sense, as it referred to economic level, occupation, and race.[10] Something that distinguished New Spain's society in Mexico was the malleability of social lines. Most of the communities included individuals who had migrated from other places, and their integration to the new site required some arrangements. Thus, the economic flow, acculturation, and racial mixture in several locations allowed certain people to pass from one ethnic category to another. Likewise, the "quality" of people was a social construction that included ethnicity, wealth, occupation, and personal behavior.

In theory, many people could improve their quality by hiding their African, Indigenous, mestizo, or mixed-blood roots by passing as "Spanish."[11] Nonetheless, as will be seen, in San Joseph del Parral some of the Spanish and Portuguese distinguished themselves from the rest not because of their presence in numbers but due to their access to economic resources and the power and influence those means provided them—although these did not preclude them from engaging in scandalous behavior.

In the second half of the seventeenth century, from the approximately 8,500 inhabitants (if the number includes Indigenous people) in San Joseph del Parral, the peninsular Spaniards represented around 400 vecinos who had a house populated with family and servants. They mainly were Andalusians (27 percent), followed in number by Portuguese (17 percent) and Asturians, Basques, Canarians, Aragonese, and Toledoans (7–9 percent), typically from rural areas. The Andalusians usually came from the ports of Seville and Cádiz, where troops left for the Indies. This phenomenon was a family chain of migrations from Spain to America, since those who arrived attracted their relatives. Many of humble social extraction were among peninsulares who attended the arms display between 1649 and 1650 in San Joseph del Parral. Few had an occupation, except for an assayer from Zaragoza and an Andalusian carpenter. Most of them came from rural places and, if they had some wealth, established themselves as merchants.[12] Likewise, among them were Spaniards who had been born in San Luis Potosí, Mexico City, and Puebla, or in parts of Nueva Galicia or Nueva Vizcaya.[13] In different parts of New Spain, Spanish individuals were called criollos. This research did not find this adjective in the archival documentation as referring to Spaniards but rather for mixed people or for those of African descent.

New Spain society first used the word "criollo" to identify Africans born in the Indies and eventually to catalog Spaniards born in New Spain.[14] In the seventeenth century, the term referred to a place of birth. The children of Spanish people born in New Spain, for example, were considered Spanish. However, as their number increased, "criollo" meant "a Spanish born in the New World." In San Joseph del Parral, more than half of the people that attended the 1650s arms display had been born in America. Up until this date, there was an economic difference between the Spanish from Europe and those born in America. Peninsular Spaniards married, had few children in their youth, and made twenty-two of the twenty-five wills. For the second part of the seventeenth century, more than half of them were born in America—most of them in New Spain and others in Nueva Vizcaya—indicating a growing number of "Spanish" criollos and, with this, a regional oligarchy force.[15]

Although Spaniards have been perceived primarily as wealthy miners, landowners, or merchants of good quality and class, the truth is that not all of them fulfilled those attributes. In mid-seventeenth century San Joseph del Parral, for example, some of them were nothing more than servants, as was a Spaniard named Andrés (no last name given).[16] Others did not follow Christian precepts. The Spaniard Damián de Ávila, for instance, did not lead a marital life as God intended; instead, "he lived scandalously with an Indian woman named María Pozole."[17] The Spaniard Pedro Robles kidnapped a woman named María Núñez.[18] The Spanish Juan Sánchez assassinated Francisco Bernal, a silversmith with whom he was playing cards, in 1641.[19] Furthermore, at times, the Spaniards made the rounds with Indigenous people or mulatos with whom they defied the law, perpetuating robberies indiscriminately. Such was the case of the Spanish Nicolás Moreno and mulato José de Carbajal when, in 1661, they were of stealing silver plates from houses. A similar case occurred in 1667 when Spaniards Felipe Pérez, Jiménez de la Higuera, Diego de Balbuena, and Simón Indio appeared in front of the authorities to respond to charges of robbery.[20]

Spanish women were not far behind in terms of economic solvency since more than one had mines and farms, as was the case of Doña Ana de Biezma.[21] Some Spanish women, on the other hand, did not escape seeing their reputation and honor diminished by being harassed by men, including Spaniards, especially when their husbands were absent. In 1642, Pedro Gónzalez, a 26-year-old merchant, was accused of "attempted adultery" with a married Spanish woman while her husband was absent. He attempted to force her, and when she rejected him, Gónzalez abused and insulted her.[22] In the same way, some Spanish women mistreated their enslaved Indigenous servants, just as Doña Francisca de Chávez had when she injured Nicolasa India in 1654.[23]

As regards the Portuguese, Spanish society considered them to be "foreigners" (not from Spain), so authorities prohibited them from trading. For this reason, the children of Portuguese born in Castile hid their parents' origin to venture into business. Among the Portuguese in America are descendants of the 6,000 Spanish Jews expelled from Spain in 1492, who emigrated to Portugal when it joined the Castilian Crown in 1580. Some returned to Seville, and others went to North Africa and the New World. After 1640, the Spanish Crown prohibited the Portuguese from emigrating because of the possibility of their being Judaizers. Authorities arrested those who were already in New Spain and confiscated their property. It was then that some arrived in the Nueva Vizcaya area. They were present in Santa Bárbara and San Joseph del Parral. In this mining town, for example, the Portuguese owned seven bakeries, a circumstance that remained for generations of families.[24] Luis Simois and Domingo de Caballo in 1705, and Don Jorge Rodriguez in 1718, among others, were active Portuguese merchants in San Joseph del Parral.[25]

The Just War against the Indigenous

Perceiving the frontier Indigenous people through a Reconquest lens was not exclusive to adelantados; it was a shared European vision. Punitive expeditions against Indigenous people occurred throughout the seventeenth century in San Joseph del Parral and other towns in the provincia. From 1652 to 1658, for example, the authorities of the mining town launched orders, petitions, and war proceedings against "the enemies of the Royal Crown," "los alzados" (rebels) who could be Indigenous Tarahumara, Tobosos, Nonoxes, Acoclames, Babanes, and Salineros, among others.[26] European inhabitants dedicated these wars "a sangre y fuego" (with blood and fire) to His Majesty or to the common good since the "enemy Indians" caused damage by committing robberies, murders, and other atrocities including the theft of women, children, and horses.[27] Apparently, appealing to the "common good" could motivate the provincia's inhabitants with enough wealth for them to get involved in La Guerra Justa to demonstrate their fealty to the Spanish Crown and the mining town and to consolidate or improve their social image. From 1649 to 1651, various residents of the provincia made contributions, some quite generous, to support Guerra Justa campaigns against the enemy Indians. For example, a neighbor of San Joseph del Parral, Doña Isabel de Urdiñola, gave twenty thousand pesos in reales to the cause.[28]

In general, most of the province neighbors with economic means generously responded to the rulers' requests as part of their campaigns against the rebels, which authorities labeled as donations to the common good and gifts were for His Majesty.[29] But His Majesty was also the owner of captured Indigenous people and had the right to sell them and receive the profit. There is a document from 1656 that indicates that Alcalde Juan de Aguilar ordered the neighbors (with money) to "visit His Majesty's carts that carry New Mexico Indians and would be sold . . . as slaves."[30] However, the alcalde's decree was totally against the royal order that Durango city made public "about not to enslave people of barbarous nations and not to send them to work without their contentment, with the purpose of keeping them in peace and including them in the Catholic faith."[31]

In San Joseph del Parral and its surroundings, the king and his European vassals were not the only ones who sold Indigenous enslaved people. Some mulato individuals engaged in war against Indigenous groups, capturing and placing them in carts. These cart owners moved the captive groups (commonly Indigenous Apaches and Mansos) from different parts of New Mexico. In 1649, for example, Andrés García Mulato and Sebastián Muñoz, cart owner and mayordomo (administrator) respectively, regularly went north of the river to reach Salinas, New Mexico, and raised "Indians, boys and girls" to sell them to the wealthy residents of San Joseph del Parral.[32] Usually, these carters requested permits from the town authority to sell Indigenous people. For example, one day in 1653, another cart owner named Juan Manso asked to sell the Apache Indians he brought in his carts. He also said:

> The Apache Indians were of the Nation that gives war to the entire kingdom of New Mexico . . . they also [engage] in battle with the Manso Indians of the North River, who are friends of the Spaniards, in whose war the Manso Indians captured many Apache Indians, who Don Luis Saldaña, son of the governor and the captain general . . . sent to rescue.[33]

As can be seen, Juan Manso used the official discourse to obtain the license that allowed him to sell Indigenous captives who were alleged to have waged violence against the inhabitants of New Mexico. Individuals such as Juan Manso captured Apache people during a war the latter held with Mansos, friends of the Spanish. That is, they captured Apache individuals during La Guerra Justa.

Furthermore, it is vital to observe that the governor's son, who apparently supported Juan Manso in selling captive Indigenous people, made the ransom order. That is an example of how the buyers were commonly Spaniards of wealth. Among them were women, such as Antonia de Urbaneja, who in 1650 asked the authorities to deliver "the Indians owed to her."[34] It seems that economically privileged people could invest their money buying "authorized slaves," who would eventually recoup the cost with many years of domestic work, in the fields, mines, or metal refineries. In 1655, for example, a vendor auctioned an Indian woman named Isabel and her two-year-old son for sale. Both were sold for 100 pesos to Capitán Juan Leal, and for that amount, they would be in slavery for ten years.[35] As with any commercial transaction, sometimes disagreements arose between sellers and buyers. In 1633, for example, someone denounced Bernardo de Los Santos for having sold some Indigenous women who already had owners.[36]

However, the periodic flight of Indigenous people did not impede Spanish vecinos in the area from continuing to try to solve the labor shortage with the repartimiento system. Archive texts reveal that the practice occurred from the seventeenth century to the middle of the eighteenth century. As the following documents demonstrate, miners and landowners searched the surrounding areas for Indigenous individuals to be used as forced laborers to make their companies profitable with the support of the viceroyalty government. From 1679 to 1720, some landowners and miners in the provincia requested the distribution of Indigenous people to be used as labor in their companies.[37] Among those landowners were some women, such as María Rosa Ortíz, who in 1725 requested thirty Indians from repartimiento to work on her farm.[38]

From 1710 to 1755, the authorities requested monetary donations or imposed contributions from inhabitants around the provincia to support guerras justas against the Indigenous. That happened to the residents of Durango in 1710, when the aid they provided was used to support Indigenous people captured and kept as prisoners of war during mobilizations. In San Juan del Río and Indé towns, around 1725, the alcaldes followed the order to "campaign" against the enemy Indians on certain days. But the residents of San Juan del Río responded with some requests: not to carry out these "raids" since they affected their commercial activities. Similarly, in 1755 the residents of San Felipe El Real de Chihuahua had to contribute and act as a physical force to "resist the barbarian Indians."[39]

La Guerra Justa, hunts or raids, authorities' campaigns or donations, and the strength of the neighbors gradually managed to achieve peace. On occasion, though, the only thing some Indigenous groups sought was peace. Something similar happened in 1704, 1708, and 1727 when the Acoclames and Cocoyomes asked authorities for a ceasefire.[40] In 1716, the Jano Indians did not ask for concord but rather announced their "surrender."[41] Whether it was a request for an accord or an announcement of defeat, the truth was that in 1712 an official escort entered the Indigenous territory of the Junta de los Ríos, significantly reducing the Apache population by 1718.[42] Neither the frequency of the hunts nor the number of Indigenous people captured is known for sure, but scholars estimate that a single expedition could capture a thousand Indians, more than enough to establish a slave market.[43] By the end of the eighteenth century, the enlightened Bourbon House still envisioned a world of "reason" with enslaved people. In 1792, it expedited a real provision about new regulations for the education, treatment, and occupations of enslaved individuals in all the Indies dominions, including the Philippines.[44]

The Life of People of African Descent

The sale of a bozal, mulato, or criollo enslaved individual functioned like the commercialization of any other object: property over which the owner had rights and exercised power (in this case, mainly in physical exploitation). On occasion, the sale transactions generated the owner's legal action because after having paid for "the merchandise," they did not receive it on time or even at all. In 1633, for example, Andrés González de Obregón filed a claim against the seller, Gregorio Carbajal, for not having turned over the enslaved Africans, Pablo and Catalina, who were husband and wife. Martín de Carbajal sued the merchant Francisco Lobato in 1640 for having resold the enslaved African person that he had already bought, and in the same year, Juan Martínez de Irigoyen and María Rodríguez denounced Sebastián de Montenegro for not fulfilling the contract sale of Diego Criollo Esclavo.[45]

Claims regarding bozales, mulatos, criollos, and Indigenous enslaved people were not limited to their commercialization. The enslaved individuals themselves began to file lawsuits where they or others denounced their owners' physical punishment. In 1634, shortly after mineral was found in the town, an enslaved individual named Blas Esclavo filed a complaint for "bad treatments" against Luis Subriel and Juan Rangel de Biezma. The latter was the founder of the mining town.[46] In 1648, Francisco Esclavo denounced his owner, Don Fernando de Valdez, "for bad treatment; his master wanting to tie him up."[47] In 1657, a neighbor accused Bartolomé Sáenz for mistreating Baltasar Negro de los Reyes and his Negra Wife.[48] At times, the masters' mistreatments culminated in the death of their enslaved servants. Such was the case in 1635 when Juan Esquivel Mestizo killed his servant Isidro Mulato Esclavo.[49] This type of violence was chancy because sometimes enslaved persons responded with the same coin. For example, that same year Alonso Mulato Esclavo killed his owner, the Spaniard Francisco González.[50]

As mentioned, in San Joseph del Parral, the sale of enslaved African-descent people occurred at least until the beginning of the second half of the eighteenth century, although the occurrence complicates itself when we consider that enslaved individuals were resold and rented. In 1651, Francisco Cañedo requested two enslaved individuals both named Domingo, who were property of Mateo Rodríguez.[51] In 1654, Juan de los Reyes Marchena requested María de Vera's slaves, a mulata and her four children.[52] In 1769, two enslaved women were sold. One was fourteen years old and was of "cocho color" (brown color). The other was nine and was of "color acollotado" (probably a derivation of the casta denomination "coyote").[53] In 1771, Atonacia Esclava and Faustina Esclava were already servants of Doña Isabel de Amparán and Juan Francisco de Miranda, but they were resold.[54] Furthermore, owners of enslaved individuals rented them as property. That was the case in 1677, when Ana Jorge and Isabel Jorge accused Antonio Rodríguez Soto of owing them the salaries of two of their enslaved men they rented to him.[55] And it seems to have been the case in 1723, when Manuel de Garay accused Pedro Mateo de los Hijuelos, Mayor Justice of Guapijuge, a town in Durango, of owing him some pesos, as Pedro had two enslaved persons, sons of María Escárcega Esclava, servant of María Méndez.[56]

During this long stretch, the enslaved person sometimes responded to abuse with means other than violence. Physical abuse, coupled with hard work and possibly a personal or family need for mobility, caused enslaved people to escape on several occasions. This problem led masters to develop control strategies, among which were branding the enslaved person's face, as Cristóbal did with Hipólito in 1641.[57] In some cases, the owners petitioned the authorities, who helped them with expeditions to locate enslaved-fugitive people and anyone involved with the escape.[58] The flight of enslaved people meant at least three investment losses for the owners: a decline in the production of their mine companies, a reduction of their pesos, and the loss of the possibility of including enslaved people as part of the assets they would inherit from their lineage.[59]

As chapter 9 will indicate, enslaved people of African descent appear as assets to inherit in a number of wills generated in the town. They were the subject of lawsuits and other problematic situations, often involving certain religious institutions and various segments of the population. But most of all, enslaved people of African descent were mine workers or domestic servants. A small number worked as coachmen, among other trades, such as in the craft industry. In 1633, Mengoreta, for example, was the servant of Sargento Mayor Juan Pérez de Bergara, while Francisco Mulato was a carpenter. In 1720, free Manuel Mulato became a coachman for one of the most important political figures in Nueva Vizcaya, Governor San Juan de Santa Cruz.[60]

Even though in the Iberian Peninsula Black people were considered to be a cursed caste and this belief supported a generalized idea that they deserved slavery, it provided ways for them to be free.[61] Las Siete Partidas was the legal code created in the thirteenth century as the legal basis for the Spanish monarchy. It stipulated that Black or white enslaved people could obtain their freedom through purchase (the most common way employed) by joining as a member of the clergy or as a donation or inheritance its owner made. In America, the Spanish Crown denied these means to the enslaved African-descent person, but only for a period.[62] In 1545, Bartolomé de las Casas initiated the debate that eventually gave the Indigenous a path to freedom. Later, the process of manumissions for enslaved Black people began. They could achieve their freedom through different legal channels, like the stipulations dictated in the code of Las Siete Partidas: purchase, inheritance, or a change the master requested. These routes increased the number of the free population and, at the same time, the desire of the viceroyalty to control African-descent and mixed people.[63]

Still, the growth in the number of free inhabitants resulted from the mixture of races, which implied the union between enslaved people and those free. For example, in San Joseph del Parral, Tarahumara women had lived in the area since the town started mining at the beginning of the seventeenth century. They mixed with bozales, and their mulato offspring were free. In fact, once they returned to their mother's place of origin, mainly from El Valle de Papigóchic in the Sierra Madre, the place had taken on the name El Valle de Santa Cruz de los Mulatos.[64] Additionally, children had the right to the freedom enjoyed by one parent, even if the other was not free. However, this situation was somewhat ambiguous. In many cases, the mixture of races was evident in physical features such as skin color and clothing. Therefore, non-Spanish individuals with light-dark skin dressed as Spaniards could improve their status or social image within their communities or before the government.

In 1648, for example, San Joseph del Parral's authorities identified the enslaved Antonio de Salazar as a "white mulato." He arrived from Mexico City to ask for his freedom, arguing he was the son of Don Benito Vázquez de Cueva, a free mulato.[65] In this case, the enslaved person had a first and last name and a racial classification made up of two categories that opposed each other. It is essential to note that the caste system in New Spain, as historian María Elena Martínez explains, took on its characteristics depending on the region and historical period.[66] Antonio de Salazar arrived from Mexico City, where the caste system and the idea of pureza de sangre took on particular characteristics: he probably had light-dark skin, dressed as a Spaniard, and his free father had first and last names. In San Joseph del Parral, the caste system was malleable. Salazar's father, Don Benito Vázquez de Cueva, bore the nickname "Don."

In medieval Spain, this title was a privilege granted only to royalty. By wearing it, noble knights who were members of the nobility wanted to distinguish themselves from the mob. In modern Spain, the title changed, as it was common for men of any class to call themselves "Don," except for the servants or the poor who worked in mechanical trades or rural areas.[67] New Spain reserved the titles of "Don" and "Doña" to Spaniards—that is, "Spaniards" who could be mestizos or of other races. Still, their countenance favored their European ancestors, from whom they took social prestige.[68] Thus, it is probable that Don Benito Vázquez de Cueva, who was a free mulato, had a "Spanish" physiognomy. With it, he "improved" his position and social image, as did his son. In addition, some African-descent enslaved individuals obtained freedom through wills, after the owner died. That was the case in 1668, when enslaved man Francisco Gallo and other enslaved people presented a demand against María de Cárdenas's testament where the deceased granted them freedom.[69]

During the seventeenth century, bozales and mulatos constituted a fifth of the population that received the sacrament of marriage. The number was significant until a certain point since they were rarely married. In addition, the data on baptisms in the town indicate that almost all the infants were born to mulato women, who usually were single mothers.[70] Those facts speak for the complex life people of African descent experienced. For example, the tailors Antonio de Talavera and Vicente Esparza were both accused of concubinaje (cohabitation). The first cohabited with a free mulato woman married to another man in 1642.[71] The second was accused of living in illicit friendship with Juana de Dios in 1743.[72] There were cases when mulato men and those of other races were interested in the same mulato woman, coming to compete for her attention in street fights or lawsuits. That was the case in 1717 when Nicolás Antonio Mulato and Juan "El Sombrero" de la Cruz-mozo engaged in a street fight over Úrsula Mulata, servant of Don Rafael de Ibarguén.[73] Or when in 1708, Tomás Indio Apache Esclavo accused Esteban Indio of kidnapping his woman, María Magdalena Mulata.[74] The cases of cohabitation with mulato women were not limited to bozal or mulato males but included concubinage relationships and even marriage with mestizo and Spanish men.[75]

Mulato women were protagonists in situations that reflected their status and the image society in San Joseph del Parral had of them. Sometimes they were accused of street brawls, as happened between Leonor de la Cruz, Ana María Balbuena, and Jusepa de Ontiveros in 1634.[76] Or as when the neighbors denounced Andrea Mulata, alias "La Palitranca," in 1716 for lack of morality, as she caused scandals while her husband was in the city of Guadalajara.[77] In another instance of male violence perpetrated against a woman, however, the merchant Gonzalo Álvarez raped María Macías Mulata in 1667.[78]

Negative perceptions and complex lifestyles did not prevent some mulato women from claiming their right to freedom on some occasions, as happened in 1641, when Agustina Mulata Esclava demanded the will of Martín Galindo, assuring that her owner granted her freedom in the document.[79] In Northern New Spain, the negative image of bozal or mulato women affected them beyond the personal since it extended to their relatives, especially their children. In 1720, for example, in the Province of Sonora, the neighbors opposed the appointment of Joaquín José de Rivera as Chief Justice because he had previously stated he was the son of a mulato woman.[80] San Joseph del Parral's wealthy spheres manifested prejudice toward people of African descent. It was usual for well-off neighbors to accuse free or enslaved bozal, mulato, or criollo individuals of theft of personal objects.[81] Similarly, on some occasions, the Holy Inquisition prosecuted mulato men and women for having had a pact with the devil.[82]

Mestizos or Padros? Indigenous or Mulatos? Coyotes or Lobos?

Typically, during the viceroyalty period, Indigenous people who were free workers lived in houses near the mining centers. In contrast, Indigenous workers and their families in southern Mexico usually lived in towns or congregations distant from the mines. The closeness between Spaniards and many Indigenous women who emigrated north of New Spain triggered miscegenation in mining areas. But the mestizo element was most pronounced in large towns of central Mexico with many Indigenous workers. Despite that fact, the mestizo percentage of the total population in the north was much more prominent due to the low density of Indigenous people.[83]

The most common racial category in the archives is mestizo or mestiza. Contrary to the situation of Indigenous and people of African descent, those individuals had last names in official records.

Among people identified as mestizos or mestizas in San Joseph del Parral was Sebastián de Alvarado, a tenatero, who in 1642 carried packages of raw metal out of the mine.[84] Juan de la Cruz, in 1651, was a mestizo owner of mines and Indigenous servants.[85] Amid women, Ana de Rentería, a single mestiza, cohabited with the mestizo Juan de León, who was married to another woman.[86] Some mestizo men had issues with the law, such as Juan Arzola, who organized prohibited games in 1671. In fact, it was typical for mestizos, along with mulatos and Indigenous individuals, to transgress the law or ordinances launched to safeguard the public order. The association between these three groups and the public and the illicit activities they sometimes carried out could have been a factor for the society of San Joseph del Parral to create a negative view of them, as reflected in ordinances or mandates' discourses.[87] But more than anything else, some primary documents show that authorities sometimes could not decide which categorization to apply to a given individual, since there is information about "Felipe Salas Mulato Indio" or "Andrés Rivers Mulato Indio" instead of "chino," which was the correct classification for this mixture in the casta system. In some cases, all racial categories were bundled in that could apply, e.g.: "Indio de la Nación Concho, o mulato, o mestizo."[88]

By the mid-sixteenth century, official documentation reflects how this system was functioning as an umbrella term for the offspring of mixed unions. Once the authorities applied casta classifications, those links began to acquire negative connotations, as the archival documents used in this book demonstrate. Mulato, for example, describes the offspring of Spanish and negro. Castizo, which appeared during the last third of the sixteenth century, applied to those born of a Spanish and mestizo (in Spain, this category had a positive connotation as it signaled good lineage and casta). Morisco was a more ambiguous classification associated with Islam, Africans, or both—although, in time, it referred to the offspring of Spanish and mulato. In the eighteenth century, casta categories included lobo, the mixture between "salta atrás" and mulato. The former resulted from unions between chino and Indio, and the latter from a Morisco with a Spanish. Coyote was the mixture of Indio with mestizo.[89]

Although the caste system was even less rigid in Northern than in Central New Spain, the documents consulted for this book reveal how the authorities in San Joseph del Parral had used all those categorizations since the sixteenth century and some that, as mentioned above, did not follow those more commonly used, such as mestizo coyote, mulato lobo, or coyote mestizo.[90] The archival documentation includes individuals identified as coyotes, Indio coyote, coyote blanco, and Morisco. The legal papers reflected both a positive and a negative image of those individuals in the community. In 1652, an ordinance accused Juan Soto Morisco of injury against an Indian.[91] In 1672, Antonio Moreno Coyote was charged with kidnapping a married woman.[92] In 1673, Franco Coyote was held to be a sacristan.[93] In 1709, someone accused Francisco Martin Lobo of robbery.[94] In 1720, Juan Martin Coyote had the same experience.[95] "El Cantero," a white coyote, was jailed for robbery and murder; he later escaped prison in Durango.[96] Nicolás de Chacras Lobo committed a robbery in 1724.[97] And in 1771, an Indio de Color Lobo falsely said he was the king of his nation and incited his people to revolt.[98]

Summary of the Diverse Mask of the Frontier

As observed, the oligarchy or mining-agricultural elite roughly solved the settlement problem for effective economic development, but the social situation was getting out of control. Spanish vecinos abused their servants, the free African population increased due to the mix of races, the caste system was malleable, and enslaved people were escaping, not to mention the area's experiencing drought, epidemics, and rebellions. In truth, this was a complex, diverse society comprised of men and women who lived in the extremes of wealth and poverty and between spiritual and profane life, as we will see.

The enslaved population, free African people, and individuals of all castas could be locals or foreigners, free or captive, domestic workers or miners, single mothers, or concubines, abused or abusers, or Indian landowners. Enslaved African-descent people who were part of the "goods" handed down in wills wished to demonstrate their calidad, in some cases even passing as "Spanish." The Spanish Crown and the Catholic Church tried to adapt their government and their religious rituals to the geographical, political, economic, and social particularities of Northern New Spain. In fact, they found fruitful land in San Joseph del Parral, a mining town with a diverse and mobile population that lacked a homogeneous culture.

This chapter provides a clearer vision of San joseph del Parral's past in terms of government, population, race composition, social conventions, labor, ideology, and Spanish cultural memory and identity. At the same time, it provokes further research about the presence of mulato communities in the Sierra Madre, where the offspring of Tarahumara women, for example, were part of the community called El Valle de la Santa Cruz de Los Mulatos. Broadly, the chapter reflects how the diverse inhabitants made the mining miracle possible and is an antechamber for the next section. The latter will cover a Spanish Baroque celebration: Carnival, a three-day celebration that uncovers the creation of a vicious but necessary mining workforce and the birth of a local culture and identity. During this celebration, individuals without last names in the archival documentation walked in procession along the dusty streets surrounded by modest houses and businesses from where everyone could see, at the top of the hill, La Negrita mine, a witness to the variety of ways those mixed peoples used rituals to transform a universal religious experience.

CHAPTER 4

CARNIVAL

A MINING TOWN UPSIDE DOWN

*During the three days of carnestolendas (Carnival), nights are a true
pleasure, with fireworks illuminating the streets of San Joseph del Parral
this year of 1649. Carnival is a special occasion not only because it is
not carried out in most cities throughout New Spain but also because it
is when many inhabitants dress in the costumes and masks they keep in
their trunks throughout the year. There is no doubt that with those getups,
more than one—even some Spanish vecinos—would try to conceal a bad
reputation for having been perpetrators of shameful crimes and for living
a scandalous private life, according to what gossiping people were saying
in the corners of the plaza mayor.*

*Spanish women, among them a few owners of mines and land,
wore the best dresses they had bought in Mexico City, Guadalajara,
or Puebla de Los Ángeles. As usual, one or two Indigenous or mulato
servants accompanied them to show off the españolas' prestige, according to some mestizas who were buying fruit water in one of the
stalls. These latter, affecting to pass as Spanish, walked around in
their Sunday dresses, which they bought from the town's seamstress.
Most of the mulato and criollo women made their dresses themselves
from scraps of fabric given to them at the church. Yet, some of them
managed to wear dresses very similar to those of the Spanish women,
as some have illicit friendships with men with resources, according to*

*the Spanish women in the main square under the shade of blankets
draped overhead.*

*Some men who call themselves españoles were drinking a glass of wine
at the cantina. Those gossipmongers talked about how often mixed individuals end up getting drunk on the wines that a merchant sells them,
how all curse, cause riots, and, late into the night and drunk, they fight,
sometimes killing each other. Meanwhile, one or two mestizos leaving
the bakery talked about having seen an Indigenous woman who tried to
go unnoticed in the crowd after fleeing jail.*

*A few of the visitors said that in this town, the carnestolendas fail to
provide enough material for a colorful or ostentatious spectacle like those
of Corpus Christi festivities in Mexico City, Puebla de Los Ángeles, and
Guadalajara, which featured floats adorned with multicolored papers,
always competing for the attention of the audience for its lavishness.
Maybe there was some truth in their judgment, said some gachupines,
since foreign chroniclers of the San Joseph del Parral Carnival could not
have described a young woman throwing flowers on balconies during a
procession, as happens in Valencia. The truth is that, in this humble town,
houses with balconies were built much later, and as for the flowers, with
God's grace and lots of water, some margaritas could bloom in the spring.*

*And so, to the rhythm of the music and songs, people of all calidades
shared space to drink, play, dance, and murmur, participating, as God
ordered, in a carnival that not even Mexico City held anymore.*

As the above pliego suelto narrates, one of the three days
of carnestolendas between February and March in 1649
could have happened as described.[1] There is only one document in San Joseph del Parral archives that addresses this religious
ritual and, perhaps as Governor Diego de Guajardo said that same
year, the town was not "worthy of drawing attention."[2] Those carnival fiestas had been organized in Europe, the Mediterranean, and
Spain. However, surprisingly, no archival documents exist either

about the Carnival occurrence in the most prominent city in New Spain, Mexico City, at least not until the late seventeenth century.[3] One reason San Joseph del Parral had Carnival days and Mexico City did not could have been the distance of the mining town from the center of power of New Spain, since it implied less control from the viceroyalty government and the Church in northern mining zones. Another cause could have been how the town was born: not formally founded and established, and with a Spanish oligarchy controlling almost all affairs, including popular events.

However, even though the mining town held a carnival before Mexico City did, this does not mean the festivity was the same as those the Spanish cities held before the Christian Era. That kind of carnival did not survive the transition from the Middle Ages to the Modern Age.[4] Instead, the essential elements of this ritual prevailed in the religious festivals of Europe that eventually arrived in America, such as outlandish clothing, masks, and theater, among others.[5] Despite the opposition of the Church and the crown, carnivalesque components arrived in New Spain and manifested more boisterously during the Corpus Christi celebration. Some members of religious orders, such as Motolinía and Fray Bartolomé de las Casas, were not sympathetic to Carnival elements. In 1540, Bishop Juan de Zumárraga, for example, suspended that celebration in Mexico City because people were wearing masks and sporting clothes of the opposite sex.[6]

And in fact, medieval-like carnivals in religious rituals were not supposed to be included per the modern "universality" of the Catholic Church. This institution, together with the Habsburg Crown, emphasized the removal of any vestige of paganism in Christian rituals when they created the Counter-Reformation, with which they arrived in America.[7] This cultural reform was gradual and differed for each religion and place. In general, its goal was to eliminate any ties to paganism. In addition, it disapproved of including the sacred in public representations of worldly nature. It attempted to prevent plays, religious festivals, and processions from forming representations of miracles, mysteries, or popular religious sermons. This reform mainly affected actors, corridas de toros, card games, magic, masks, taverns, and anything that could lead to a manifestation of paganism.[8]

During that time, the Spanish Crown envisioned a religious-cultural reform to shape its hegemony. This motivation led it not to hesitate to modify the form, manner, and place where popular cultural events would occur. Thus, Carnival and theater significantly changed during the sixteenth century. The Spanish Crown believed that these instances, generally oriented toward the recreation of the ordinary people, could be more useful if they acted as intermediaries between their government and the inhabitants. The transformations that Carnival and theater underwent in Europe are present in chronicles that address Carnival and other festivals. Authors describe how ordinary people still appear at those events, not as active participants but as spectators. For the crown, public rites represented a means to show power and to make social distinctions more evident. Proof of this intention was the design of exclusive theatrical works for royalty performed in the private enclosure of the Madrid palace. But there were also occasions when the Spanish Crown staged theater performances from the palace gardens for ordinary people, thus trying to reaffirm social differences and teach obedience.[9] Gradually, religious events and rituals replaced profane public entertainment, as happened with the proliferation of autos-da-fé, for example.[10]

Considering the history of Carnival and carnivalesque elements and practices in Europe and particularly in Spain, this chapter examines the only document in the AMHP-UTEP that deals with the town's oldest festive ritual found to date. It occurred in the mid-seventeenth century, between February and March 1649, and it informs about the three days of carnestolendas, the carnival time that would launch the Lenten season. The archival document is a proclamation the alcalde mayor gave one day before the festivity to the population and, particularly, to mining and service workers (free and enslaved Indigenous, African-descent, and mixed people) about how they should participate and behave during those three holy days. The analysis reflects how most segments of society, from the government and the militia to the workers, started forming a local culture. The examination of the archival document consists of locating ambiguous words, terms, ideas, and events and placing them in historical context. Just as chapters 1 and 3 reveal the coexistence of at least two historical "voices"—medieval and modern ideologies and practices in Northern New Spain—this chapter underscores how by merging some essential elements of the carnival itself with medieval and modern ideologies, mining and service workers began to forge a local cultural identity.

The Carnival of 1649: Between Pragmatism and Custom Law

The active involvement of non-Spanish inhabitants in the religious ritual of San Joseph del Parral was a slow and thorny process. Once agriculture and mining consolidated in the provincia, and there was sufficient population, the local government continued with a crucial task: to consolidate its hegemony. The first part of the proclamation of Alcalde Mayor Juan Fernández de Carrión, offered on February 11, 1649, states "that there has been in many years before, it is commanded, that every day of carnestolendas includes corridas de toros (bullfights) in the public square."[11] In this statement, the alcalde communicates that "many years" ago the local government had been fulfilling a social duty: the organization of the carnival. Since the mining town was unofficially formed around 1632, he could have implied that the authorities had organized the festivity for at least seventeen years. However, with the statement "many years before," he could also indicate a more remote and imprecise time, as if the event itself and the duty of the government to carry it out had been part of an ancient Spanish in Spain and transferred to San Joseph del Parral.

Perhaps the alcalde Fernandez de Carrión was partially correct with the two possible meanings. This old ritual, the carnival, and most public celebrations, included bullfighting, which originated in the Middle Ages. The custom prevailed until it was part of the Spanish Baroque expression and was very popular in Valladolid during the seventeenth century. Although corridas de toros were supposed to be public amusement, for the royal government those were forms of evasion: a tool they used to keep order in public celebrations.[12] Corridas de toros persisted in America. In Mexico City, at the end of the sixteenth century, for example, society experienced corridas de toros when celebrating:

> The entry of a new Viceroy, the swearing in of a monarch, the happy delivery of a queen, the weddings of the kings, the canonization of a saint . . . [those] were more than enough reasons for the quiet vassals of the King of Spain to surrender to the virile exercise [of] . . . spearing wild cattle before an enthusiastic crowd.[13]

Besides those royal and religious occasions, it was also customary to offer bullfighting for most of the festive days in the liturgical calendar all over the viceroyalty of Mexico.[14] If this diversion was a popular amusement, in vogue in the prevailing metropolis of Mexico City and throughout New Spain, it is not surprising that the alcalde offered it up as an entertainment in San Joseph del Parral.

At the same time, the phrase "there has been in many years before" could have referred to a custom. In Spanish Iberia, "custom" was a legal concept rooted in the medieval period, when the peninsula was a plural society of Catholic, Muslim, and Jewish municipalities that coexisted through the recognition of local culture and political autonomy. Thus, the coexistence of Spanish law and local custom, in combination with legal plurality, resulted in an elastic and complex Iberian legal apparatus.[15] Modified in the

Indies Laws, codified in three articles in the New Laws of 1542, and addressed in the Compilation of the Laws of the Indies in 1680, Spaniards created a version of "custom" law practice for Spanish America. The Laws of the Indies, among other concerns, indicated that Indigenous customs should continue if those were not contradictory to the Spanish faith. Likewise, the most critical resource for the Laws of the Indies was the Política Indiana of 1647 (Indian Policy manuscript). It was a continuation of Las Siete Partidas, the legal code created in the thirteenth century as a legal basis for the Spanish monarchy to balance royal authority with respect for local custom. During the viceroyalty, Oaxaca's authorities used "custom" as a rhetorical strategy, for example. Furthermore, in several remote places of New Spain borders, the Indian Policy became a resource for mayors who, not sufficiently educated in law, used any textual help to order their municipalities, employing a combination of local custom and pragmatism.[16] Even though is not possible to assure that Alcalde Fernández de Carrión had the Política Indiana of 1647 at hand when he delivered his discourse, due to the date of its publication, it is probable that the content of the Indian Policy was well known in governmental affairs. In sum, with the expression "there has been in many years before," the alcalde was alluding to both medieval and modern Spanish traditions and not to the local customs of San Joseph del Parral, if those had already existed.

However, considering that, ordinarily in San Joseph del Parral alcaldes came from the local oligarchy, it is worth asking if Fernández de Carrión had personal interests in his role as administrator. As mentioned, San Joseph del Parral did not have a council as did the rest of the towns and villages in New Spain. Following the form of government of the Castilian municipalities, in America, the authorities formed cabildos mainly of councilors and mayors who were in charge of regulating local public institutions, such as the administration of justice or the management of municipal funds, among other areas of public service.[17] However, in the mining towns of New Spain, the government functioned differently.[18] In the sixteenth and seventeenth centuries, the Viceroyalty of New Spain divided itself into reinos (kingdoms), which in turn divided into major mayoralties (a minor district in a vast territory). Thus, the mining town of San Joseph del Parral was a minor district under a mayor's jurisdiction in which the governor of El Reino de La Nueva Vizcaya appointed the alcalde mayor. That was how Fernández de Carrión came to occupy this office. Apart from regulating public festivals, his duties included administering justice and repartimientos, collecting tribute, and serving as a war captain, among other responsibilities. He had some latitude, such as appointing lieutenants, but at the same time, he had specific prohibitions, such as the impediment of placing businesses or properties under his name.[19]

Fernández de Carrión carried various public responsibilities and had a certain level of freedom, making him the most influential figure in the town, not only as alcalde but also as a war captain. It was a prominent position within northern mining centers. The Spanish Crown granted the role, but not with good will because, in reality, it could not pay for an adequate military defense in the peripheral areas. For precisely this reason, the crown distributed military appointments to Spaniards who inhabited those remote places in Northern New Spain. For example, when a landowner obtained a military rank, the crown allowed him to combine military, civil, economic, and ecclesiastical functions in his town. On many occasions, rich and powerful men, as apparently was Fernández de Carrión, exploited these functions.[20]

Still, even though his position as mayor had exclusions, it turns out that Fernández de Carrión owned a mine called La Cobriza. Moreover, he had a smelter hacienda called Santa Ana, located in El Valle de San Bartolomé, where he had also been alcalde mayor. He also governed a town called Cuencamé in 1646. Likewise, besides having the rank of military general, he was later appointed lieutenant governor. Under this position, he cornered the town's trade, created a monopoly on the sale of wine, and had establishments for card games. Among his assets were at least twenty enslaved people of African descent and a good number of servants.[21] Given this scenario, it is most likely that Fernández de Carrión's speech revealed a cultural memory based on Spanish medieval customs, ideas, and practices that advanced his interests.

The speech gets more complicated as he goes on and mentions the role mine workers should play during the carnival. In the second part of the discourse, he states, ". . . so that all the people of service and mines gather in the square and congregate and entertain themselves in the fiesta."[22] In this portion, the alcalde gave the idea that he was inviting all people "of service and mines"—the workers—to have fun in the plaza mayor. In public events, people of all races and calidades shared this space, an essential public spot in any town in the viceroyalty since it was there where authorities announced and celebrated the most significant religious and civil events. Knowing that New Spain government's most common interest in mine workers was to control them, it is strange that Alcalde Fernández de Carrión wanted to offer them such an entertainment. But, as Cheryl E. Martin explains, yearly public festivals were an opportunity to stage social and political hierarchies. Workers expected diversions from labor routines, and local leaders understood that festivities were an essential part of that arrangement.[23] Moreover, the scarcity of mine workers in mining towns could have motivated Fernández de Carrión to demonstrate that he was fulfilling his duty: providing workers with entertainment and dissuading them from fleeing or emigrating.[24] Nonetheless, it is essential to question: How did he do it? That is, what was the ideology behind the government apparatus? The oligarchy did not act alone. It needed a facilitator to exercise its power and manipulate and control workers: the Baroque Catholic Church.

Spanish Baroque: Carnestolendas' Pious Mask

Although Spanish Baroque thought underwent modifications when transferred to America, it maintained its universal ideas and practices through Catholic institutions and rituals. It was not a set of defined and stable instruments and practices in New Spain. Instead, it emerged from a religion that promoted its dogma through the visual. Baroque devotions were visible acts of veneration toward divine figures, simultaneously revealing the individual's inner state.[25] The Catholic Church was the leading promoter and sponsor of baroque art. The church compound was the ideal space to teach obedience and hierarchies. In paintings, murals, and altarpieces, the Celestial Court communicated the order of an immovable scale that celebrated the triumph of orthodoxy and the emperor.[26] Apart from striking the viewer with religious objects of baroque art, the religious ritual was perhaps the most powerful visual element, as it included the active participation of individuals and the community. Furthermore, it was the most helpful resource with which the Catholic Church taught the practice of devotion toward God and to the figure closest to him: the king of Spain. To a greater or lesser extent, the baroque religious ritual followed Mexico City's model, and the archival documents show that in San Joseph del Parral, people performed it according to their local circumstances.[27]

Carnestolendas included a spiritual element. The faithful celebrated on holy days, the initial part of Lent. The long season culminated with the Corpus Christi Mass, the most significant ritual in the Christian world. As stated, no chronicles narrate how San Joseph del Parral celebrated this festivity. Secondary sources generally present this ritual in Mexico City as a divine space where all people, regardless of race, calidad, or occupation, coincided inside the church building and with the ideology that guided all aspects of spiritual and social life. How might the pagan and spiritual worlds relate to each other?

Spanish Baroque thought ordered the Christian world according to hierarchies. These invisible divisions manifested on the church grounds during the Mass ritual, when the faithful observed the decorations, paintings, altarpieces, and other spaces that showed the divine order of the cosmos. The godly figures were always seen in high spots, indicating that God was the supreme and fearsome being, and Christian mortals were lesser beings unable to curb their passions. That is why they needed an intermediary to guide and help them to obtain indulgences and, with those, to exit purgatory sooner.[28] Lent's most religiously significant celebration within that structure was the Corpus Christi Mass. In Mexico City and Guadalajara, in villages and towns, the Catholic Church was the space where the faithful witnessed the very essence of Christianity on a stage: the bread and wine, the body and blood of Christ present.[29] For this wisdom, this sacred site was the most intimate, blessed, in sum, the most baroque. It was there where God and the saints manifested themselves physically since their presence "emanated" through objects, images, rituals, and the Eucharist. That was the microcosm of what was supposed to be Heaven or Glory: the promised place where mortals could live eternally after death.[30]

The organizers communicated this image employing a theatricality that strategically illuminated paintings, altarpieces, chandeliers, Marian images, and the tormented faces of Saints dressed in costumes of delicate fabrics and vibrant colors. All that was a whole visual composition aimed to transmit the promise of eternal life to the faithful.[31] The church's visual composition was central to baroque spaces in Catholic religious rituals. Since most "lesser" members were illiterate, the Catholic Church and the viceroyalty government used that configuration to educate the unfortunate faithful. It was how the sanctified space established an agreement on the meaning of the divine, instructing people to worship it. Religion provided guidelines for social behavior and offered a cultural pattern for the ritual.[32]

In the middle of the seventeenth century, New Spain society enjoyed the splendor and drama Baroque Catholicism brought with it in various rituals, Masses and religious festivals being perfect venues to promote collective devotion.[33] At the same time, all this theatricality had one more message attached: mortals needed authority to guide them in life and assure them a place in Heaven after death.[34] As Curcio-Nagy explains, the celebration of Corpus Christi, the entry of a new viceroy, or the oath of the new monarch were ideal occasions to show the vassals the greatness, not only of the Catholic Church but also that of its viceroyalty rulers. These events were crucial to shaping, presenting, teaching, and carrying out political and social control, consolidating a cultural hegemony that led to the submission of the castas and, at the same time, promoting the acceptance of the political agenda of a Spanish elite that "deserved" to govern under the protection of the Catholic religion.[35]

Nonetheless, in Northern New Spain, solidifying a cultural hegemony was peculiar. The Provincia de Santa Bárbara experienced migrations, enslaved people's escapes, Indios enemigos' wars, lack of labor force, unfriendly climate and geography, and the lack of a cabildo, among other issues. All those elements made the area unstable and unpredictable for mine owners and the oligarchy regarding workforce supply, but also for the Catholic Church attracting and retaining devout Christian members. Considering all these misfortunes, the Church and the viceroyalty authorities shaped various negative images of non-Spanish people that suited their needs.

Carnestolendas' Barbarian Mask

In another document, dated March 28, 1649, probably on a Palm Sunday (the first day of Holy Week), alcalde Fernández de Carrión demonstrated his military power by ordering the Spanish vecinos to defend the territory, as stipulated in the vecino contract that recognized them as such:

In as much as the order of the governors and captains have observed the holy weeks, all the vecinos and other Spanish people walk in military form to be ready for all the cases and things that His Majesty may need. It is ordered, except for people over 60 years of age, to drop their capes at Easter and walk with sword and dagger.[36]

Even though the alcalde did not specify which "cases and things" could have led the vecinos to defend His Majesty's territory, it is possible to deduce that he was referring to the "enemies of the crown," the alzados, the rebel Indigenous attacks and uprisings that, as we observed in the previous chapter, could have been an essential part of the imagination and the cultural memory of the inhabitants of San Joseph del Parral. The discovery of silver around the 1630s attracted a lot of Spaniards, provoking the reaction of the Native groups in the area, who, in 1645, attacked Spanish establishments and many carts that transported silver to the south of New Spain. At the same time, the Tobosos Indians, along with the Conchos, Cabezas, Mamites, Salineros, Julimes, and Colorados, destroyed the mission of San Francisco de Conchos, supposedly as a sign of rejection of sedentary life.[37]

The Indigenous uprisings continued for several more years. In 1645 there was a revolt among the Tarahumara community that culminated in the death of forty Indios of paz and several Spaniards. In 1652, these same Indigenous groups rose up, killing the missionary and the Indigenous Christians of Misión de San Francisco de Borja. The military campaigns against Tarahumaras and Tobosos in the zone of Tarahumara Alta ended in 1653 with the leader's capture. Nonetheless, those who took refuge in the Bolsón de Mapimí occasionally went out to assault cars that traveled the Camino Real from Durango to Parral.[38] In his discourse, the alcalde did not mention the Indian attacks. Still, it is feasible to posit that he was addressing a violent environment that could take place during the carnestolendas. This celebration favored the civilized vision of the Spanish vecinos while rejecting those who could act against the viceroyalty order.

With the third part of the mayor's discourse, the image of Fernández de Carrión and the people of service and mines gets more complex. In this portion, he disapproved and emphasized the inappropriate behavior of the mine and service workers while, at the same time, inviting them to entertain themselves with the corridas de toros. However, it seems that he had everything planned and under control. During the three days of carnestolendas, he imposed on the workers a condition on holidays, that "there should be no deaths, blasphemies, and serious riots that among those people usually happens on those days . . . so that what is customary continues."[39] As observed in the previous chapter, the inhabitants did not always consider racial barriers or social rules in daily life. Some primary sources have indicated that mestizos, Indigenous people, negros, and mulatos met and conspired to commit robberies and other crimes. The documents also reveal that some mulato women have had "bad – masculine – friends" (including Spaniards), and apparently, they were many of the mothers of illegitimate children. The records also provide examples of Spaniards accused of adultery with mulato women. Men and women gathered to consume intoxicating drinks and play in establishments dedicated to this entertainment. In criminal cases, files show that people of all castas, from Spaniards to mulatos to Indigenous, killed each other.[40] Actually, the atmosphere of the carnival that was about to start in 1649 depended on all members of society. However, Fernández de Carrión demarcated a line between the uncivilized workers and the people of calidad, the Spanish.

Fernández de Carrión's discourse had still other contradictions. In the document, he suggests that one of the intentions of the carnival festivities was to gather and entertain service and mine workers— that is, "those people" that blasphemed, killed, and rebelled—but he did not want them to misbehave. If the authority knew what to expect from "those people" in the festivities, why invest time, effort, and money in them? Everything indicates that the alcalde (representing the viceroyalty government) and the Church needed them. As some scholars explain, public disobedience could signal the encounter between two opposing realms, both required to make up a massive ritual.

Philosopher Mikhail Bakhtin offers a valuable concept to examine the struggle between two divergent groups: he calls it "carnival." For him, the battle between two factions is to establish and challenge a socio-political-cultural hegemony. Bakhtin presents carnival as a social system that commonly carries a subtext: because public celebrations contain carnival elements and because the fiesta occurs at a time and in a space in which the individual does not exist except in the community, the collectivity can challenge the socio-political-cultural organization.[41] Gonzalo Soto Posada adds that the carnival itself implies an invitation to dissent because, without transgression, there is no laughter, nor its manifestation par excellence: carnival.[42] More directly, historian Curcio-Nagy echoes those thinkers, asserting that the colonial festivals in Mexico City occurred outside the "normal" space and time, where participants and spectators were more receptive to social, cultural, and religious concepts and meanings.[43]

To some extent, these scholars' schemes suggest that religious and civic festivities are necessary to bring together two different worlds. One group has the potential to oppose as it enters the festive atmosphere and can open doors to the expression of contrary ideas, thoughts, or experiences that are against the ones legally established. The other group, the "civilized" one, can contribute to this disobedience-like ambiance by having an official and constant view, which will inevitably cause the community to transgress it. Following those ideas, it is possible to argue that in San Joseph del Parral, authorities and workers needed each other during the carnival celebration. That is, the alcalde organized and established the rules workers were supposed to transgress during the carnestolendas. In fact, the combination of carnival elements, the presence of diverse non-Spanish groups, corridas de toros, and alcohol could have been a dangerous mixture for a northern area where "enemy" Indigenous people carried a long history of rebellions. Furthermore, during the carnival, people of African descent could join the Indigenous to commit delinquent acts or to plot an uprising against the Spanish people, as had happened on several occasions in Mexico City.[44]

Carnestolendas' Vicious Mask

One can say that New Spain society, like medieval Spain, was defined based on the presence of the "other." In Iberia, the "other" were the Jews and Muslims, whereas in America they were Indigenous groups, people of African descent, and those of mixed race. For the Church, government, oligarchy, and Spanish elite of San Joseph del Parral to occupy the highest place in society it was necessary to fabricate a social class, not only a lower and submissive one, but also a rebellious and vicious one. Alcalde Fernández de Carrión's third part of the discourse about the carnestolendas in 1649 alludes to that fabrication. That day in February, his discourse continued saying, ". . . that no merchant of this town in the three days of carnestolendas sell wine to Indians, negros, mestizos or mulatos, or other people in mining and service."[45]

Those words indicate that the prohibition was directed only to mining and service people, that is, to Indians, negros, mestizos, or mulatos, not to Spaniards, perhaps because the latter perceived themselves as civilized and moderated their consumption of wine, which at the same time symbolized their Catholic heritage and the cultural essence of the Spanish diet. But the alcalde's discourse suggests that non-Spanish groups, especially the Indigenous ones, were naturally inclined to overconsume alcoholic beverages, which was indeed a vice, a sign of uncivilized behavior that could easily lead to fights and crime.[46]

Fernández de Carrión did not consider the drinking habits of Natives before the Spanish arrived to be part of the cultural heritage and diet, worthy of divine significance. Usually, Indigenous groups in central and south New Spain drank fermented beverages in their rituals and used them to replace water in times of scarcity and as medicine. More than anything, the widespread custom of drinking among pre-Hispanic Indigenous groups occurred in ceremonies dedicated to harvesting and rain, at births, weddings, funerals, and celebrations of specific deities.[47] In the north, the different Indigenous groups that comprised the Chichimecas were scattered over vast geography and drank agave juice to replace water. Maybe that was why they included it in their rituals dedicated to the deceased and captives. As previously observed, the Loma de San Gabriel Chalchihuites people who during the eleventh and fourteenth centuries lived at the foot of the Sierra Madre Occidental drank a wine made of mezcal during their ceremonies.[48] Tarahumaras used to hold meetings and drank tesguino, a liquor made from fermented corn and herbs. During the encounter, they performed a ritual to ask their divinity for a good harvest, rain, protection against lightning, and good health.[49] The Jesuit religious order later noticed that the Indigenous Tepehuanes liked to involve themselves in the festivities of the Holy Week with dances in the churches' courtyards. When they finished and were away from the missions, Tepehuanes carried out the ritual of drinking alcohol at night.[50] Thus, everything indicates that, on the one hand, these Indigenous people joined the Catholic ritual imposed on them. On the other hand, they did not stop practicing their own.

The ignorance about or lack of interest in Indigenous people's cultural and religious traditions made it very convenient for the Spanish elite and the local government to impose the Catholic ritual and perpetuate the vision of the Indians as "barbarous" but pious. Alcalde Fernández de Carrión and the Spanish elite did not even consider that Catholic Spain had already experienced the struggle between excess and moderation during religious festivities in *El Libro del buen amor* (*The Book of Good Love*), by the Archpriest of Hita, which deals with the struggle between Don Carnal (the flesh) and Doña Cuaresma (symbolizing Lent). This book reflects the Spanish cultural-religious tradition of its time. It tells of the battle on Tuesday before Ash Wednesday. That day, Don Carnal enjoys drinking wine, eating delicacies, and listening to music, surrounded by wealth and luxury, until Doña Cuaresma arrives. An army of edible animals from the sea followed her and defeated Don Carnal's troops. Thus, for the next forty days, the forces of Lent reign and dispel Carnival. When Easter Sunday arrives, Lent leaves the throne so that carnality and love can regain their places in the Christian world.[51] The prose book's earliest version is from 1330, considered a significant fourteenth-century Spanish manuscript. It reflects humans' struggle between opposing forces that face each other during the most significant festivity in the Catholic tradition.

The metaphor of the carnival suggests the need for two adversaries to exist, and that is how Bakhtin's carnival theory echoes de Hita's book. Alcalde Fernández de Carrión's discourse reflected it as well. He suggested the need for the carnal side and invited the mixed and vicious workforce to face the Christian power. In the last part of his discourse, Fernández de Carrión gave workers a vicious face, and with it, he reaffirmed the Spanish elite's negative perceptions of the traits of mixed people. The alcalde's words resonate with the idea of Irving Leonard: that the local government has used this poor behavior to ensure the stability of the hierarchical order. In other words, the existence of a group that is socially smaller "affirms" the order that the group that considers itself superior has established.[52]

By prohibiting local merchants from selling alcohol to all these people, Fernández de Carrión's speech takes on strong overtones that expose another facet of Spanish Baroque ideology. Irving Leonard indicates that the profusion of ethnic detail and hierarchy are typical characteristics of baroque thought in seventeenth-century New Spain. Official proclamations reflect the government's emphasis on the community's racial makeup to ensure stability. The author adds that when the official documents referred not to one but to several ethnic compositions, which highlight details about skin color or features, the speeches placed the various ethnic groups in a "baroque caldera" (cauldron). It was the precise space for these groups to occupy and to complete the logical division by hierarchy.[53] The third part of Fernández de Carrión's statement reflected this idea when he deposited Indians, negros, mestizos, mulatos, and other service people in a baroque caldera, a spot where social dissonance was not as strong as the division that existed between it and the Spanish elite.

The archival document about the carnival fiesta in San Joseph del Parral is integral to Northern New Spain's history. Everything indicates that in the middle of the seventeenth century, not all towns, villages, or even Mexico City celebrated the carnestolendas. However, around 1670, authorities began restricting carnival customs in religious celebrations throughout New Spain. The decision to limit those practices reflected the concerns the government and the Catholic Church had about the uprisings of some ethnic groups, which had already occurred in the past and were increasing in those times.[54] That decision implies that the cities' representatives failed to control the uncivilized behavior during the religious festivities. Still, a question remains: whether or not by eliminating carnival elements in fiestas, the Spanish, Indigenous, people of African descent, mestizos, and more mixed people would no longer curse, make disturbances, kill each other, or use intoxicating drinks in religious rituals.

Recount of a Town Upside Down

We do not know if there were more carnestolendas days in San Joseph del Parral before or after the one examined. However, after

analyzing and placing the text in a historical context, we can conclude that more carnival celebrations might have occurred. As the
archival document informs, in San Joseph del Parral the carnestolendas were part of the Catholic ritual that served the local government to create, communicate, and highlight Spanish customs and
cultural memories. The Catholic Church contributed by molding a
pious community of workers and simultaneously enhancing the oligarchy and government's cultural hegemony. The Catholic Church,
the viceroyalty government, and the Spanish oligarchy thus brought
into and imposed the Catholic ritual on this mining town.

The ambiguity of the discourse and the various historical voices
reveal how the town society divided itself into two main social
classes, Spanish and non-Spanish; in two times, medieval and modern; and under one ideology, the Spanish Baroque. What seems
clear is that Alcalde Fernández de Carrión needed the presence of
those workers to legitimize his position, to emphasize and reaffirm
hierarchies, and, in short, to do what was customary in the town
according to his European conception about the term. Furthermore,
in his discourse he made people of service and mines rebellious
workers, which was a convenient image for the Catholic Church and
its baroque practices and ideas. That was why it welcomed the "sin-
ners," the ones who could not control their instincts, the ones who
needed more guidance in life and death, and the ones it needed to
perform its rituals for the orderly terrestrial and celestial kingdoms.

Although the documents do not inform about the active participation of Indigenous, negros, mulatos, mestizos, and mixed
people, we can appreciate it through the images or the "masks" the
authorities and the Catholic Church fashioned for them. Those
two forces carried the tools for those vassals to challenge the same
socio-political-cultural Spanish hegemony. Curcio-Nagy believes
that the Habsburg Crown somehow contributed to the emergence
of a popular "street" culture. Determined to manifest to the world
the intrinsic, if not divine, relationship between the king and God,

the crown did not measure the expenses involved in the fiestas they organized to commemorate the sovereign's events (death, births, marriages, birthdays).[55] In sum, by emphasizing the inappropriate workers' behavior, Fernández de Carrión reinforced the negative image of the labor force: vicious but necessary. Nonetheless, the performances of diverse participants assembled in the plaza mayor, amusing themselves with corridas de toros, was a foundation for creating a local identity, culture, and memory as the government and the Church left the door open to tolerance, syncretism, and local cultural diversity. As the coming chapters will unveil, even though the alcalde emphasized those customs that were of Spanish origin after seventeen years of the town's formation, the non-Spanish community had already initiated their own.

CHAPTER 5

NATURALES AND PARDOS COFRADÍAS

A LOCAL TASTE OF THE UNIVERSAL CHURCH

It was the first day of November in 1669 when almost all people in San Joseph del Parral departed early to meet in the plaza mayor. Some left their old relatives at home as the alcalde had indicated, and with good reason: they did not have the energy to march in military style in the religious procession that was about to start to receive the Virgen del Rayo, who came from Minas Nuevas town. The militia waited for the participants before La Parroquia de San José. The captain instructed the officers to line up in a row. All wore uniforms and war weapons, except for one who probably forgot his knife in the tavern the night before. The captain approached him, took off the man's beret, and threw it in his face, reminding him that, for not bringing the weapons with him, he owed the mayor twelve pesos.

While people waited for the signal to march, a gale suddenly passed, leaving behind thick gray clouds. Everyone looked at the sky with mouths and eyes open. At that moment, it seemed the community's memory awoke because all began to talk about "the miracle" they witnessed seven years before, "when a terrible storm came as if it had been the very fury of God." Among the groups, there were various versions of that miraculous event. Still, all agreed that one day in August, the brothers of La Cofradía de Nuestra Señora de La Candelaria de Los Naturales carried out a procession through the town. They were begging alms to contribute to the alcalde's office to combat the enemies of the town and the crown, the fearsome barbarous Indigenous tribes. The mayordomos of the cofradía were raising the figure of the Virgin when suddenly, a terrible storm broke out. Angry lightning began to strike on the outskirts of the village. The partakers did not know what to do when a rayo (lightning bolt) struck the face of the Virgen de la Candelaria, leaving her holy visage marked forever. People said that it was for this motive that the Naturales brothers changed the name of their virgin, their Marian advocation; from that day, they named her "Virgen del Rayo" since her face was marked with the fury of the sky. The inhabitants would never forget that day when the divine figure interposed to be the one who received the lightning strike rather than her faithful servants. That is how years ago, the Virgen de la Candelaria, or the "new" Virgen del Rayo, saved San Joseph del Parral from being destroyed by the fury of God.

This pliego suelto used two primary sources. One is an archival piece employed to portray how in 1669, the alcalde mayor's office continued to intervene in the town's religious rituals, adding a military element to the pilgrimage of the Virgen del Rayo.[1] The document does not state why the inhabitants and cofradías had to get involved with the army on a day dedicated to a Marian advocation.[2] The town's miracle, on the other hand, is part of a relatively recent legend narrated around the 1990s by Father Hilario Echevarría, San Joseph del Parral's priest.[3] The legend describes how, due to a miracle, the Virgen de la Candelaria became the Virgen del Rayo. As mentioned in chapter 1, La Virgen de La Candelaria was the Marian advocation for La Cofradía de Los Naturales, the Indigenous groups called Mexicanos or Mexicaneros who were transferred from Central New Spain to Northern New

Spain to serve as an "example" of Christian behavior to Indigenous Conchos and Tepehuanes in El Valle de San Bartolomé during the early years of the mining town's formation.

As previously noted, this book is interested in the mining town's two cofradías whose names refer to their members' race. Primary sources reveal how the two brotherhoods emerged and evolved differently over time. The variances relate to the members' arrival time in the mining town, place of origin, and race. One of the main questions is why the Naturales' cofradía still plays a significant role in the town's cultural past, whereas the Pardos' brotherhood does not. In addressing this question, this chapter detects the heteroglossia in La Cofradía de Los Naturales' primary sources: two sociohistorical languages with a unique meaning, one from the mid-seventeenth century and one from the present time. Those two languages underscore the creation of a legend that continues to symbolize the baroque order, where European culture still occupied the highest place. As for La Cofradía de Los Pardos, this chapter analyzes some documents that set a precedent for the confraternity's emphasis on perseverance, recognition, and ancestral memory, decisive values that eventually could indicate the creation or recreation of African culture.

The immersion of religious brotherhoods in communities' social issues has its roots in the Middle Ages. Since that time, as a religious institution, the cofradía has been one of the primary vehicles for educating the population about Christianity.[4] During the twelfth and thirteenth centuries, the cofradías of clergy proliferated in the Spanish territory. Among them, hospital cofradías stood out. Those entities cared for leprosy patients in the eleventh century. Penitential brotherhoods also existed; their members explicitly shared the Passion of Christ and the Virgin's pains in acts of penance, as the Brothers of the Penance of Christ did in Salamanca. Meanwhile, cofradías dedicated to workers, later called gremios (guilds), emerged along with the phenomenon of professional solidarity throughout Europe. This version maintained a religious element but at a secondary level. The artisanal development that occurred in Castilla and León, for example, led artisans to establish cofradías to protect their interests as workers.[5]

However, those religious institutions had an essential feminine-familiar element at their core: the Virgin Mary. Back then, the atmosphere of sin, guilt, and condemnation strengthened with the cult of the Immaculate Conception. During the twelfth century, devotion to the Virgin Mary spread and became humanized by multiplying of images with different Marian advocations: Virgin of the Remedies, Virgin of Mercy, and many others. In general, the name referred to the assisting tasks the organizations or cofradías performed.[6] In itself, devotion to Mary calls for veneration, love, invocation, and imitation, concentrating on proclaiming her mystery: the divine dispensation of original sin and the miracle of giving birth without losing her virginity. That was why she occupied a different level among all the saints, and she required veneration, imitation, and celebration. Seville, and the rest of the Spanish territory, celebrated various Marian advocations, including Virgen de los Dolores and Virgen del Rosario. She was the holder of various dedications in churches and cofradías. Her image was worthy of respect; if grievances occurred during the festivities offered to them, communities interpreted those wrongs as serious insults.[7]

During the late Middle Ages, in all the Catholic states of Europe, figures of wealth and power took enriched churches and created pious charities for hospitals. In most cases, religious orders organized them. Over time, the establishment of pious works and capellanías was not exclusive to powerful men; it spread and became popular among urban people. The urban cofradías' function was largely to instruct people in Christianity. These arose from mendicant orders like that of San Francisco. In this way, the organization of cofradías oriented to hospitality and charity proliferated, but lay cofradías started as well, primarily organized in terms of trade.

These had a socioeconomic line, although they maintained their spiritual nature.[8]

The cofradía molded to be the most effective tool in disseminating the ideology of the Universal Catholic Church in the New World. Except for running guilds (non-Spanish people were prohibited from engaging in most trades), in America, those religious institutions inherited the service character that congregations consolidated in medieval Europe. Their communities raised funds to repair or build churches, carry out public works, maintain hospices, and bury the abandoned dead, among other social aid activities.[9] In America, the brotherhoods' spirit of service was also included in the baroque element that distinguished universal Catholicism: the idea that one had to live well to die better. This ideology is reflected in those religious societies' efforts to obtain indulgences or "dispensations" of sins that the pope granted to the congregations. The cofradías distributed indulgences among the brothers in exchange for attending Mass, praying, offering spiritual talks, caring for the sick, and other Christian efforts they made in the community. Thus, cofradías also gave comfort and the assurance of eternal life to those on the verge of death. The religious organization supported their members financially so that they had a dignified burial at the time of their death.[10]

Naturales' Cofradía

Throughout New Spain, Indigenous cofradías functioned as a vehicle for evangelization. Indigenous people obtained all the benefits these institutions provided to their members. However, there were more advantages for confraternities that practiced what historian Laura Dierksmeier identifies as "Nahua Christianity" or "Nahua Catholicism." Usually located in Central Mexico, Indigenous cofradías were popular in centers such as Michoacán, Oaxaca, Yucatán, and Jalisco, among other places. Members' adherence helped advance the social status and positions of power in both religious and community spheres. It is estimated that the source of those brotherhoods' empowerment centered on their religious hybridity, the mixture of Spanish and pre-Hispanic religion. Customarily, those brotherhoods kept records in Nahuatl writing, with finances recorded in Aztec currencies. Furthermore, those Indigenous confraternities were allowed to elect their leaders without Spanish intervention or oversight. On occasion, Indigenous brothers assisted in providing sacraments in remote rural areas without a priest. Historians debate the extent of Indigenous confraternities' benefits, advantages, and autonomy: whether those privileges were used to recreate pre-Hispanic nobility hierarchies or to express genuine commitment to an individual leader, although, as Dierksmeier points out, the Spanish viceroyalty did not recognize such Indigenous positions.[11]

Indigenous brotherhoods in Northern New Spain have a distinct history. In Nueva Vizcaya, the absence of sedentary and elite Indigenous communities, the decline in Native groups' numbers due to illnesses brought by Europeans, and the impossibility of congregate Indians in mission pueblos incited Spaniards to transfer Indigenous peoples of "paz" (peace people), also called Mexicanos or Mexicaneros, from the center of the viceroyalty to serve as "examples" to Indigenous peoples in northern areas. They arrived in families and already had a Christian formation and Marian identity. That was how they settled in El Valle de San Bartolomé and continued with their brotherhood, La Cofradía de Nuestra Señora de La Candelaria de Los Naturales.

Considering the advantages Indigenous confraternities had in central and south New Spain, this chapter questions whether the status of "Indígenas de paz" and the form and manner of their arrival at the provincia granted Indigenous Mexicanos some benefits as well as merits to be the protagonist of a local legend that Father Hilario Echevarría narrated around the 1990s. The Tlaxcaltecas arrived from Central Mexico in northeastern New Spain with granted benefits. María Isabel Monroy Castillo explains how the Tlaxcalteca council agreed to the transfer of Tlaxcalteca families, but not without first providing the viceregal government with a list of conditions, among which the following stand out: the 400 families had the same privileges in force as in Tlaxcala; settlers and their descendants would be deemed hidalgos, lower nobility, free of tribute and personal services, rode on horseback, carried arms, and provided with clothing and food for two years.[12] There are no primary sources that inform about Indigenous Mexicanos receiving privileges as those Tlaxcaltecas in San Joseph del Parral, but as indicated in chapter 1, in 1632, Gregorio Francisco Indio Mexicano was recorded as holding a land title; in 1634, Juan Francisco Indio Naborío listed his foundry farm and ranch in his testament; in 1665, Miguel Franco Indio and Juan Francisco Indio listed properties as well; and in 1673, Juan Diego Indio registered his land.[13]

At the same time, the history of the Cofradía de Nuestra Señora de la Candelaria is wrapped in vagueness due to the scarcity of archival sources, a trait that has culminated in a legend that local chroniclers and priests, and some historians, created. Robert West's book, for example, mentions how Indigenous people were "brought from central Mexico" to San Joseph del Parral. This piece of data comes from Zacarías Márquez Terrazas, a chronicler who edited and wrote the introduction and notes for West's book. In a footnote, Márquez Terrazas mentions how the AMHP contains miners' salary books that inform about Indigenous people brought from central Mexico identified as "Mexicaneros" (Tarascos and Tlaxcaltecas) who formed the town Huexótitan, a Jesuit mission.[14] However, as stated, the transfer of Indigenous groups from Central Mexico to the Provincia de Santa Bárbara did not include Tlaxcaltecas.[15] Nonetheless, according to Márquez Terrazas, those Indigenous individuals brought the devotion of Nuestra Señora de la Candelaria to San Joseph del Parral. However, he does not specify whether the Indigenous group came to the mining town from Huexotitlán or from Central Mexico—that is, if they arrived first in Huexotitlán and eventually moved to San Joseph del Parral or if part of the group arrived in San Joseph del Parral or El Valle de San Bartolomé from Central Mexico. Márquez Terrazas continues by saying that the confraternity members formed the first hospital for Indians, and later (late seventeenth century), they changed the name of their Virgin de la Candelaria to Nuestra Señora del Rayo.[16]

Márquez Terrazas expands on this issue in a book of his co-authorship and repeats that the Indigenous people transferred to the north were Mexicanos, Tlaxcaltecas, and Tarascos, and were already hispanized. He also says these were a vital labor sector in the mining camps and were called "naborío Indians."[17] The author even gives precise detail about the individual who funded the "Hospital for the Natives" in the town in 1632, when San Joseph del Parral was just formed. According to him, the person was a Tlaxcalteca Indian named Domingo Sebastián who, next to the hospital, built his house located on the hill of the neighborhood called Triana.[18] The quote Márquez Terrazas offers to support his assertion reads as follows:

> In a guide he wrote about trips to Mexico, Philip Terry already mentions the hospice construction by a Tlaxcalteca Indian 'who brought a pure gold ingot every Saturday to cover with its value the salary of the workers in the construction of the church weekly.' Imagination surpasses reality, but Philip Terry, finally a Saxon, and from his harvest, gobbles up the conclusion of the story: when the construction of temple finished, the Spanish commander apprehended the Indian, threatening him to show the place from which he took the gold, and since the Indian refused, he was subjected to cruel torture until he died in torment. According to Terry, the mine was lost forever, but he [Philip Terry] added a grain of sand to the 'Black Legend.'[19]

After Márquez Terrazas cites Philip Terry's manuscript, he continues with priest Hilario Echevarría's oral story, included in the second part of the pliego suelto that opens this chapter. Hilario Echevarría's chronicle is about a procession that occurred on August 12, 1661. The participants aimed to collect alms to combat the Indigenous enemies that attacked the area. Suddenly, a tempest arrived, and when a flash of lightning was about to hit the faithful mortals, the Virgen de Nuestra Señora de la Candelaria interposed herself to receive a strike in her face. Then, "those present and absent were impressed by the prodigy, and since then, the parralenses (people born in San Joseph del Parral) called her Nuestra Señora del Rayo." The author explains that they preferred this new name for the supplications and miracles "since she did not badly serve them."[20] Then, Hilario Echevarría's oral narrative describes how the Virgin helped the inhabitants in war affairs: "Not for nothing, the governor, Don Martín de Alday, declared this Virgin la Generala [feminine of military general] of his armies, putting the insignia on her chest . . . in gratitude for the help . . . against the uprising Indians." For this account, Márquez Terrazas cites Rubén Rocha Chávez's book, which also includes the priest Echevarría's oral story.[21]

Márquez Terrazas's effort to insert the Virgen del Rayo in wars between the Spanish and rebellious Indigenous groups is evident, an image he also aims to incorporate into the parralenses' cultural memory. The question is the motivation behind the fusion between the religious and the profane, between "peaceful" Indians and Spaniards, with a feminine religious figure in the middle, between past and present.

To analyze the involvement of La Cofradía de Nuestra Señora de La Candelaria de Los Naturales in San Joseph del Parral's Catholic rituals and to reveal additional aspects that could help illuminate the history of this congregation, it is necessary to make a regression in time and base the inquiry on the primary sources that begin with the foundation of the cofradía. The affair occurred on February 5, 1634, before Mr. Juan Robledo, priest, vecino, vicar, and ecclesiastical judge in the town, who said:

> Appeared the Naturales who attend and reside in town [San Joseph del Parral] saying they have accumulated a capital with the title and vocation of Nuestra Señora de La Candelaria and asked . . . the elections of new officers for the service and care of the capital. They elected Domingo Sebastián and Baltasar García and Nicolás. Likewise, the Naturales, having their books . . . promised to attend the hospital augmentation with all care and vigilance.[22]

After the protocol, the Naturales brothers immediately confirmed the elections and lit a candle to those elected.

A document issued in 1642 identifies Baltasar García as "a living Indio married to Mariana India." He was killed by Francisco Calahorra the same year.[23] I located no further information on Domingo Sebastián. Still, this document agrees with Márquez Terrazas's assertion about Domingo Sebastián being the originator of Virgen de la Candelaria's hospital. That same year, 1634, the Naturales brothers appeared before the priest and vicar Juan Robledo. They reported on some expenses made in the health care of some Indigenous people who lived there. They said they had invested "in the repair of the sick and other necessities for the hospital." At that time, Francisco Gregorio and Andrés García acted as the mayordomos, and they added that, on the day of the Mass of the Assumption, they spent two pesos and a tostón on buying candles for the mourners, six reales that they gave to a sick brother, a real for a candle for a suffering sister, and two tomines for an afflicted Christian.[24] Information on the religious festivals of this congregation appears in a document dating from 1637. It says:

. . . having had the Hospital de la Candelaria, which was a foundation in said town [San Joseph del Parral], the laborío Indians at their request [request permission] to celebrate the festival of Nuestra Señora de la Candelaria and having celebrated it as every year between, said the Naturales.[25]

However, after 1662, the date on which, according to the priest Hilario Echevarría, the name of the Virgen de la Candelaria was changed to the Virgen del Rayo, archival sources no longer mention La Cofradía de Los Naturales, only its hospital. For example, a document states that on February 16, 1694:

In San Joseph del Parral, Hipólito de Echevarría, Vicar and Ecclesiastical Judge of this jurisdiction and administrator of the assets of the Holy Image of Nuestra Señora del Rayo, which is in the Hospital of Nuestra Señora de La Candelaria de Los Naturales in this town, I order that whatever is collected from the alms of said most holy image be delivered to the depositary the Vicar appointed, so that he may have them in deposit.[26]

This information suggests that the hospital preserved the cofradía's original name, while the latter changed its name from Virgen de la Candelaria to Virgen del Rayo. However, there is a reference to a public event in the town in a 1669 archival document that hints that this Marian advocation no longer belonged exclusively to La Cofradía de Los Naturales but also served as the protective image of the entire town, a new role that gave her and the mining site a local identity.

On November 1, 1669, the alcalde mayor, General Don Juan Hurtado de Castilla, ordered all the town's residents to go out to receive the Virgen del Rayo. They would not go unattended, but the militia should accompany them. As the military marched through the streets, loading their weapons of war, people were supposed to come out and join them. The alcalde ordered individuals from ages fifteen to fifty to join; otherwise, a penalty of twelve pesos would be assessed.[27] The document does not indicate the purpose of the army's intervention in this religious act. But Márquez Terrazas suggests a fusion between the religious figure and the government apparatus when in his book he mentioned how the governor declared La Virgen del Rayo as La Generala of his armies.

This event could have occurred around 1704, since the AMHP-UTEP document mentions Governor de Alday as the author of some campaigns against the enemy Indigenous people.[28] According to these sources, La Cofradía de Nuestra Señora de La Candelaria's members, the Naturales brothers, adapted their Marian devotion to the local environment by changing the name of their brotherhood to la Virgen del Rayo. Historian Sara Sánchez de Olmo proposes that New Spanish Marianism led to the creation of the collective conscience of a religious "we" that carried a strong local character, and the devotion to the Marian image was, at the same time, adherence to the immediate space that contained it.[29]

Then, what do the archival records and the legend about La Virgen del Rayo communicate? Could the local government have appropriated the miracle of Nuestra Señora del Rayo to give the town a miracle and a local memory with medieval resonance? Naming the Virgin "La Generala" of Spanish armies that fought against the Indigenous "enemies" merits questioning the meaning or meanings that "local" had at that time for both the authorities and the cofradía. Everything indicates that at least two local expressions could have existed in those times in the mining town: encouraged by religious and government officials, the faithful brothers created the new name for their Marian advocation because they needed eternal salvation and a local identity. The former allowed the brothers to do it because of their need to consolidate a hegemony with a cultural memory of the Reconquest and to give a local taste to the universality of the Catholic Church and the crown. In sum, with the name change that arose from a town's environmental event, the congregation of the Virgen del Rayo acquired a new northern identity that inserted itself into the local religious culture. As archival documents and the current legend evidence attest, the local Spanish elite appropriated the divine image to manifest a cultural memory of medieval origin that appeared "local." Eventually, some historians and local chroniclers included the history of this cofradía in San Joseph del Parral's cultural memory that, to this day, continues to contain, and in some ways praise, the Spanish experience in the Reconquest.

Historians agree that membership in both Indigenous and Afro-Mexican cofradías had additional benefits for their communities, such as the possibility to obtain mechanisms of resistance, adaptation, and conservation of their culture that existed before Spanish rule.[30] They also could achieve individual participation in acts of devotion and charity and in groups where they obtained spiritual and monetary support at the time of death.[31] An additional advantage for those religious institutions, in general, was that, since they were the living image of devotion to the sacred and sacrificed for the common good, they usually received the admiration of the people. This gesture gave them prestige and honor.[32] It seems that La Cofradía de La Candelaria de Los Naturales/ La Cofradía del Rayo enjoyed and stills carrying prestige, honor, and admiration through its legend. The question that remains is whether La Cofradía de La Purísima Inmaculada Concepción de Los Pardos enjoyed the same admiration as did the Naturales' brotherhood.

Pardos' Cofradía

In contrast to that of Indigenous people, Black brotherhoods' presence in the Catholic world is longstanding; it goes back to Africa. In fact, the earliest Black/Afro-Brazilian confraternities surged during the fifteenth century in the Portuguese world (the west coast of Africa and Brazil). As medieval confraternities, Catholic lay brotherhoods of African descendants included social care for their members in life and death, including support to dependent survivors, Masses for the deceased's souls, and legal aid to purchase freedom.[33] At the same time, before the massive transatlantic trade, African enslaved people were part of Spanish cultural and religious life. They received Catholic Church sacraments, could be buried in parish cemeteries, be part of confraternities, and involve themselves in rituals.[34]

If this previous experience was an advantage for people of African descent in New Spain, it is a motivating interrogative. Joan C. Bristol indicates that in the African diaspora, a crucial form of Christian practice came from participation in Catholic brotherhoods. According to the historian, those institutions, mostly in Brazil and the Caribbean, provided their members with a sense of corporate identity that was based in ideas about a shared African origin.[35] What is certain is that Spanish legislation from as early as 1542 forbade enslaved individuals to congregate after sunset in numbers exceeding three.[36] Furthermore, in New Spain hierarchical society African people were at the bottom of social and racial categories. That status affected cofradías' identity, social image, and performance.

Enslaved Black people funded brotherhoods as early as 1572. Although those were an important socialization venue, there were also occasions for rebellions. As mentioned, perhaps the previous experience at Hispaniola served African people to be aware of and react against the abuses with which they lived as enslaved workers. Some scholars support the idea of Black brotherhoods in Mexico City being instances for rebellion. Around 1612, in those religious institutions, Afro-Mexicans were able to recreate and preserve certain cultural elements at the time they interacted with other ethnic groups, and rebellion was among those cultural components.[37] What is certain is that viceroyalty authorities judged

Black confraternities a threat to public order. In 1612, for example, there were rumors in Mexico City about a slave conspiracy planned in Afro-confraternities.[38] A similar occurrence happened in 1623, and in both instances, the brotherhoods were suspended.[39] Actually, there were African enslaved people through the sixteenth and seventeenth centuries who fought to create for themselves an autonomous life. Some escaped and established settlements called "palenques" in the mountains. Self-styled "Cimarrones," those Afro-Mexicans were the most successful African-descent individuals in maintaining vestiges of an African cultural past, according to some historians.[40]

Other researchers consider that from the early sixteenth throughout the seventeenth century, African enslaved people in New Spain were encouraged to found confraternities, which were key institutions to cultivate communal ties around a shared sense of corporate identity. Those communal ties meant connections to other ethnicities, mostly Indigenous, where Black cofrades were able to perpetuate the social and cultural practices they brought with them from Africa.[41] Historian Miguel A. Valerio, for example, recognizes Black sovereignty of Afro-Mexicans through a 1610 performance in Mexico City. He analyzes Black kings' enactments as an imitation of an Angola–Kongo Kingdom ceremony mixed with that of European origin. He identifies it as Afro-Baroque culture that demonstrates three Afro-Mexican agency traditions: cultural, social, and political.[42]

In San Joseph del Parral, the Pardo brothers did not escape the negative perception other Black confraternities received throughout New Spain. In fact, we can say that it faced several barriers, probably because of its diverse ethnic composition and for being a mining cofradía. This brotherhood was part of a mining hacienda owned by the provincia's oligarch. However, the Pardo brothers were resilient toward the obstacles the elite placed in front of them, perhaps motivated by the Catholic Baroque need to lead a good life that would ensure them a place in that hierarchical society and in Heaven after death. This research finds that the Pardo brothers tried to improve their image by participating in the town's religious ritual.

In making this claim, this book questions historian Nicole von Germeten when affirming that La Cofradía de La Purísima Inmaculada Concepción de Los Pardos did not have the success other Black cofradías had in New Spain.[43] She examines, compares, and contrasts confraternities made of Blacks or mulatos in Valladolid, Mexico City, and San Joseph del Parral. In Germeten's view, La Cofradía de Los Pardos, which was quite active throughout the San Joseph del Parral viceroyalty period, did not have the same success as the other mulato brotherhoods in Valladolid or Mexico City. The historian suggests that the elements that accounted for the latter's achievement stemmed from their being in urban centers, where there was a greater concentration of people of African origin, where they had a better economic level, and where they were allowed to live more peacefully than in other places. Regarding La Cofradía de Los Pardos, Germeten indicates that the factors that contributed to its failure in San Joseph del Parral were the constant attacks of rebellious Indian tribes, isolation, poverty, a floating population, and the excessive control of the mining elite.[44] This book refutes Germeten's conclusion about the Pardos' cofradía after analyzing primary sources that evidence its active involvement in the universal Catholic ritual, one through which it consolidated a cultural memory and identity, when they showed efforts of preserving African ideas and practices. Thus, during the second half of the seventeenth century, a time of Spanish Baroque and its religious fervor, the Pardo bothers transformed the universal Catholic ritual into a space of constant struggle.

Negros, mulatos, mestizos, and Indigenous were the brothers who integrated La Cofradía de La Purísima Inmaculada Concepción de Los Pardos. Mestizos were mainly from various parts of the northern zone. They arrived in the Provincia de Santa Bárbara at different times by will or force to alleviate the labor shortage on the mining estates. Nicole von Germeten suggests that the Pardos' cofradía was to some extent unique, since it was not composed solely of people of African descent, like the Black or mulato brotherhoods in the rest of New Spain.[45] Dierksmeier supports Germeten's assertion when indicating that in Mexico City or Puebla de Los Ángeles, most confraternities were of a single ethnic composition due to their large populations of Spanish, mestizo, Indigenous, mulato, and Black people.[46] Therefore, if Germeten compares two Black confraternities in two large cities, Valladolid and Mexico City, with a Pardo brotherhood in a small town such as San Joseph del Parral, it is evident that the latter will be "unique." Nonetheless, the city of Zacatecas, a city closer to San Joseph del Parral, had a cofradía composed of free and enslaved people of African descent. It was La Cofradía de San Juan de La Penitencia, which was founded in 1635, and whose history could enrich our inquiry about the Pardos brotherhood's distinctiveness.

Historian Lara Mancuso explains how La Cofradía de San Juan de La Penitencia asked permission to organize a procession on a day when no other cofradía in the mining town would do it. Mancuso believes that this petition for the performance's exclusiveness could indicate that this brotherhood was exclusively for Black individuals and that they did not feel connected to Spanish and Indigenous confraternities. Even though free mulatos probably lived in peripheral neighborhoods and Indian pueblos, and worked along with Indigenous, mestizos, and Spanish people in the mines, according to Mancuso, the confraternity of San Juan de la Penitencia's identity was not based on place of living or occupation. Instead, the brotherhood's identity was built in the ethnic group sense, that maybe fomented a shared group identity among them. This cofradía was in a precarious condition by 1742 and disappeared a few years later as its members abandoned it.[47] We can conclude that time and space were determinants for individuals, groups, and towns to organize and design a modus vivendi. Zacatecas' mining flourished years before San Joseph del Parral, and the zone had different circumstances regarding local Indigenous groups and the arrival of African enslaved individuals, for example.

Furthermore, it is necessary to clarify what kind of racial category "Pardo" refers to. It is true that in New Spain the interpretation of ethnic classifications derived from local customs, the nature of the work people did, skin color, physical features, quality, and honor. For the Afro-Mexican population, the most common categories were negro or mulato, which referred to an African heritage that had not been "mixed." Mulato referred to a person of African and Spanish origin. "Pardo" spoke of a person resulting from a mixture of African and Indigenous heritage (also mulato if they had lighter than black skin).[48] Assigning the adjective "pardos" to La Cofradía de La Inmaculada Concepción makes sense since its members, as the primary documents demonstrate, were identified as negros, mulatos, and Indigenous individuals. Nonetheless, we must consider that common ethnic or racial classification was mostly visual; therefore, we are referring to skin color. Mulato skin, for example, was the result of the mixture between white and Black people; mestizo skin was the consequence of the union between whites and Indians; and "pardo" referred to a skin color derived from unions between Blacks and Indigenous peoples, although these designations also took into account African physical features and cultural customs.[49] Nonetheless, the fact that San Joseph del Parral had a Pardo cofradía born in a mining area complicates its name. Mancuso explains that mining cofradías in New Spain experienced and witnessed migration and job and economic instability, not to mention the abuse of the elite (land and mine owners), among other aspects.[50] These conditions may have worked to bring together individuals of different ethnicities to the Pardos' cofradía in San Joseph del Parral.

What is crucial to observe is that from approximately the year 1656, most Pardo brothers hold Christian names and surnames in the archival documentation, in contrast with some Indigenous and Africans and their descendants in Santa Bárbara and El Valle de San Bartolomé at the end of the sixteenth century. Nonetheless, it is complicated to arrive at conclusions regarding African-descent people's use of Christian last names. Historian Colin Palmer, for example, indicates that all African enslaved people in Mexico were given a first name and were identified by it. Some had a last name, but it was usually that of their masters and, when they were acknowledged as criollos, ladinos, or bozales, that meant they were in the process of being acculturated.[51] Considering that by 1650 San Joseph del Parral had around 1,100 enslaved bozales and criollo African people who started arriving around 1632, we could question whether some of those enslaved individuals were among the Pardo brothers and used their owners' last names.[52] Due to the absence of primary documentation, it is challenging to determine who was enslaved and who was not precisely because some free individuals kept their masters' last names.

In its beginnings, the Pardo cofradía was integrated by Indigenous, mestizo, negro, and mulato individuals, all workers of the silver refining estate of Don Francisco Montaño de la Cueva. He was an oligarch who established himself in the town before it was formed in 1630. Apart from having an Indigenous and mestizo labor force, this man bought some enslaved African people to work on his farm (he was among the 80 percent of the residents of the town who bought enslaved Black people around 1632–1657). Being a devotee of the Virgin of the Immaculate Conception, he had a chapel dedicated to this Marian advocation on his hacienda, for which he held an annual festival. His workers were involved in the celebration. During those years, the fiesta did not associate itself with any cofradía. When Francisco Montaño de la Cueva died in 1647, he bequeathed the hacienda to his nephew, Felipe de la Cueva, who continued to organize the celebrations for the Virgin in the same hacienda.[53]

After participating in those celebrations, workers began to conceive of forming their own cofradía. They wanted the pope to recognize their brotherhood, the one they had already established in the Hospital San Juan de Dios where they dedicated their lives to Christian tasks.[54] The pope's recognition was imperative for the Pardo brothers to continue as a religious group, not only because with it they would consolidate a social place but also for financial reasons. Usually, when cofradías did not have sufficient resources, they could ask for alms in their respective towns or receive financial help from their churches to organize their religious rituals. However, the Pardos' cofradía could not do it because it was not independent; the pope had not recognized it yet. Therefore, they had to solve their economic issues as best they could. For example, around 1650, mayordomo Pedro Martí appeared before the judge to claim three silver bars uncovered on a farm in Sonora. Sebastián González de Valdés had offered the congregation those bars more than twenty years before. After Valdés's death, the farm in Sonora passed into other hands, but Martí said the cofradía had not forgotten Valdes's gift.[55]

It is assumed that the Pardo workers of de la Cueva continued as an "unofficial" brotherhood at the Hospital de San Juan de Dios, where they formed as such and adopted the racial category of "pardos" in their name. But their fate as a religious congregation radically changed in 1699. It happened that the hospital was run by the religious order of San Juan de Dios. By 1681, it raised funds to build a proper structure, and three years later it settled in the hospital. This place offered care to mulatos, Indigenous, and mestizos who suffered ailments related to their work in the mines. However, the religious order left the town in 1699. Historians believe that this was when Don Felipe de la Cueva's Pardo workers / "unofficial" brotherhood took the hospital's reins, thus completely disassociating the brotherhood from Don Felipe's hacienda.[56] Perhaps the separation was a key factor in their trying to improve their image and achieve more active participation in the religious ritual, as we will see in chapter 8. But before that could happen, the Pardo brothers had to endure their fate as an unendorsed-hacienda congregation. As we will see, the documentation illustrates how the line between those individuals and their congregation was threadlike, especially for those who served as mayordomos. Their individual and the brotherhood's reputation suffered if someone accused them of committing a fault. The truth was that, unfortunately, if the acquisition of indulgences depended on cofradías members' good Christian conduct, then during much of the seventeenth century, the Pardo brothers had a well-earned "fast pass" to purgatory.

The first protagonist of La Cofradía de Los Pardos' drama was Antonio Narváez. He was considered a free mulato and worked on Don Felipe de la Cueva Villamayor's hacienda. In 1656, he received a loan of 120 pesos from sergeant major Don Valerio Cortés del Rey. It is unknown how Narváez got involved with this man or why he needed the loan he requested. The fact was that Narváez was giving the corresponding payments stipulated in the voucher he signed, but in 1660 he stopped doing so. Cortés del Rey then filed a lawsuit in court, as Narváez still owed him 90 pesos and 6 tomines. Narváez appeared before the judge, confessed to owing that amount to the sergeant, and said he would pay. But as the months passed, that day did not come. Cortés del Rey asked the justice to imprison his debtor. Narváez returned and appeared before the judge. He alleged that he could not collect the amount because he was a poor man who supported himself in his work. He said his acquaintances could attest to that fact and corroborate that he had only a road horse and a mare with a total value of 50 pesos under his belt. So, he would pay the rest of the money he owed to Cortés del Rey in la primera raya (the next payday).[57] No archival document revealed whether Narváez finished paying his debt. What stands out in this mulato allegation is that in front of the authority, to his favor, he used the image the town had of him: a poor worker of a mining estate. In addition, he offered the testimony of his acquaintances, which may indicate that he was aware of the importance of the reputation and social image of everyone in the community.

Another document dating from 1672 shows how the social image of an individual could also harm or benefit the Pardos' cofradía. That year, someone filed a complaint against Juan de Dios Vargas, a mestizo and a Pardo brother. He committed the crime of uttering palabras mayores (inflammatory words) against the reputation of a Spanish woman who, furthermore, was married. This fact reached the ears of the alcalde, who immediately ordered an investigation. Several witnesses appeared to testify. One of them said he had seen Vargas throwing a stone at the Spanish woman. The witness said that the woman called Vargas "shameless," to which he replied that he was going to "break her mouth," that "she was the shameless one," and that she was also a "whore." The rest of the witnesses concurred with this statement. The result was an order to imprison Vargas. Once in jail, the authorities accepted his testimony. He said that he had been "out of his mind with a married woman" and that he had "little guilt" since she had yelled at him earlier, saying he was "a shameless chichimeca dog." Vargas's allegation did not spare him from being punished with twenty-three lashes.[58] These two cases, the mayordomo-mulato debtor and the "shameless" mestizo-Pardo brother, did not help the cofradía to build good standing. Nor were these behaviors favorable to the lousy reputation of mining and hacienda workers. In these years, the congregation members had enough to do to change the entire town's opinion of them.

In 1675, a representative of bishop Don Diego de Medrano visited San Joseph del Parral. During his stay, Medrano tried to determine whether La Cofradía de La Purísima Inmaculada Concepción de Los Pardos or La Cofradía de La Virgen de La Candelaria de Los Naturales / La Cofradía de Nuestra Señora del Rayo would hold the insignia that was to be used in processions and public cars. Everything indicates that this was the first time the Pardos began to share the emblem year after year with the La Cofradía de Los Naturales, beginning in January of the following year. The visitor recommended that the mayordomos of the two cofradías meet in the house of Don Juan del Candano, beneficiary priest of the town, so they could raffle for the honor of wearing the logo. The person who carried out the draw was the Pardo mayordomo Antonio Narváez, accompanied by his brothers Baltasar de los Reyes (an enslaved Black person), Diego Hernández, and Sebastián Antonio. Also at the meeting were Juan Domingo and Pedro Martin, mayordomos of La Cofradía de Nuestra Señora de La Candelaria de Los Naturales / La Cofradía de Nuestra Señora del Rayo. That afternoon, the lucky brothers were the Naturales.[59] Even though the Pardo bothers were not fortunate that day, the occasion was an excellent opportunity for them to be noticed and perhaps made a positive impression on the bishop's visitor since he would consider their wearing the symbol for the following festivals and processions. The gesture was significant due to the negative image of some Pardo brothers and mayordomos in previous years. However, it did not mean the Pardo brothers' life improved. Baltazar de Los Reyes (the enslaved Pardo brother), for example, appeared before the judge a few years after that meeting to ask for another "master" since the one he had, Don Bartolomé Sáenz, whipped and mistreated him and his wife.[60] Either way, the recognition the religious visitor gave him placed the congregation in the public environment of the town.

It happened that the following year of 1676, on December 8, La Cofradía de La Purísima Inmaculada Concepción de Los Pardos organized the procession to celebrate its Virgin. The brothers took the figure out of the chapel in Don Felipe de la Cueva's hacienda to the parade. Sadly, suddenly, and not knowing how, it ended up on the ground during the walk. According to mayordomo Narváez's report, he and his brothers were honoring the Virgin as they did yearly. He added that the Pardos who carried the image did so with solemnity when suddenly a servant of Don Felipe de la Cueva,

Antonio de Urrecha, entered the path that led the procession and "snatched the image from the brother who was carrying it, with much scandal in the town." Narváez argued that the Pardo brothers were concerned about the damage that Urrecha may have done to their reina (virgin) and the disturbance that may have occurred among people of service and mines. After exposing the facts, Narváez petitioned the authorities for Urrecha to come forward and give testimony about what happened.[61]

Urrecha appeared on December 10. According to him, the Pardos carried the image of the Virgin precariously. He testified that the wind was mighty that day. So, he had advised mulato Narváez and other Pardo members not to take the Virgin in the procession, as it had to be treated with reverence and conveyed only "in the hands of a priest." He concluded by saying the mulatos had acted indecently. At no time did he clarify whether or not he threw the image, but he did say that the Pardos were not "clean" enough to carry the Virgin. In addition, Urrecha questioned the right of the Pardos to appear before the judge, especially with Narváez as the leader, since, he said, "this mulato is a reckless, incapable, and crude person." Narváez dropped the case when Urrecha demanded him a new testimony. For some reason not stated in the document, he said he could not speak for all the members of the cofradía.[62]

Everything indicated that, by this time, the Pardos were securing a more respectable place in the town. Don Felipe de la Cueva's mining hacienda did not enjoy the sympathy of its servants and workers. Urrecha's testimony suggested the Virgin's image did not belong to the Pardo mayordomos, whom he described as "impure." For this reason, he considered mine workers had no right to go to court. However, Narváez not only had access to the judge, but the latter considered his request and summoned Urrecha to give testimony. Thus, regardless of the attitude and hostile actions taken towards the Pardos' cofradía, in these years they had the freedom to resort to authority, express themselves, and make requests. Even though the brothers continued facing challenges, they were very close to getting something that they had wanted for a long time.

In 1677, La Cofradía de La Inmaculada Concepción de Los Pardos finally strengthened its position in San Joseph del Parral society when they finally received official approval from the pope to hold their fiestas in de la Cueva's chapel. Probably proud that the pope approved their request, the mayordomos, including the mulato Narváez, posted the papal response on the chapel door.[63] However, the Bulla Pontificia the pope granted did not resolve the negative attitude that Don Felipe de la Cueva's employees and relatives continued to have toward La Cofradía de Los Pardos. In December 1687, Narváez was already in another lawsuit with Don Cristóbal Villamayor, nephew of Felipe Montaño de la Cueva. The main issue was determining who was responsible for the chapel of the Virgin of the Immaculate Conception and the religious objects kept in the mining hacienda. The allegation was that the Pardo brothers had acquired those objects through theft. In short, the lawsuit accused Narváez of stealing and taking relics to the chapel. During the investigation, several community members testified on his behalf, evidencing his excellent character as "a man of good faith and reputation, very well known in the town." The witnesses added that "he attended the governor's palace and private houses for fiestas and celebrations" and, in addition, he gave "silver objects and jewelry to the church." With these testimonies, Narváez was declared innocent of the charge.[64]

By this time, Narváez was well regarded in his community and apparently among some social circles. In fact, within the cofradías and in New Spain society in general, the figure of the mayor-domo conferred a certain status since when carrying out his daily activities pertinent to the congregation, this individual had to deal with ecclesiastical and governmental authorities and members of the Spanish elite. This type of contact could have added positive characteristics to his image in the social sphere, such as projecting a specific influence and receiving some privileges, as happened with mayordomo Narváez, who attended elite meetings. In addition, within the religious fervor that existed at that time, the cofradías' mayordomos should have a social image that reflected their Marian devotion and their sacrifice for the good of others. Thus, it is not surprising that mayordomos customarily received people's admiration, a condition that gave them prestige and honor. However, due to their bad reputation, for the Pardos' cofradía—made up of Indians, negros, mulatos, and mestizos—having and maintaining a good image was doubly tricky and vital at the same time.

Review of the Local Taste to the Universal Church

Together, La Cofradía de Nuestra Señora de La Candelaria de Los Naturales and La Cofradía de La Purísima Inmaculada Concepción de Los Pardos reveal what San Joseph del Parral looked like in the seventeenth century. It was a period of relative freedom for non-Spanish groups involved in Catholic ritual to create or recreate identities through local events perceived as miracles, or to obtain an official license and exhibit it in a public space as a symbol of both an ancient African and a new or renewed local character, and a right to belong to a religious institution and a mining town. The Naturales' and Pardos' cofradías also reveal their Virgins' need to be local. That is how the town witnessed the birth of two collective consciences by employing a Marian advocation.

Nonetheless, we observed how the oligarchy reacted differently toward the two ethnic confraternities. The Indigenous Mexicanos came to the village as "Indians of peace" to serve as an example to the barbarian Indigenous of the late sixteenth century, who eventually fled and took refuge in adjacent areas that were difficult to access. Perhaps the absence of a local Indian elite was advantageous for the Native Mexicanos since they occupied a practically unclaimed space in the town. The Pardos themselves were people of different races. Some of them were of African or Indigenous descent, enslaved or free workers in mining haciendas that the oligarchy controlled. This chapter indicates how the Pardo cofradía had just begun a struggle that, as the following chapters will show, would prevail until the end of the eighteenth century. Placing the pope's license on the parish doors was the first step to representing a complex diasporic experience that signaled a creation or recreation of African culture in Northern New Spain that, still, has not counted as part of the cultural memory of today's city of Hidalgo del Parral.

In this regard, Márquez Terrazas includes the legend of a "Tlaxcalteca" virgin whom lightning turned into a warrior and who was in favor of the Spanish elite and against the Indigenous "uprisings" of the north. However, Márquez Terrazas does not mention that Philip Terry, the author he cites in his book, fails to identify the Indigenous miner Gregorio Sebastián, the founder of the Cofradía de La Candelaria, as Tlaxcalteca. Furthermore, Márquez Terrazas does not mention that, according to Terry, it was "the Indigenous people" of Parral and not Governor Don Martín de Alday who acknowledged the Virgen del Rayo as "the chosen one" since they were proud of the stoicism its founder showed (the Indigenous miner, Domingo Sebastián) to build it.[65] This information invites the question whether, even in the present time, some historians and local chroniclers reconfigure Indigenous' legends, myths, or stories to reaffirm a "local" cultural memory while the history of medieval Spain is "revived."

In any case, the two religious institutions this chapter examined reveal that in the seventeenth century, at least two non-Spanish groups that inhabited the area involved themselves in Catholic rituals. Nicole von Germeten presents La Cofradía de La Inmaculada Concepción de Los Pardos as "unsuccessful" when comparing it with the cofradías of Blacks and mulatos in the cities of Mexico City and Valladolid, places with more significant resources housing a greater number of people of African origin.[66] Regarding Germeten's vision, Herman L. Bennett points out that revisionist historians (he includes Germeten) have focused on investigating Afro-Mexican groups from two extremes, either as sixteenth-century enslaved individuals or as characters of a history of social mobility of the eighteenth century.[67] Bennett believes that under this extremist scheme, people of African descent appear as objects. The author invites us to consider that if the Afro-Mexican community starred in its historical drama, it was precisely in the seventeenth century. This chapter accurately showed that in this century, both the Naturales' and Pardos' cofradías were, in fact, in charge of their drama in San Joseph del Parral despite the small but powerful oligarchy. However, as chapter 8 will demonstrate, the Pardos' cofradía was more assertive in claiming a place in the cultural sphere of the mining town during the eighteenth century. Whether that phenomenon was due to maturity as a brotherhood, which could indicate the creation of a local identity, is a possibility that we will explore later, as the following two chapters cover the evident changes the eighteenth century brought with the Bourbon Crown's enlightenment ideas and how those affected the Naturales' and Pardos' confraternities and the mining town's festive life in general.

CHAPTER 6

NATURALES´AND PARDOS´COFRADÍAS

A ROTA FORTUNAE AT THE TURN OF THE EIGHTEENTH CENTURY

The year 1788 dawned one morning at the end of July amid a wind that smelled of change, stirring the minds of the inhabitants who yearned for the abundance of the previous years. Four Pardo brothers were silently stationed in la plaza mayor, before the alcalde's office, perhaps thinking, "Nothing is like before." With a mien of an absence of joy they joined the "town's claims" long line. Suddenly, Doña María Rosa Ortíz's representative arrived and entered the building, skipping the line. Nobody said a word. A frowning merchant known as Pedro Domínguez said that Doña María had been requesting fifty repartimiento Indians for her hacienda for some time. After a chain of bad words, he explained to the few who were listening to him that he was in line because of people like Doña María. "How is that?" someone asked. "She wants repartimiento Indians. We have raids against Indians. That damages my commerce," he answered. Another man who was seven spots before him yelled that Salineros Indians and other Indigenous groups were asking for peace, but none said a word, probably because they did not know if he was asking a question or making a statement.

As the sun changed position overhead, some individuals approached the Pardo bothers to ask, with a hopeful tone, if they had news about the remate (auction) of corridas de toros, then they continued walking while shaking their heads in a resigned gesture of "nothing yet." What better way to forget about life's vicissitudes once in a while than a fiesta with corridas de toros? More than a week had passed, and the Pardos and the inhabitants were at God's will, still waiting for a solution because they no longer had the Church and the government's support on their side as they had before. The new Bourbon king felt farther away than ever. Many people wondered what he had against the holidays. A curandera claimed the monarch urgently needed a limpia de espíritu (a cleansing for the spirit) so that he would not be a bitter king.

The Pardo brothers broke the silence from time to time to rehearse the scene that one of them would perform before the judge. Once it was their turn, the mayordomo went to the office. With eloquence, he asked permission to announce the auction of a corrida de toros. He explained how the auction was the only way to carry out the religious festival for their Holy Virgin in January of the following year, since the pesos were as absent as the Bourbon king. When the Pardo mayordomo went out, he assured his Pardo brothers and the rest of the inquisitive folks that he had played his role very well in front of the authorities; he mentioned the mining decline and their compromise with their ancestors and the Virgin. In short, he believed he represented her civil and Christian role as never before. As the Pardos continued talking, the town crier came running and announced to all that a vecino had proffered a good sum of pesos for the Pardos' remate. The Pardos jumped and hugged each other, and little by little, the wind spread their joy throughout the vicinity.

The pliego suelto above portrays the atmosphere in which people in San Joseph del Parral lived under the Bourbon reforms. The crown entered the scene in the early 1700s, launching a series of economic, political, and social reforms that, among other outcomes, significantly affected the Catholic ritual in Spain and America. Even though those transformations, as merchandise and news, arrived late to Northern New Spain, frontier people eventually learned the truth: the Habsburg Crown left the empire in decline. It was in debt and had poor production and deplorable trade in America as powerful imperial rivals (England, France, and Austria) challenged it. With this unfortunate heritage, the Bourbons' struggle to revive the empire started in 1713, as soon as it officially assumed power. The reforms did not come out of nowhere. Before the Bourbon House arrived at the Crown of Spain, the Age of Enlightenment had manifested in Europe and its ideas spread out with the wind. It was a cultural and intellectual movement that, from the end of the seventeenth century until well into the eighteenth century, used "reason" as a weapon to end ignorance and superstition.

The Enlightenment, the manifestation of the spirit that dares to think for itself according to philosopher Immanuel Kant, came to Spain mainly from France, Italy, England, and Central Europe. Juan José of Austria, the illegitimate brother of Carlos II (King of Spain, 1665–1700), had extended his stay abroad in his minister's position. He acquired and spread new ideas and attitudes in Spain during these trips. For example, he created a pre-enlightened environment by establishing a private academy at the court and protecting foreign intellectuals very close to his new projects. Juan José de Austria was also an advisor to Carlos II who, influenced by the new ideas of these "novice" intellectuals, undertook the task of recovering the critical sense, overcoming scholasticism, and shortening the scientific delay that separated Spain from the other nations.[1] Nonetheless, Carlos the Second's effort did not help much to solve the crown's problems when he left in 1700. The Bourbon reign began with Felipe V in 1700. However, he abdicated in 1724 in favor of his son Luis I, who died that the same year. Felipe V then resumed the crown.[2]

The most faithful admirers and representatives of the Enlightenment, though, were Fernando VI (1746–1759) and Carlos

III (1759–1788), who spread new and modern ideas to move Spain forward, at home and aboard. For the Bourbon crown, the Kantian philosophy was an invitation to an individualistic education that encompassed economic, religious, political, social, and cultural qualities. Motivated by the deterioration of the kingdom at home and abroad in form of epidemics, demography, economy, and foreign policy, among other tragedies, Kantian ideas fostered the crown's main purposes: to preserve the empire, recover authority, and increase the treasury with new administrative measures.[3]

The result was a series of changes that affected the social, political, and economic facets of Spain and its American possessions. The transformations were more palpable in the festival arena since new edicts restricted public participation. Bourbon government officials set out to reduce, limit, or even eradicate popular religious dramas, pilgrimages, dances, and corridas de toros, for example. This control also reached some religious institutions, such as cofradías and capellanías, two spheres that until then had managed to bring together various social segments under the same Catholic Baroque purpose: to live well to die even better.

This chapter examines how the Bourbon reforms altered the participation of cofradías de Pardos and Naturales in the Catholic ritual. The lack of economic support from the Church and the government altered how they organized and carried out their festivities. The archival documents reveal how those brotherhoods accommodated the modifications the Bourbon reforms brought to continue participating in the religious life of the mining town and, with it, to have an honorable image, a sense of community, and practical and spiritual support. In doing so, they transformed the universal Catholic ritual that was trying to welcome an illustrated ideology without success, since some medieval and baroque elements resisted change. Analyzing archival documents as "colonial texts" allows us to underscore their multiple meanings, and through their contextualization to identify various historical voices that reveal how the

Spanish empire tried to transform its subjects, and how the latter used the same discourse to advance their purposes.

As mentioned, the Bourbon reforms' primary drive was to end ignorance and superstition at home and abroad. The endeavor manifested itself mainly in eliminating the vulgar and irrational components in religious celebrations, replacing them with pious demonstrations that would mold a new type of (mainly male) population oriented to be better workers and better heads of family. In Spain and America, festive life was restricted.[4] In Mexico City, the government no longer tolerated more profane celebrations, much less during Easter or Christmas. In 1769, for example, authorities banned public performances, fireworks, and alcohol. They regulated entertainments' duration as well: the events had to end in the afternoon and not last for many days. Furthermore, by 1771, the reforms prohibited the inclusion of new festivals in the liturgical calendar.[5] The alterations in Mexico City's festive life portray a government interested in ordering, reclaiming, and reconquering public space. In the Bourbon Crown's mind, unregulated public celebrations were occasions for an "inappropriate" mix of classes, sexes, and ethnicities, disorders that were against the idealized, hierarchical, ordered society the Bourbons had in mind. To achieve this model, the masses must be disciplined and productive for the state and for the society in general through attention to church, home, and work.[6]

This situation existed alongside the economic slowness that Mexico City experienced, a premise that the Bourbon House used in its favor. This city witnessed high prices and inflation, especially in the last quarter of the eighteenth century. The increase in population, and peasants without work migrating to the new mining miracle, San Felipe El Real de Chihuahua, gave rise to a crisis in which the Bourbons acquired the necessary pretext to distribute the burden of economic festivals on the inhabitants. For example, the crown limited the donation of funds to specific partakers. Thus, groups without financial solvency and high social status eventually disappeared from the celebrations. In any case, for the Bourbon Crown it was necessary to focus on getting the empire out of the economic predicament it was in, but that responsibility also belonged to the industrious inhabitants the crown was in the process of reforming.[7]

In Mexico City and throughout New Spain, Bourbon authorities exhorted rulers and inhabitants to practice moderation at public festivals. The atmosphere of austerity emerged even in the celebrations dedicated to the royalty. Previously, those were a source of pride for their ostentation. By the end of the eighteenth century, they had to be sparing and sober. Thus did Don Manuel Antonio Flores Maldonado Martínez de Angulo y Bodquín, Viceroy, Governor, and Captain General of New Spain, announce it in 1789. To carry out the ceremony that would commemorate the death of Carlos III (1788), he said: "On the 14th day of the last December, at about four in the morning, the precious life of our Catholic monarch, Don Carlos III, ended (may God rest his soul)." He added that he oversaw delivering the news of the monarch's death:

> . . . to the public of this capital and of all the cities and places of these domains, with the usual formalities, authority, and pomp in such unfortunate events, and that in the same way, the funerals and suffrages are celebrated for the soul of our deceased monarch. . . . The neighbors and inhabitants of this kingdom, men and women, must dress in rigorous mourning for six months, under the penalty of 50 pesos . . . except the Indians attending to their poverty and relief . . . understanding the same with the solemn and miserable poor people . . . entrust to God with prayers and suffrages the soul of the King Our Lord . . . that the royal spirit of His Majesty declared in the Royal Order mentioned before . . . to the throne [of Carlos III], as in funeral demonstrations . . . no more expenses be made than the very precise, so that the

excesses do not turn into vanity or profane acts that should only be aimed at religion, and a sincere manifestation of the fidelity and love of the vassals to the sovereign.[8]

Whether all the cities and towns of New Spain followed the precise recommendations of Maldonado Martínez is unknown. Still, his insistence on foregoing excessive spending and leading a life of devotion toward the Church and the monarch is evident in his discourse. This new approach to festive life suggests a distance between the Church and the crown. The relationship between those two entities had been solid and necessary to consolidate the Spanish empire's hegemony in America. Then, as we will see, it is not strange that the gradual gap between those two forces affected American cofradías in many modes.

The new religious orientation the Bourbon Crown wanted to implement would have involved the collaboration of the Catholic Church, especially to instruct the cofradías about the recent provisions, which during the seventeenth century oversaw disseminating and maintaining the Catholic Baroque cult of the universal Church. But the Bourbon regime did not concur. Some enlightened sectors of the Bourbon government blamed the Catholic Church precisely for exacerbating a baroque ideology that cultivated ignorance and superstition in the America's masses. Thus, authorities decided that the cofradías would be better held under royal jurisdiction. That meant that from then on, the brotherhoods would give an account of their activities, especially economic ones, to the government, since another of its objectives, perhaps the central one, was to protect the royalties of the crown.[9]

Since the mid-eighteenth century, the Bourbon Crown asked itself where to place the Church in its new project: inside or outside? While it resolved this issue, it progressively implemented measures to reduce religious institutions' power. In 1767, for example, the crown expelled the Jesuits from all Spain and its territories, including the Americas. In 1786, it began to control the administration of the diezmo (tithe).[10] Moreover, in 1795, it initiated the suspension of the ecclesiastical jurisdiction.[11] Thus, everything indicated that the place of the Church was going to be "outside." This situation impacted the cofradías since the Church provided them with moral and financial support; it paid expenses related to religious events. Faced with such a situation, the cofradías had to seek this type of support from sources outside the Church, as La Cofradía de Los Pardos did.

La Cofradía de Los Pardos: From One Remate to Another

In San José del Parral around 1788, La Cofradía de La Purísima Inmaculada Concepción de Los Pardos was experiencing economic shortages. At that time, neither the Church nor the local government economically supported the religious cofradías in organizing celebrations. For this motive, one day in July of that year, the mayordomos José Muñoz and Leandro Mosqueda chose to auction corridas de toros to offer the profit in the form of a fiesta for their Virgin in January of the following year. With those intentions, the Pardo brothers appeared before the judge. They said they had sworn to hold:

> . . . the church, corridas de toros, and other public celebrations every year . . . until the decline of this mineral seized them; however, in fulfillment of our promise, although overcoming many difficulties, the said festivities were held on the first of January of this year, and wishing as we wish that they continue in the coming January, and the cofradía nor we have funds to support the increased expenses to build the plaza and enable corridas de toros [we ask] that the plaza be published and auctioned at the highest bidder . . . for the pious costs of its erection . . . remaining for the benefit of the bidder the product of the tablados [wood platform].[12]

Authorities announced the remate in the plaza mayor. The town crier had been shouting for several days about the auction of corridas de toros for the benefit of La Cofradía de Los Pardos and the required sum of money. If the Pardo brothers were lucky, the congregation would receive several offers; the remate would be awarded to the individual who offered them the most money. In a few days, the Pardo brothers received an offer from an individual. From then on, this person would supervise all the expenses in organizing and staging the corridas de toros during the holidays. In return, this person had the right to keep a portion of the profits from selling the tickets—that is, after making the corresponding tax payment to the crown.[13]

Given their success that year with the remate, the Pardo brothers requested it again in July 1789. Once more, claiming their state of poverty, they added that they needed support "so that this devotion does not faint, and after paying the expenses and its function, there remains a surplus to benefit the repairs of the temple of the soberana [Virgin] . . . the remate is announced for a term of thirty days in the same way as in the past year."[14] On August 30, the authorities awarded the auction of corridas de toros to Don Pedro Medina and Don Cayetano Cano, residents of Santa Bárbara. They bid 210 pesos for six years, promising to give each year the same amount to La Cofradía de Los Pardos. These men contributed the pledged amount for four consecutive years until 1794, with two years remaining in fulfillment of the deal. Faced with the prospect of a shortfall, the alcalde decided that he would auction again the corridas de toros for the Pardo brothers so they could organize their fiesta the year of 1795.[15] After several proclamations made during January 1794, it was not until February of the following year when a bidder appeared, Don Joaquín Antonio Ruíz de Cevallos, who offered to give the Pardo brothers 100 pesos for the next corridas de toros. But as the offer was insufficient, the town crier announced the auction again, inviting the population to enhance the bid. On

March 1, Don Joaquín de Ávila appeared to make a deal for two years, offering to give 200 pesos each year to benefit La Cofradía de Los Pardos.[16]

As can be seen, the Pardo brothers adapted their discourse and practices according to the new reality they faced resulting from the Bourbon reforms. They strategically used the economic crises in their favor to advance their objectives. It gives the impression that they agreed to mention and highlight to the alcalde "the decline of the mineral," that is, funds, to request and obtain an auction that would not only help them to pay for their festivity expenses but also to reserve some pesos to repair the temple. Although the auctions of corridas de toros and other types of entertainment included in religious festivals supported the government's public spending, it was also a way, perhaps the only one in these times, for this cofradía to continue practicing their "sworn" rituals.

Even though the Pardos' cofradía remained subject to the oligarchy's control, the proximity to other towns gave it advantages when organizing the corridas de toros because, as seen in this case, goodwill and wealth could come from neighbors in surrounding places. While Bourbon reforms reduced the cofradías' access to economic resources to sustain their festivities, in San Joseph del Parral the government allowed the Pardo brothers to auction corridas de toros, with which proceeds they could continue joining the religious ritual, even though the event evidently preserved "pagan" elements of the baroque religiosity.

The Cofradía of Naturales in the Bourbons' Eyes

La Cofradía de La Virgen del Rayo, which until 1662 was La Cofradía de Nuestra Señora de La Candelaria de Los Naturales, had a different experience from that of the Pardo brothers in the same year of 1788. The Naturales brothers honored their Marian devotion, a celebration on the three days of Easter Pentecost. During that time, they used to carry the statue of the Virgen del Rayo from

San Joseph del Parral to Minas Nuevas. One day that year, they went to the priest to apply for the required license to organize the pilgrimage. After listening to them, the prelate was reluctant to accede to their request. He explained that it was harmful to raise the statue of the Virgin in that mining town of Minas Nuevas, in addition to the fact that the festivity itself meant many expenses. Before the clergyman's resolution, the brothers left. However, in a few days, they met with some neighbors and find a solution.[17]

At the meeting, they agreed to make some important variations on how to execute some events in their congregation. For example, they decided to abolish the ancient custom of taking the Virgen del Rayo to Minas Nuevas. From that date on, "the ecclesiastical function always had to be carried out in the town's parish church." They also modified the mode in which they made their mayordomos' elections. From then on, they would write the names of all members who had not previously been mayordomos on pieces of paper. These they would put into envelopes to select at random. Lastly, the name of the individual who appeared more than three times would be the next mayordomo. Furthermore, they agreed they would not offer refreshments or treats the next time they announced their festival. For them, it was sufficient that the inhabitants would listen to the ring of the church bells to celebrate the news.[18]

Those modifications indicate that, as had the Pardo brothers, the Naturales brothers were obliged to adapt to the new local circumstances. Although on that occasion they did not change the name of their Marian advocation, they decided to make some significant reformations that perhaps were advantageous for them as well; taking their Virgin to the town of Minas Nuevas perhaps did represent a significant expense for the congregation. Furthermore, changing the election process for mayordomos and the new, more austere way of announcing their celebration spoke of a quite independent attitude, especially when this freedom of decision and action compares itself with the limitations La Cofradía de Los Pardos faced.

After analyzing the documents involving Pardos' and Naturales' cofradías, it is vital to question two aspects regarding the new provisions of the Bourbon Crown for the cofradías. The Pardo brothers requested a license from the local authority to offer a corrida de toros that would allow them to celebrate their Virgin. In contrast, the Naturales brothers asked the priest for permission to organize the pilgrimage for their reina. While the prelate's speech reflected the new Bourbons' effort to reduce public spending, at the same time his intervention lends itself to questioning how effective and consistent the new Bourbon edicts were in regulating the cofradías. Who would control them: the royal jurisdiction, the Church, or both? Also, supposing the local government and the Church echoed the Bourbons' approach to eliminating pagan, irrational, or baroque elements in religious events, why did the provincial government support La Cofradía de Los Pardos to auction corridas de toros, a pagan public activity? Likewise, the question arises as to why the Church continued allowing La Cofradía de Los Naturales to organize a public celebration that prioritized its Marian advocation and not the monarchy.

Perhaps the most straightforward answer is that those types of exceptions or adjustments tended to occur frequently in towns, villages, and cities of New Spain, where the participants, the government, cofradías, and the Church negotiated their interests according to the local context. But the intervention of universal forces "in conflict," the Catholic religion and the Bourbon Crown, could lead to a more complex response, especially in clarifying whether the Catholic Baroque ritual of the seventeenth century prevailed, adjusted, transformed, or died with the birth and development of the Bourbon reforms of the eighteenth century.

It is evident that the Catholic Baroque ritual of New Spain, the exuberant pious expression of the divine and the hierarchical space from which God ruled, was not an autonomous idea or practice. On the contrary, it arose and depended on the relationship the

Catholic Church and the Habsburg Crown established before they set foot on American soil. These two universal forces joined and inserted the Spanish Baroque into the Catholic ritual. Since this type of relationship did not exist during the Bourbons' reign, it is difficult to determine the permanence, transformation, or end of Catholic Baroque ritual after the Bourbon reforms. This chapter reveals the ambiguous atmosphere the cofradías faced when organizing religious festivities during those times, as at least three historical voices were competing for the faithful/vassal attention: the Baroque Catholic Church, the Baroque Habsburgs, and the "Illustrated" Bourbons.

An Overview of Cofradías' Adaptation to the Bourbon Reforms

The Bourbon Crown had difficulty ending superstition and ignorance in New Spain. It was particularly problematic in San Joseph del Parral, a mining town that did not welcome "reason" with open arms. Partakers in the Catholic ritual continued seeing festive life through the Spanish Baroque lens. However, the archival documents reveal how Pardos' and Naturales' cofradías adapted to the new regulations. To ecclesiastical and governmental authorities, they represented themselves according to the role the Catholic Church and the crown gave them, even though the former two had an ambiguous relationship. The brothers appeared before the judge as obedient vassals of the Bourbon House asking permission to organize events with Spanish Baroque components: pilgrimages for religious figures and religious fiestas that included corridas de toros. In that sense, the two brotherhoods altered both the universal Catholic Baroque ritual and the Bourbon religious reforms and persevered as religious institutions, contrary to what happened to many confraternities in Mexico City that completely disappeared from the Catholic ritual scenario. And, perhaps the Pardo and Naturales brothers noticed that despite the dismissal the crown expressed for the ignorant and superstitious practices of Baroque Catholicism, it still needed them, as did the Habsburgs: as its vassals, to consolidate a very much needed hegemony.

CHAPTER 7

A TOWN IN QUICKSAND

BETWEEN BAROQUE FERVOR AND ENLIGHTENED REASON

On Sunday, July 10, 1763, the town crier communicated the new orders the jurisdiction judge drew up because of the provisions of the Royal Justice. He did it before la plaza mayor, just when the faithful Christians of San Joseph del Parral were leaving the day's Mass. All heard the edicts restricting card games or any other games during public holidays or working days. Failure to comply with these provisions would provoke a penalty of ten pesos and jail for the person who officiated said games and the players. That day, Don Benito Sortia and Justino Álvarez gave thanks to God after the town crier stopped his shouting because when they go to Mass it is not to hear banalities but poetry, music for the living soul, that young men wrote and recited eloquently in the middle of the plaza mayor.

But it seemed that most of the inhabitants ignored both the poetry and the new regulations. Now, almost a year later, the alcalde learned that someone in the town often organized card games at his home during holidays and even on workdays. One recent night, this authority and other Spanish vecinos showed up at Rafael Sierra's house to accuse him of having officiated those games at his jacal. He did not know how to answer when asked if he had not heard about the new protocols that were announced a year before. Perhaps he thought of excusing himself,

153

saying he had been absent for over a year, but his neighbors could attest otherwise. Maybe it also crossed his mind to claim that he was sick the day of the announcement, but again, anyone in town could confirm that he, indeed, attended Mass that day.

While Sierra was racking his brains, wondering what to say, the alcalde and his companions entered and encountered some men of various calidades playing cards at Sierra's jacal. All of them, along with Sierra, were directed to jail. Juan Pedro Talamantes, Pedro García, Juan Agustín de Mijares, Fermín Urrieta, Prudencio Gardea, Cayetano Gallardo, Juan Agustín Martínez, Antonio Naranjo, and Sierra himself, all downcast, heard the admonishment. It stated that they would be reprimanded for not complying with the regulations of the Royal Justice and for participating in those games. The reason given for the reproof was that "from them emanated the fact that people of such nature undressed and were left without clothes and money." Following three days of being in jail, Mijares broke his silence and, after making the sign of the Holy Cross, he promised to tell the truth. He said that for three days, Sierra had invited him to play, and he had since lost some tools, a handkerchief, a pair of silver-buckled spurs, his cape, riding sleeves, his knife, and a pair of breeches. So, Mijares' statement supported the alcalde's allegation: in Sierra's case nudity, literally, was the result of this type of entertainment among people of such nature.[1] Don Benito Soria and Justino Álvarez agreed completely with the alcalde and commented how delighted they were with the merchants guild's efforts to bring high art to such a noble province and mining town, as some retablos and paintings were about to arrive to illustrate this demonstrable ignorance among ordinary people.

The pliego suelto above characterizes the effect Bourbon reforms had on workers in San Joseph del Parral during the last third of the seventeenth century.[2] It reveals how deeply the Enlightenment ideology penetrated the Bourbon Crown and its attempts to improve the conditions of its most highly praised revenue

154

element: mining. The scene exposes how the Bourbon reforms tried to end superstition and ignorance and welcomed "reason" to improve the mining industry. This chapter examines how global and local changes impacted workers' festive life. The Bourbon House's interest in Northern New Spain's mining productivity generated a new powerful social actor: the guild of miners. With the support of civil and ecclesiastical authorities, this entity struggled to control the workforce and public celebrations in the entire provincia. Rather than analytical, this chapter is informative about the changes this area experimented with from about the mid-eighteenth century, which will serve as historical context for the remaining chapters.

By 1750, the mining town of San Joseph del Parral was no longer the same in terms of the composition of inhabitants and mining wealth. During the second half of the seventeenth century and the beginning of the eighteenth, the provincia experienced an increase in towns and inhabitants.[3] Even if, until the beginning of the eighteenth century, most of the population in San Joseph del Parral had been Indigenous, the blending of Indigenous people, mulatos, negros, mestizos, and other mixed people caused an increase in the mulato and mestizo population around 1750. Although on this date the baptism books noted a more significant number of mestizos than mulatos, this could have been the result of miscegenation. The racial lines between the two groups were thin and difficult to define. The baptism books gave the category of mestizo to almost all those recorded, although some of these were mulatos.[4]

Regarding mineral wealth, in the 1720s San Joseph del Parral began a period of decline that lasted until 1750. The causes were various. Among them was the discovery of mines at Real de San Francisco de Cuéllar, later called San Felipe El Real de Chihuahua. Formally instituted as a villa in 1718, with a cabildo and acting as the new capital of Nueva Vizcaya for most of the eighteenth century, the location unsurprisingly attracted many people, including the governors of La Nueva Vizcaya, who now preferred it to

Durango.[5] The discovery of mines at this site caused many San Joseph del Parral inhabitants to migrate to this prosperous villa, which reduced the mining town's workforce. During the bonanzas that San Francisco de Cuéllar experienced (1718–1725, 1730–1734, 1748–1751), entrepreneurs abandoned various mines in San Joseph del Parral and several merchants, along with their money, went to the new "mining miracle" that was taking place nearby.[6]

However, the mining bonanzas that San Francisco de Cuéllar enjoyed ended in the early 1750s, just as mining revived in San Joseph del Parral. By this time, people discovered new metal veins in the town. This situation improved the supply of quicksilver, the mineral with which miners extracted the metal and that had been difficult to distribute in previous years. Still, as of this date, the Camino Real was commercially connected with different points of New Spain by various routes. Towards the south and the north, the Camino Real reached Santa Fe and Sonora, respectively, while to the west, a road left the town to Sinaloa. Thus, these circumstances helped San Joseph del Parral to have a slight recovery in the mining-commercial activity, but it did not return to its former splendor, despite the efforts of the Bourbon Crown.[7]

The discovery of new veins in San Joseph del Parral coincided with the implementation of Bourbon reforms. The promoter of these new regulations was José Gálvez, visitador general (inspector) to New Spain from 1765 to 1771. Between 1765 and 1786, Gálvez defined and applied economic reforms to make mining productive. This man saw mining as the origin and sole source of the metals that gave spirit and movement to all human occupations and universal commerce. With this mentality, he organized the miners into a guild with the jurisdiction (its courts) of mining-related disputes. He also managed to lower the price of quicksilver, and with this shift production increased, freeing mining from commercial control. Furthermore, the 1778 Free Trade Decree abolished the old monopoly of Cádiz, opening the Spanish market to all South America, except Venezuela. From then on, the main ports of the peninsula traded freely with America, granting economic independence to miners and merchants.[8] This series of initiatives applied almost immediately in San Joseph del Parral. The archival documents attest to an economic boom among the mining class, showing that at that time, their presence, especially their power, could be more clearly stated under the guild council they formed.

The new status that mining entrepreneurs acquired, thanks to the promotion of mining production, served them to manipulate various issues in their favor, so much so that they did not hesitate to intervene in everything that, in their opinion, or hindered mining production. At the community level, they intervened in organizing public festivities to control service and mine workers further. In 1766, for example, Judge Joaquín de Colla granted an order for the suspension of festivals that Don Miguel de la Fuente, a resident of the San Joseph del Parral, requested, saying that:

> Together with the authority and assistance of His Majesty, to bring a retablo [an altarpiece] that at the expense of this trade [guild] . . . brought from Mexico to Parral . . . an ornament for el Templo de la Sagrada Compañía de Jesús. It was determined [by the guild and some miners] that . . . there would be no corridas de toros, so that the sale of products from the stalls and card games could paid the altarpiece . . . that due to the notable damages that those [fiestas de toros] cause to the mining trade . . . which is currently in decline [due to] this type of festivities . . . service people are prone to them due to their diversions . . . ruin of families and other consequences . . . better [is to] pay the money owed for the altarpiece.[9]

Apparently, the men of commerce and mines of San Joseph del Parral were doing charitable work for La Compañía de Jesús by taking charge of the cost of the altarpiece brought from Mexico City. According to Colla, the economic rewards of mining were suffering a setback, which was part of the justification for requesting the cancellation of corridas de toros but not for card games. It seems that by eliminating corridas de toros, people would spend more money on stalls' merchandise and card games, and those proceeds would cover the altarpiece's payment. According to Colla, service people harmed the mining industry and their families by organizing the corridas de toros. So, it was better for these mining and merchant men to manage and profit from card games, for their cause was noble.

It is unknown who covered the payment of some paintings and altarpieces that La Compañía de Jesús kept in the town of San Jerónimo de Huejotitán. In 1666, this mission had three canvases brought from Mexico. The same happened with another altarpiece, also transported from Mexico in 1680 to the San José parish.[10] However, in 1766, the men of commerce and mines were very interested in giving a gift to La Compañía de Jesús. At the same time, they wanted to control the expenses that the service people made in such harmful festivities, both for the mining industry and the workers' families. The interference of rich and powerful men and the members of the mining council increased and took on different tones as the century progressed.

A primary document from 1794 informs about comedy actors who came from San Felipe El Real de Chihuahua to perform at San Joseph del Parral, where authorities did not welcome them. An official document from the Bishop of Durango communicated that:

> The corresponding measures against the current comedians . . . abuses that the comedians of Chihuahua committed in the performance of their comedies, and that it is known that they are themselves in this town still performing their comedies . . . so that they suspend the performances, and

the due providences are dictated so that they are fulfilled, and the faithful do not make scandals and make mistakes against the faith.[11]

The bishop's response to end the eighteenth-century comedians' performances contrasts with mid-seventeenth accounts. In *Historia de la Nuevo México*, Captain Gaspar de Villagrá mentions that some northern regions experienced theatrical performances from around the year 1640. In canto XIV, he tells of late-sixteenth-century civil festivities held in the El Paso del Norte area, where a captain performed a comedy. In canto XVI, on the other hand, he mentions that in New Mexico, the army conducted a drama of the Battle between Moors and Christians around the same time, which included dialogues. In addition, in 1691, a peninsular-type comedy was staged in Durango entitled "El dichoso bandolero" (The Happy Bandit), one of many comedies performed every year outside a convent during viceroyalty times.[12]

There are also indications of dramatic poetry performances in Santa Fe, New Mexico, during the celebration of the swearing in of Fernando VI in 1748. The town of Santa Eulalia, Chihuahua, held a loa (a praise in form of poetry) during the visit of the Bishop of Durango in 1760. Santa Fe, New Mexico, offered the inhabitants a zarzuela (Spanish opera) season with an eighteenth-century tornadilla (Spanish popular song) titled "El solterito" (The Single Man).[13] And even San Joseph del Parral had some poets. A document on the "Patronage of San Francisco Javier in Nueva Vizcaya," dating from 1669, mentions the creation of panegyrics and poems in the place.[14]

New Spain also included satire in the form of parades, songs, poems, and parodies, especially during the seventeenth century. In Mexico City, for example, groups met at night in the streets or in taverns where they performed parodies about government officials and clergy. Fringe groups used anonymous satire as a form of political communication and as an act of defiance. Satire became a way of challenging the official discourse of the New Spain elite, questioning the idea of "good government." Satirists ordinarily emphasized the disorder, frailty, and incompetence of the officers who ruled the colony, including the greed, hypocrisy, cruelty, and arrogance of the king himself.[15] In Mexico City's mid-eighteenth-century context, the public tolerated and, to some extent, expected satire. Curcio-Nagy indicates that resistance to change signified the new way of demonstrating the purity that the Bourbon Crown was trying to impose. So, government reformers attempted to mitigate that reluctance toward "the new" by allowing satire in plays and theatrical comedies.[16]

In 1795, San Joseph del Parral's mining guild held a meeting to decide on certain actions: to have greater control over public life and the performance of workers throughout the provincia. The guild aspired to remove any obstacle that might harm the mining company. The council asked the rest of the territorial mining bodies to report clearly and methodically which issues they considered unfavorable to mining development in the area. The participants also had to explain why they considered them "burdensome." Besides that, they needed to give an account of the number of inhabitants, mines, and people operating; the names of mines' owners; the number quicksilver smelting farms; and an indication as to whether mining was productive or not in their localities.[17] In short, the mining council wanted almost total control of the area.

The council's request to the territorial bodies expressing "matters" that could damage metallurgical development was an attempt to make their interference in public life more decisive and consistent. But, as noted above, the Catholic Church was not far behind in contributing to the reforms that were in full swing. One day in August of that same year, the Bishop of Durango issued a proclamation stating that "the servants of mines and estates can go to their jobs on holidays at sunset."[18] This communication arrived late and incomplete in San Joseph del Parral for unknown motives.

So, to formalize and complete it, the local government needed to consult about the rest of its content with councilors or alcaldes of neighboring towns. The authorities made inquiries in Guanajuato, Pachuca, and Zacatecas, which in turn delivered the information that had been lacking as follows. That is, in those places,

> At sunset, the workers did not go to any acts of religion to sanctify the festivities. Instead, they went to forbidden games, dishonest gatherings, and the detriment . . . of the mines; that night and the next one, they lost the wages they had to earn the entire week, [and by leaving] . . . in hunger and need women and family, worse consequences followed.[19]

The discourse suggests that the bishop's mandate intended to protect mining industry interests. First, it justified why the authorities resolved that the mining workers return to work after the festivities, which in these times ended at dusk. As the workers did not go to religious events but engaged in unethical activities, it was more profitable for them and the mining industry to return to work. Then, the edict justified Don Fernando Alfaro and other miners from San Joseph del Parral driving their workers to work at sunset, taking a step beyond the bishop's recommendation. San Joseph del Parral authorities also ordered some leading miners to read the mandate in front of them, perhaps as an attempt to establish a common rule among all mining workers.

However, the bishop's mandate does not mean the mining union had not controlled public events in the past to benefit metal production. Sometimes the oligarchs or the Spanish elite asked the Archbishopric of Durango for a list of official holidays they should keep, probably as an attempt to discard and not allow workers to attend those that were not strictly endorsed.[20] After the formation of the miners' council, however, those individuals had greater freedom to exercise control over public events throughout the provincia.

On occasion, they even interpreted or adapted mandates, allowing them to practically take workers bodily and bring them back to the workplace once the festivity ended. These types of actions and attitudes continued and reached extremes. In 1790, for example, the mining council requested authorization for the mines not to close at night, nor before and after the festivities.[21] By 1799, they suspended nocturnal religious processions throughout the provincia.[22] The Catholic Church supported and embraced the new Bourbon proposals to make a more dynamic worker, especially in mining. In America, the Catholic Church altered the liturgical calendar so that it coincided with the Bourbons' enlightened vision of ordered cities, whose concern centered on the waste of time and resources public celebrations yielded. Hence, it seems that the relationship between the Church and the crown was ambiguous, although both manipulated mining, workers, religious institutions, and society in general.[23]

San Joseph del Parral closed out the eighteenth century by officially receiving the category of villa in 1802, and by 1809, the mining town organized a celebration for royalty for the first time: a festivity for King Fernando VII. Neither the local authority nor the Church sponsored the celebration. It was Don Cesario Sánchez, a Spanish neighbor of the Villa de San Joseph del Parral, who in April offered to finance this royal celebration. He claimed to have had news that several cities in New Spain would celebrate the king in the coming month of May. He added,

> I find myself . . . it is a duty to take on my own the whole of the arrangement of them [the festivals], for their effect as corresponds to the bullring and other precise maneuvers for what the position that seems admissible is intended to do, considering that I was given . . . some luces [money] from the product to fix my offer.[24]

Sánchez presented 1,200 pesos on the condition of charging kitchen stalls and public entertainment. He asked for wood to surround the plaza where the corridas de toros would occur. Sánchez got everything he asked for, but the authorities warned him that corridas de toros had to end at a "judicious time."[25] This celebration is not recorded in archival documents. However, besides kitchen and entertainment stalls, which could have included card games, raffles, and comedies or theatrical works, there were also corridas de toros. These and other entertainments constituted everything the enlightened crown was supposed to disapprove. As already observed, the Bourbon House emphasized royal ceremonies. Still, it did not mention that in towns or villages such as San Joseph del Parral, the inhabitants had the ingrained habit of organizing and attending corridas de toros, one of the many "Habsburgs' customs" the Bourbon House wanted to eradicate.

Account of a Town in Transition: Between Baroque Fervor and Enlightened Reason

The local government, the Church, and the mining council's efforts to control public festivals to create industrious workers had several universal and local aspects in their favor. In the second half of the eighteenth century, San Joseph del Parral was "lucky" to be a town flourishing in mining. Visitor Gálvez's vision of this company—as he expresses, as "the spirit and movement of human occupations and universal commerce"—must have had an essential impact on the mining elite. Grouped into a council that enjoyed jurisdiction, the descendants of the oligarchs of the seventeenth century had the power to manipulate the mining business. The Catholic Church joined them and, although its claims were unclear, it showed its interest in maintaining the Marian cult. At the same time, the aim of the local government and the mining elite was to take advantage of public baroque entertainment. They used the profits in works they considered truly Christian, like buying altarpieces to embellish and educate inhabitants on their duties as Catholics and mine workers.

CHAPTER 8

PARDOS' FIESTAS

A CAROUSEL IN A
DIASPORIC FRONTIER

It was January 8, 1747, another feast day in San Joseph del Parral. On this occasion, La Cofradía de la Purísima Inmaculada Concepción de Los Pardos celebrated its reina as they had sworn to their Pardo ancestors to do long ago. After Mass, the town crier announced the most attractive amusements that would take place during the day: corridas de toros and the representation of the Battle between Moors and Christians. Months before, the cofrades held elections to determine who would be the actors. The spectators were going to resolve the bets they made at the tavern some nights before. Some bet on Francisco Javier and others on Joseph Ortega to be the Great Turk.

Only because of his tattered shoes, people perceived that the Great Turk was Francisco Javier Pacheco. As the gamblers argued about their bets, Francisco Javier calmly walked around the main square. As he waited for his companions, he tried to frighten passersby with his deep gaze, accentuated by the charcoal placed around his eyes and the red turban that hours before his wife had wrapped around his head. An old gachupín commented that he also walked with gestures of bravery and power, as in the wars in Alpujarras, a region in Andalusia, Spain, around 1568. A girl was on the point of asking him if he was in that war when the rest of the brothers arrived: Francisco Javier Méndez, who would act as an ensign; Domingo, who would play the captain of the Moors; Joseph Ortega, who would represent a captain; and Clemente, who would act as lieutenant of the Moors.

The Great Turk joined them and, as a group, they walked around the square, greeting the crowd already beginning to head to the esplanade where the performance would take place. The brothers kept going around. They believed that arriving when people had located themselves around the stage was advantageous. They enjoyed knowing that while the audience was waiting, they would surprise it by coming in together, making evil faces, and raising their wooden swords high, waiting for those who would act as Christians to arrive. And they did it. They seemed to take their roles very seriously, as if they truly believed they would fight the great battle against the Christian warriors of the Reconquest. The crying of some of the children in the crowd did not subside, even though their mothers repeatedly told them that everything was make-believe, that the Great Turk was none other than Francisco, a "fallen" neighbor who, by dressing like a Turk and being one of the Pardo brothers, believed that his reputation as a thief would evaporate, like the steam that came out of the pots of atole (hot corn beverage) that some women were stirring in the kitchen stalls that cold day in January.[1]

As this pliego suelto presents, in the middle of the eighteenth century, the Pardo brothers continued to fight their own "battle" in a theatrical space that had the potential to confuse the real with the imaginary. That is what Linda Curcio suggests when stating that those kinds of festivities occurred in "abnormal" time and space.[2] In either of the two spheres, those cofrades likely continued to try to gain a place in a San Joseph del Parral hierarchical society that insisted on making them look inferior. But by then, these brothers had more tools with which to defend their right to participate in religious observances in the community. Apparently, their ancestors' efforts left their mark since, throughout the eighteenth century, they finally organized religious fiestas as God commanded. It was not an easy task, much less when the Pardos finally formalized their cofradía with the pope's recognition, at a time when the Bourbon reforms were knocking on the door.

As previously observed, during the seventeenth century, the oligarchy that monopolized and controlled the mining town in almost all areas placed the people of service and mines (workers) in a baroque vessel. The powerful had a more significant involvement in the organization of religious events, which adversely affected the Pardos' cofradía. The oligarchy and the Spanish elite's negative image of this congregation did not change in the eighteenth century. In fact, it took on a new connotation since, under the influence of enlightened ideas that favored order, reason, and progress, the Pardos might have represented an impediment to executing those beliefs. However, perhaps those in power never realized that, in many ways, the Pardo brothers by this time were no longer the same.

The censuses between 1739 and 1788 indicate that twenty-five individuals registered as mayordomos of various cofradías were mestizos, Indigenous people, and mulatos. All were free and mostly mine workers, specialized traders, tailors, shoemakers, wood gatherers, and candle artisans, all with nuclear families.[3] The increased number among those individuals who were free did not mean they had left behind their usual recreations, though. In San Joseph del Parral, there was a tavern or meeting center located on La Calle de Los Ladrones (Thieves' Street) where negros, mulatos, Indigenous, and mixed people congregated to socialize and to do business.[4] The street's name is one of the manifestations indicating that the negative image of these individuals continued to be an issue. It is precisely that perception the Cofradía of Pardos had to overcome throughout the eighteenth century.

This chapter reveals the tension between the Pardos' confraternity and the Spanish elite. It examines the requests the former made to the local authorities to organize celebrations for their Virgen Inmaculada. Seventeenth-century archival files referenced in chapter 5 showed the discursive sagacity and the negotiating capacity the Pardos employed to be part of the town's festive life. In fact, with their persistence, they obtained the approval of the pope, procuring an official document that granted them formal status as a religious organization and let them disassociate themselves from an oligarch's hacienda minera (mining estate). This chapter further illustrates how in the eighteenth century this congregation approached the local council and the Spanish elite with new and sophisticated negotiation tools that this investigation identifies as social theatricality, heteroglossia, and an acculturated discourse, that ultimately allowed it to re-create and consolidate a cultural identity.

In 1723, Juan Gamboa y Bernabé, mayordomo of La Cofradía de Los Pardos, appeared before the mayor, General Don José Montero de Aguilar, on behalf of Antonio de Venegas Peralta, Manuel García, Francisco Escárcega, Antonio Talamantes, Joseph Rentería, Pedro López, and the rest of the Pardo brothers, and on behalf of all he said,

> We appear before you and say that the festivities, which are endowed and sworn, of the purest Virgin, having just been celebrated in Parral in other past times and having stopped celebrating in the time of five years, causing the Cofradías to have fallen in this town, and at the present time find us with some means [money/resources] for the celebration of these festivals as usual on occasions that there have been means to celebrate them . . . [we ask] to grant us a license for the celebration . . . that by giving the said license we promise to celebrate the next coming January 6, 1724, which is celebrated with mass, sermon, comedy, and corridas de toros that the same captains of Moors and Christians, and

the rest mentioned in the above offer for said celebration, and we look forward to your greatness.[5]

The Pardo brothers' discourse reveals the coexistence of various historical voices and specific value in words and phrases they used in their favor. Before requesting permission to organize their event, they justified why they wanted to do it: because their festivities were endowed and sworn in, they had financial means, and it was their custom. After declaring their motives, they suggested some advantages the community and the authorities could gain by permitting them to organize the celebration: the brotherhood would provide an occasion for public entertainment with Mass and sermon, comedy, and corridas de toros. They also highlighted why the authorities would grant them consent: (due to) the greatness of the mayor's office. Furthermore, their festivity included the representation of the Battle between Moors and Christians, a significative element of the Spanish elite's cultural memory: the Reconquest.

The persuasive elements the Pardos included in their discourse indicate how the brothers accomplished what Juan Villegas identifies as a "social theatricality": how social sectors represent themselves on the social scene and how that representation encodes their perception of the world. Villegas proposes that in self-representation, social beings consciously or unconsciously act as if they were in the theater. This includes the way they dress, the position they occupy in space, gestures, voice, and other elements that indicate a "staging" in which all those involved decipher different signs, both in what they connote (imply) and in what they denote (signify).[6] The Pardos crafted their discourse (the element that implies the staging of a conscious social-theatrical performance) within a cultural context that contained a system of codes that society shared during that time. The document includes some signs that the local authority was competent to decipher and exposes the ability of the members of the cofradía to manipulate these signs in their speech, an ability that expanded and became complicated as the eighteenth century progressed.

Nonetheless, even though the Pardo brothers represented themselves in the social scene, that day the alcalde postponed granting them the license until someone could confirm whether it was true that the cofradía had had the custom of organizing religious festivals in the town. Yes, the alcalde's response is unusual. If he was not aware of the Pardo confraternity's involvement in the town's past religious life—perhaps because he recently arrived from another place—he could have asked anyone in his office to corroborate the information the brotherhood provided. Instead, he prolonged the petition requesting such corroboration. While the cofrades look for a witness, we can learn some details about the individuals involved in the matter. The Pardo brother Francisco Escárcega, for example, was a mestizo who had three major cattle sites, three minor ones, and six caballerías (horse stables) of land in San Francisco de Conchos.[7] Antonio Venegas Peralta, in 1724, was a mulato master blacksmith.[8] Alcalde General Montero de Aguilar belonged to the mining elite; by 1725 he had a mine among his assets, as did alcalde Fernández de Carrión some years before. There were some particulars against Montero Aguilar's reputation, however. In 1727, he was imprisoned for losing court documents and pesos debt. In addition, that same year, he escaped from jail.[9]

Going back to the Pardos' petition, a few days later an acquaintance, Joseph Martínez Muñoz, appeared before the mayor. He affirmed that the cofradía offered celebrations to its reina Virgen Inmaculada in the plazuela (smaller than a main plaza/main square) de San Juan de Dios for more than thirty years.[10] Although there is no primary documentation about the festivity taking place, we can assume the alcalde granted the Pardos permission to celebrate their reina. But as time passed by, the confraternity encountered more and more problems.

Twenty-two years later, in 1745, the Spanish vecinos appeared before the ecclesiastical authority to declare themselves against the festivities the Pardos organized. In a few days, there was an official statement explaining how at their annual celebrations in the plazuela of San Juan de Dios:

> there were incongruities to society and more [absurdities]. But, like that, by custom, as by being sworn [the festivities], to end the uncomfortable situations and offenses to God that are made in said plazuela, far away from the downtown, I command the alcalde that the Pardos carry out these corridas de toros, comedies, and other [amusements], in the plaza mayor . . . to show them their obedience to their superiors, although the celebration of said festivities must have an effect on serving God.[11]

The document does not specify what type of "incongruities" the Pardos manifested in the annual fiestas. Still, it is not difficult to deduce that those referred to the negative image Pardo brothers and other mixed people had in the town, and to some damaging events that did not help them portray a positive social image. On December 9, 1731, a murder occurred during the festivity La Cofradía de Los Pardos allotted to its Virgin Inmaculada. Isabel Selosio, a woman who lived in the town of Las Ánimas, went to the celebration in the company of her husband, Captain Vicente Sáenz. On the way home, she claimed some Indians assaulted them and finally killed Sáenz.[12] Although the Pardo brothers were not the protagonists, the violent act happened during their fiesta, probably creating an unfavorable panorama for their cofradía.

However, despite the Spanish vecinos' turning to the Church to complain about the "incongruities" in the Pardos' yearly celebrations, the authorities' resolution was to move the Pardos fiestas to the plaza major, rather than preventing them altogether. This fact leads one to question whether the authorities changed the location of the Pardos' fiestas because they valued the Pardos' "customs" and being "sworn:" two powerful signs about their religious and civic commitment. In reality, moving the corridas de toros, comedies, and other entertainment to the plaza mayor had advantages for the Pardo brothers since the place was bigger and more accessible and popular than the plazuela. Also, it is important to note that the ecclesiastical authority "ordered" the alcalde to make this change, an action that indicates that by 1745, the Church continued intervening in matters related to the cofradías, although it was not supposed to under the Bourbon reforms.

Then, it is not surprising that on January 20, 1746, alcalde José del Puente y Andrade made official the change of place where the Pardos' celebration would be held the following year: from the plazuela de San Juan de Dios to the plaza mayor. This alteration did not affect the Pardos' enthusiasm for organizing celebrations of the Virgen de la Inmaculada. On the contrary, that same year, they requested formal permission from the alcalde to arrange the festival for the following year (1747). In that instance, they said they had already started planning and shaping the representation of the Battle between the Moors and Christians. The alcalde agreed to grant them the license, not without first instructing the Pardos that the holiday must comply with the obligation and duty of offering Mass and sermon.[13] To this point, in the two documents analyzed, the Pardo brothers mention the Battle of the Moors and Christians as a comedy they staged and acted. This detail invites the conjecture of whether there was a popular taste for this type of spectacle in the town and if the Pardo brothers took advantage of such a public performance.

In the Viceroyalty of New Spain, representations of the Battle of the Moors and Christians occurred almost as early as the arrival of the Spanish. In his essay "Conquest of Rodas," Fray Bartolomé de las Casas narrates a mock representation of Moors and Christians that took place in Mexico City in 1539: "There were fake theaters big as towers in the Plaza de México. . . . There were castles and a wooden city that Indians fought on the outside and those on the inside defended; there were large ships with their sails that sailed through the square as if they were by water, going by land."[14] In this scene, the friar described the natives of central Mexico acting as Moors, but in the Spanish peninsula, that role fell to the Spaniards. Over there, the important religious festivals of the liturgical calendar almost always included the Battle of the Moors and Christians as the expression of the struggle that the Spanish had waged against the Arabs, although, as Max Harris points out, those battles existed since the Middle Ages.[15]

In modern times, this dance became a mock battle that lasted several days, requiring a very elaborate stage apparatus that included the embellishment of wooden fortresses and the participation of many actors.[16] From modern Spain to Mexico City, then to Northern New Spain, there was a significant change in the actors who performed the roles of Moors in this dance. Karoline Cook points out that at the end of the sixteenth century, the Indigenous Chichimecas of the north appeared as conquered Moors in dances commemorating the Spanish victory at the Battle of Lepanto. Regarding these "new actors," Cook suggests that in Northern New Spain, the Battle of the Moors and Christians recovered an important Spanish cultural memory. According to the historian, the image the Spanish had of the Muslims and Moors influenced their perception of the Indigenous people since, in the sixteenth century, both the Arabs and the Chichimecas were seminomadic in Spain's eyes.[17]

Thus, whether the recreation of the Moors and Christians' battle conveyed a "plausible credibility" in Northern New Spain is worth questioning. Although in that remote area Arab individuals were not present to join, there were seminomadic actors on hand who played the Moors: Indigenous Chichimecas. However, it is important to consider the visual statement the Pardos (negros, mulatos, Indigenous people, and mestizos) made when performing the battle in San Joseph del Parral. Perhaps, through their "pardo" skin color that carried medieval Spanish ideas of paganism, slavery, and nomadism, they awoke a Spanish cultural memory. Still, they used their image as "Pardos" to their advantage: to take possession of this performance in San Joseph del Parral.

In this humble town, it is doubtful that representations were like those Fray Bartolomé de las Casas narrates. However, the fact that the Pardo brothers selected the actors for the battle a year in advance may indicate that this mock battle was essential for the cofradía. Perhaps for the same reason, they needed time to find material resources to mount the performance in the best possible way. For example, once the Pardos obtained permission for the festivity, they would be able to organize it in 1747. Pardo mayordomo Francisco Pacheco, a free mulato, appeared again before the alcalde to request monetary aid. He said,

> It is customary in the town that every year the fiesta of the Inmaculada Concepción is celebrated, the expenses the Pardos covered, for which they choose and appoint two [Pardos] with the title of mayordomos to collect alms that the faithful offered, supplied and complemented [said alms giving] of their own eagerness and work, because fortune none of them had, what is missing for the celebration that consists of solemn Mass, sermon, adornment of the temple, three days of corridas de toros, in which the invention and celebration of Christians and Moors is also customary, in which a captain with the appellation of Great Turk is named.[18]

This document also informs about the Pardo brothers' using signs that, when associated, reveal the presence of various voices or sociohistorical tensions and conflicts.[19] In that social scenario, the Pardo brothers' discourse reflects the parallel use of different words/signs such as "custom, begging, supplying, eagerness, work, solemn Mass, and invention." Those words' semantics refer to that time's political, social, cultural, and religious values that, when put together, project the tension and historical conflicts between the Pardos and the Spanish elite. For example, when mulato Pacheco expressed "It is customary in the town that every year the fiesta of the Inmaculada Concepción is celebrated," he implied the custom was not only theirs but belonging to all the people of the mining town. By integrating the entire community in his claim, the mayordomo emphasized that, by requesting a license to collect alms, they were doing a service for the local society. After that, he highlighted that of all the cofradías of the town, the Pardos' brotherhood was the one that had the custom of organizing and carrying out the invention of the Battle of the Moors and Christians.[20] This plea is significant for the Pardos since it implied that they were the only ones in the history of the mining town who had the "invention," the "innovation," and the "design" of such theatrical battles. In this way, it seems that the mayordomo was trying to insert La Cofradía de Los Pardos not only within local history but also in the Spanish Christian past.

During the sixteenth century, as was true for most regions that surrounded the Mediterranean, Spain experienced the birth of commercial theater, which began because of an economic crisis experienced between 1576 and 1593. That was when the Spanish Crown could not fully control the manifestation of cultural activities oriented to the people. The brotherhoods, to continue aiding the inmates in hospitals, began to organize a kind of commercial theater to raise funds to financially relieve their institutions. Eventually, this type of theater was successful among the urban population, as it fulfilled their sentimental and ideological expectations. The playwrights of the time appealed, then, not to a real or elitist audience, but to a public one. Some of the themes in the dramas were about nostalgia for a certain place or region, or an evocation of the Middle Ages.[21]

In considering African enslaved people's exposure to Christianity, we must remember that African slavery was part of Iberia's universe since the fifteenth century, with the Portuguese slave trade, with a gradual increase in African presence in Lisbon and Seville by the turn of the sixteenth century. A 1565 census showed an increase of Africans (among them Moors and Moriscos) living in Seville, Cádiz, Málaga, Cartagena, and Granada. We learned how those enslaved peoples were active in religious endeavors by being members of cofradías, for example.[22] Therefore, it is worth asking whether the theatrical experience among people of African descent, from Iberia to the Americas, was a fusion between Catholicism and African culture. Even though we cannot trace the Pardo brothers' path back to Africa, Iberia, the Atlantic, or New Spain, when in their discourse they represent themselves as the "inventors" of theatrical representations in the mining town, it could be possible to question if they recreated that experience and inclination for those artistic and cultural manifestations from past experiences.

Furthermore, those theatrical representations contained an important Spanish cultural memory: the Reconquest. The apparent visual element within that memory realm was the Moor skin color that could have been like that of the Pardo brothers. In a sense, those cofrades were performing and representing figures of Spain's past that prompted and associated with them a glorious memory and assured their higher social position and power. However, as we will see, the Pardo brothers did not have anything settled yet. They could indeed convince the authorities this time about the value of their involvement in the town's religious festivities, but soon they faced another obstacle.

Once again, in the same year of 1746, the Spanish vecinos presented a petition to eliminate corridas de toros in the town. In the request, they stated that for a long time, San Joseph del Parral had experienced hardship, scarcity, and poverty, and:

> ... if this is common and transcendent to all, more particularly it is appreciated in the Pardos of the referred town, these are all so miserable that they do not have the faculties even to maintain themselves, needing to be desarraigados del lugar [uprooted] to provide food, and now in such a situation, to that add the exorbitant expenses of a corridas de toros ... that the neighbors and residents are not distracted and annihilated with the title of festivities, inventions, and other celebrations, even if they seem to be in favor of the common good ... that such agitation of corridas de toros is against good customs, for giving the neighbors less time to worship and reverence, that by attending this [corridas de toros], the most essential [element] was ignored: the Mass.[23]

The statement suggests that the tactic of the Spanish vecinos consisted of making the authorities notice that the tragedy people in town were living through was much worse for the Pardos, since they were so "miserable." Their proof was that to support themselves, the Pardos had to leave town. The word "desarraigado" has a negative connotation. It implies that individuals leave behind the place where they were born, where they grew up and had jobs, where their parents and remains of the dead are, and, finally, where everything "the people" gave them exists. In this context, it was likely that the vecinos of San Joseph del Parral considered the Pardos ungrateful for everything that constituted being from a place. Putting aside their need to seek means to survive outside the town, the vecinos remarked on the hierarchical division between themselves and the Pardos, highlighting how the immoral habits of the latter deprived inhabitants of enjoying the spiritual benefit of the Mass on feast days.

The Spanish vecinos also referred to the poverty and scarcity of the town. Those situations could have referred to the famine, epidemics, and droughts experienced in the area from 1737 to 1740.[24] Likewise, Spanish vecinos probably had a conflict of interest. If these calamities threatened their financial resources, they had to intervene to control public celebrations. At the same time, it is worthy of note that by requesting the cancellation of those events, the vecinos exhibited disapproval of the mayor's decision since he had already given the Pardos the license to organize corridas de toros and the Mass as part of the celebration.

This situation exemplifies Spanish vecinos' power in regulating the religious ritual. On that occasion, they managed to get the alcalde to issue an official order in December 1746. It prohibited corridas de toros during the fiesta for the Virgen Inmaculada, despite the fact that such had been the Pardos' custom:

> . . . so that the days of [corridas de] toros are extinguished . . . [due to the] poverty of the town . . . by the present command . . . other mayordomos are not encouraged or urged to do corridas de toros, despite the custom . . . that there are only church celebrations so that there will not be corridas de toros from now on . . . whoever does not obey . . . [will receive a] fine of one hundred pesos and one month in jail.[25]

There is no reference in the archive to whether the festivity included corridas de toros in 1747. The question was whether those corridas de toros would disappear forever from the mining town.

In 1773, Pardo mayordomo Antonio Ynurcio, accompanied by Ignacio Panal, Domingo Sáenz, Pacasio Montoya, Alejandro Betances, and Máximo Escudero, requested a license from the mayor to organize their annual feast. In the hearing, they said that all of them were:

vecinos of San Joseph del Parral, of Pardo class, lend-
ing a voice and cause for others . . . in ancient years they
swore to annually celebrate and solemnize the Inmaculada
Concepción Nuestra Reina y Señora, la siempre [always]
Virgen María, with demonstrative rejoices of public festivals,
of corridas de toros and others [rejoices], with the worship
and dedication that their short capacities allowed them . . .
and unfortunately this benefit has been forgotten, the cult
and celebration not being performed with the care and joy
that our predecessor brothers had promised and sworn to
continue . . . and thus, timid for having experienced in this
kingdom the calamities and hostilities of enemy Indians,
we have considered all those of humble class, having been
the motive to suffer these misfortunes . . . we have had to
fulfill what was sworn by our predecessor brothers.[26]

From the outset, this speech displays how the Pardo brothers tried
to affirm a position they believed they occupied in the community: they were also vecinos. Even though in these times, the word
could identify the place of residence of any individual or group,
the Pardo brothers integrated a word charged with sociohistorical
significance during their performance before the civic authority.
As already observed in other official documents, the Spanish elite
in San Joseph del Parral used the word "vecino" to highlight social
hierarchies. In a previous primary source, they mentioned how the
Pardos' festivities were harmful to "all vecinos and residents of the
town." This phrase signals a differentiation between vecinos and
residents (citizens vs. inhabitants).[27] Furthermore, as previously
stated, in the Provincia de Santa Bárbara, the status of vecino was
reserved for individuals with sufficient economic resources to have
a populated house, especially during the first years of settlement in
the area.[28] It is impossible to affirm that by 1773, the Spanish elite
or the Pardo brothers continued to understand the term vecino as it

had been in the middle of the seventeenth century. Still, it is notable that the Pardo mayordomos began their speech by identifying themselves as vecinos.

In the same way, through the discourse, the Pardos recognized and declared the class to which they belonged, "de clase Pardos," suggesting they accepted their social position in that hierarchical community. However, it seems they disagreed with the Spanish elite's negative image of them. Rather than being "scandalous, miserable, and with little fear of God," that day, they acted as true Christians. With their discourse and performance, the Pardo brothers made a public statement about their values, which basically were the same as those of the "Spanish class." They showed how they, like all the vecinos of the town, also felt bewildered by the calamities and hostilities the enemy Indians carried out, and even more for being of "humble class" and "having been the motive to suffer these misfortunes."

At the same time, in this discourse, the Pardo brothers mention their predecessors at least twice: "the cult and celebration not being performed with the care and joy that our predecessor brothers had promised and sworn to continue" and "we have had to fulfill what was sworn by our predecessor brothers." This research considers that reference to ancestors within a group of people of African descent being significant. Dr. Jacob Olupona, expert in indigenous African religions, asserts that for African families, clans, and tribes, ancestors and ancestral spirits act as guardians of morality. Even when Africans are emancipated from their metaphysical beliefs, they continue to make room for their ancestors; they look after their descendants' welfare and expect their cooperation in return. That is, Africans practice ancestors' appeasement offerings to attain security for the living but, besides the self-protective measure, it is an affirmation of essential values: self-discipline and respect for authority that form the moral basis for society.[29] But was the African meaning of ancestors or ancestral spirits the same for people before and after coming to America? Were Africans able to conserve their beliefs when removed from their ancestral lands and people? Even though there are no definite answers, some historians have tried to respond to those questions and have arrived at some conclusions.

In fact, this book presents the topic in the introduction with historian James Sweet's query: To what extent were specific African cultural practices transferred across the broader diaspora and how were these practices transformed? The scholar mentions that Western Christianity did not destroy Central African (e.g., present-day Angola, Congo, Gabon, and Zambia) core beliefs and practices, among which are religion and cosmology based on the division between the world of the living and the world of the spirits, with particular emphasis on the importance of ancestral spirits. Sweet asserts that the relocation of African core beliefs was possible due to the arrival of African people in coherent cultural groups that shared much in common: language, kinship, and religion, among other cultural elements. [30] Following Sweet's assertions, John Thornton explains that in large regions, more than a few enslaved individuals were able to find members of their own nation with whom they could communicate and, in this way, transmitted and maintained the African culture they brought with them, although there is not such a thing as an "intact" African culture. Thornton makes this statement following an anthropologist's definition of culture: a lifeway for a society that includes, among other elements, kinship, political structure, language and literature, art, music, dance, and religion that are not fixed; those can change as people interact with other cultures. Therefore, kinship, for example, was not a fixed system; it played a role in areas where African families formed, and criollo generations developed with a different structure from that of Africa. [31]

Kinship historian Herman Bennett proposes a similar African cultural alteration occurrence in Mexico City when saying that Africans continued practicing their own religions in the New World

181

but under a "captivity" context, as an act of defiance where they were no longer Africans but performing as ethnicities: Angolan or Kongo, for example, an exhibition of Afro-Creole consciousness.[32] Frank T. Proctor III adds that it was possible that the newly arrived Africans developed a new sense of self upon their arrival in Mexico City through the interaction with enslaved individuals from similar regions in Africa. Through those interactions, they could have redefined new diasporic ethnic identities and became identified by terms such as Angolan or Congo.[33] Through the African diaspora, the captivity context provoked African men and women of religion to act as intermediaries between the realms of oppression and oppressors, ending up as leaders as a mechanism of self-perpetuation.[34] Furthermore, in Mexico, due to Spaniards paying more attention to the spiritual conversion of Indigenous peoples, it was not possible for them to eradicate African traditional beliefs; an evident example is the number of cases in Inquisition archives that deal with African-descent people's "pacts with the devil."[35] To close, Joan Bristol offers a balanced view of Black confraternities' preserving African culture in Mexico City when saying that, if on one side Afro Mexicans possessed an African consciousness and practiced African-influenced rituals, there were no sites of African-based practices like those confraternities in Brazil and the Caribbean.[36]

For the Pardo brothers in eighteenth-century San Joseph del Parral, the question remains: Is there a significance in bringing their ancestors into a discourse whose goal is to convince authorities to grant them permission to organize a festivity? There is no document in the archive from another brotherhood to compare to the Pardos' discourse, and this fact relates to what Bennett identifies as Africans performing under a captivity context. It is not precisely that the Pardo brothers were enslaved, but the authorities and society questioned their moral values for being Pardos—that is, people of African descent. We can say that if not literally under a captivity context, Pardos were under a figurative captivity context, as they were practically attacked by authorities and society. Bringing their ancestors into the discussion was perhaps an attempt to demonstrate they had values and, most importantly, a past. Was this an African past?

If we apply Thornton's culture definition, we can propose that the Pardos' past was a reconfigured African past, one that was exposed to a variety of influences through time and space. If we consider the fact that African enslaved individuals came mainly from West Africa to New Spain and from there to San Joseph del Parral, and that those individuals usually found members of their nations with whom to face the cultural change, it is probable they transmitted and preserved core beliefs such as the one that provided a moral basis for African societies: ancestors' spirits, their guardians of morality. If it is true that we cannot talk about an African consciousness in San Joseph del Parral as being similar to those manifested in Brazil and the Caribbean, and perhaps not even as those in the rest of New Spain, we can propose that the Pardos were able to create or recreate a new sense of self, a new diasporic identity that responded to the challenges Northern New Spain imposed on them. In the eighteenth century, this new diasporic ethnic identity was that of the Pardo class (poor), vecinos, and "inventors" of the Battle between Moors and Christians, a theatrical custom. All those characteristics refer to an adaptation to Spanish ways while performing as an ancient African people of religion, the intermediaries between the oppressors and the oppressed, and by conserving and perpetuating a belief and practice that was at the heart of African culture: the world of spirits and ancestors. This diasporic frontier identity becomes more complex as the Pardos continued using the Spanish ideology in their favor, as for instance mentioning the "hostility of the enemy Indians" as one of the causes for the town not being able to organize religious celebrations. As time passed, they responded in a similar manner to the rest of challenges that society inflicted on them.

In the same 1773 document, Pardo mayordomo Antonio Ynurcio continued the discourse, saying, ". . . the celebration and solemnity of these festivities are carried out in cities, towns, villages, and mining towns by all faithful Christians, and only in this kingdom [of Nueva] Vizcaya that, being the most prominent, such forgetfulness must be noticed."[37] It can be asserted that Ynurcio appealed to the Spanish elite's pride with the idea of it not keeping up with the rest of the cities and mining towns in New Spain regarding festive life. That was how the Pardos' cofradía questioned the mayor's office's duty and religious commitment. Were the Pardo brothers suggesting they were more devoted Christians than the Spanish people? Ynurcio's discourse thus complicates but at the same time enriches the Pardos' diasporic frontier identity by integrating an "acculturated" religious discourse, in some respects similar to that Guaman Poma de Ayala made in his 1615 pictorial manuscript, *El primer nueva crónica y buen gobierno*. Belonging to the Indigenous elite, in this chronicle Poma de Ayala uses pictures and written discourse as strategies to draw attention to the mistreatment of Indigenous Inca people under the Spaniards' hands. One of the tactics was to adopt the discursive model of oratory the missionaries used. It was the first instrument of acculturation used among the Indigenous people. In his chronicle, Poma de Ayala marks certain concepts, a lexical selection, and some inflections and accents, just as the missionaries were supposed to teach them and as the Natives learned. He also used other types of discourse (legal, humanistic, historical, and dramatic, among others) to embed his message in an "acceptable" way and according to the historical context in which he lived. The new Incas committed to reestablish the mercy and social justice their ancestors once enjoyed.[38] With his pictorial images and written discourse, Poma de Ayala insisted on suggesting that the "new Incas" were even more Christian than the Spaniards themselves.

La Cofradía de Los Pardos continued integrating some of Poma de Ayala's discourse tools in that same performance in 1773 when saying that:

Our Catholic monarch, Don Carlos III, may Our God save him and make him prosper in blissful victories, monarch of this mining town of Parral, determined to dispatch his superior certificate so that all his domains and lordships could be sworn with equal joy and plausible rejoicing as universal patron of all the monarchy, La Inmaculada Concepción Nuestra Soberana Reina y Señora La Virgen María, these motives and others that, in order not to tire your prudent attention, we omit, leaving to your discreet understanding the purpose that moves us.[39]

Through their speech, the Pardo brothers projected themselves and their predecessors as good Christians. They were aware of the religious developments in Spain, and they knew about the devotion Carlos III had for the same Marian devotion as theirs: la Virgen de la Inmaculada Concepción. Indeed, in 1762, King Carlos III proclaimed this celestial figure as the official patron saint of Spain. He declared she would be celebrated at home and abroad, with three sermons and three comedies, not to mention the music.[40] Having provided these details, perhaps the Pardos wanted to accentuate that they shared the Marian devotion of la Virgen Inmaculada with the king of Spain. Also, they were up to date with the most relevant events of the Christian community, as the local authorities and the Spanish elite were also supposed to be. And they openly manifested their devotion and commitment to the monarch's Virgin.

Everything indicates that the Pardos' theatricality brought good fortune because, in November 1773, the authorities permitted them to hold their festivity in January of the following year. The document indicated that the alcalde gave them the license due to "The old-fashioned custom of their ancestors of solemnizing the Illustrious Mystery of the Conception, in the Grace of Mary, Our Lady of the Universal Patron Saint of Spain, by virtue of the Royal Decree of our King and Lord, Don Carlos III."[41] As can be seen, the alcalde described La Cofradía de Los Pardos' custom as "old-fashioned," that is, venerable, in which they solemnized not only the Virgin's image but also "the Illustrious Mystery of the Conception." In this content, the authorities paraphrased the discourse the Pardos just gave. However, it is remarkable they mentioned it and by doing so recognized that the Pardos' custom came from their ancestors who, in this case and under this "Spanish" context, was not of African origin but Christian, Spanish, Catholic, universal, and royal. How could two different groups explain the same event differently? As Thornton points out, during the sixteenth and seventeenth centuries, the religious experience was not simply an intellectual conception but a series of ideas and images that individuals received from "non-worldly beings." In any case, the humans' role was to interpret those images and ideas. In this sense, religious philosophy was not precisely the creator of religion, revelations and interpretations were. Those divine revelations and human interpretations were what religions had in common. Therefore, even though African and European people had different religious systems of knowledge, they had some major ideas in common, such as the acceptance of a basic religious reality: there is another unseen world, and human revelations are essential to know it.[42]

After obtaining approval for their request, the Pardos took another vital step toward something they had been building toward for years. They begged the mayor to give them written testimony about "having renewed the custom that their predecessors had until the year 1754, when the last festivity was verified up to the present, which was nineteen years of intermission and forgetfulness of the festival."[43] It is unknown whether the authorities gave them the testimony. Still, this request demonstrates the interest the Pardo brothers had since the previous century in keeping a record of having carried out a noble and ancient work for the cofradía, and that they were paying attention to its future. The Pardos thus used religious discourse to obtain, for the first time, a written testimony that validated their efforts. Was this labor a characteristic we should add to the Pardos' diasporic frontier identity and, as a consequence, a sign of having created or recreated a cultural memory and identity that their predecessor brothers, such as Antonio de Narváez, constituted and supported since the previous century?

For the next nine years, the Pardos continued to solicit permits to organize their annual celebrations. In 1782, the staging element was their performance as "children and neighbors of this Royal Town." They also again used religious-acculturated discourse, demonstrating lexicon selection, inflections, and accents in certain words and phrases loaded with cultural significance. Those were: "having remembered their devotion," "the oath to their ancestors," "at the convenience of the Royal Order of our Catholic monarch Don Carlos III, may God keep," and "as experienced in many cities, towns, and places of the Kingdom."[44] Sadly, after the authorities had granted them a license, the mining and trade guild requested the cancellation of the Pardos' celebration a few weeks later. Don Gabriel Apodaca, deputy for commerce, Don Benito Sánchez de la Barra, and Don Juan José Aldama, deputies of the mining guild, said these celebrations were damaging and causing harm, much more because of the scarcity of grain in the town.[45] The guilds may have been correct in their assertion that the lack of grain indicated a threat of famine, which was the main motivation to cancel the Pardos' fiesta, but the brothers did not concur with this determination.

A few days later, Antonio Ynurcio and "many others from his Cofradía" appeared before the judge to plead, "Please call a general meeting of both guilds, with the assistance of deputies and the priest" so that "they may revoke the permission, because if you do not give it to them [the notification for the meeting], we will protest for it to happen, and will ask and claim what is in our interest."[46] As we can appreciate, in this part of the discourse, mayordomo Ynurcio's attitude is no longer submissive or meek; he is demanding and warning, which could have been a sign of a "legal consciousness," an insight to navigating viceroyalty life. That is how historian Bennett identifies Africans in New Spain: through the establishment of family and friendship networks, African-descent people became aware of the legal system. This knowledge allowed them to pursue autonomy using law in their defense.[47]

It seems that we must add this legal consciousness trait to the Pardos' diasporic frontier identity, and perhaps that was why the judge paid attention to Mayordomo Ynurcio's request and ordered an official notification to the trade and mining union's representatives about the Pardos' cofradía requesting their appearance. However, these gentlemen refused to attend the meeting. Faced with this reluctance, in the same document the judge decided "not to disturb the peace and quietude among the people . . . the convocation of the meeting the Pardos are requesting should be omitted and notify it to them." Apparently, the Pardos civilly accepted the meeting's cancellation, but they begged this authority "to give them a testimony of these proceedings for the purposes that suit them."[48]

It is important to note that Antonio Ynurcio, one of the "renovators of the custom of his predecessor brothers," was still an active member of the Cofradía de los Pardos by 1782. It seems that this mayordomo acted as an African man of religion: as an intermediary between the oppressors and the oppressed. He actively collaborated in designing the discourses' strategies to request the cofradía's permissions. It was he who, on two occasions, solicited written testimony from the alcalde and the judge's resolutions and declared that the mayordomos were willing to continue "claiming" if they disagreed with the official decrees. However, in five years, as we will see, that was not going to be necessary.

In 1787, thanks to the jurisdiction and other benefits visitor José Gálvez granted, the San Joseph del Parral mining union had powers to determine whether the town festivals were harmful to the mining body, the town, and the entire provincia. So that year, the Pardo brothers requested that this guild organize their fiesta and, surprisingly, obtained a favorable response almost on the instant. On that occasion, again, they used some of their discursive strategies, although those were not the main ones that influenced the decision of the mining union, since the guild was pursuing its interests. After requesting the petition, the mining union stated that,

> The corridas de toros that the Pardos pretend to solemnize during the function of the Mystery of the Immaculate Conception . . . far from harming this mining industry, it promises the benefits that I will state: in the days from Easter to Christmas, the miners and their crews are so used to having fun, that they usually close all the mines. Corruption has been introduced . . . [and] some amusements in this season that . . . now we justly hope will be repressed. . . . The fatality of the previous years [has] dispelled a multitude of miners and workers away from this town, for whose cause the work of many mines is suspended . . . the aforementioned festivals give hope that from the multitude of people who attend, several settle down for the cultivation of mines and all.[49]

This declaration was made public, and a few days later, the deputy delegate of the Royal Treasury, Don Manuel Rodríguez, stated that:

> . . . because people have received news of the festivities with applause . . . wishing to contribute to the two pious ends to which they are directed, [and] with them they can raise their spirits after so many calamities, [I] . . . order that the Pardos be granted the proceeds of the tablados of the square . . . for the benefit of the temple of San Juan de Dios.[50]

Likewise, Rodríguez approved that the Pardos make the nomination of the Great Turk and Captain of the Moors for the representation of the Battle between Moors and Christians, as was their custom. The document includes a long list of Pardos' names, in which Luis Gardea would act as the Great Turk, José Julián Pico de Grulla as Captain Moro, and Yxineo Mosqueda as the Christian captain. After accepting their respective positions, these Pardos, in turn, appointed their Moorish and Christian lieutenants, as well as those who would serve as soldiers.[51]

It is more than evident that the mining union's will and generosity toward La Cofradía de Los Pardos were due to its interest in attracting workers. As Martin shows in her study on San Felipe El Real de Chihuahua in the eighteenth century, towns' festivals were an opportunity to attract workers who came to the festivities of surrounding places and hopefully would settle in the town and integrate into the mine labor market.[52] At the same time, the Bourbon reforms, to some extent, benefited the mining guild since the latter had full power and freedom to manipulate the festive atmosphere in its favor, much more when San Joseph del Parral experienced "calamities" that made workers emigrate. Although the mining union did not mention what kind of misfortunes the town had experienced, these were likely related to the declaration a mining and commerce deputy made in 1790. This man gave official news about the deep poverty the mining town was experiencing due to the attacks of Apache Indians, causing a reduction in mining production.[53]

It seems that in 1787, economic interests allowed this union to make exceptions to the enlightened reforms the Bourbon Crown introduced to control religious festivals. It can be said that by this date, Spanish Baroque elements mixed with the atmosphere of "Enlightened Reason." Those made possible the return of old practices to the scene: the plaza mayor was the stage of corridas de toros and performances of Battles between Moors and Christians but also of lawsuits, abuse of alcoholic beverages, and other "incongruities" that occurred during the Pardos' fiestas. Even so, as the archival text indicates, the inhabitants of the mining town welcomed the news about the upcoming celebration of the Pardo brothers with applause in times of hardship.

Account of the Battle Between the Pardo Brothers and the Town Council

In the Battle of the Moors and Christians, the Pardos' weapons were wooden swords; before authorities, their armaments were words. This chapter demonstrated how they used discursive tools on the social scene to continue participating in a religious ritual and in so doing not only created a new diasporic frontier identity but also transformed the Catholic universal ritual. Oscillating between the Baroque and the Enlighted ideas, throughout the eighteenth century, the Pardo brothers demonstrated that instead of being a fiasco they were able to navigate and negotiate their status in the mining town. In the seventeenth century they took a big step in obtaining papal license for their confraternity, and during their discourses in the following century they made sure to publicly recognize their ancestors' compromise to honor their brotherhood's Marian advocation. This diasporic frontier identity is a manifestation of a Northern New Spain local culture, a hybrid character made up of Spanish, Indigenous, African, mulato, criollo, mestizo, and mixed beliefs and customs. Although the members of La Cofradía de La Purísima Inmaculada Concepción de Los Pardos were not sure about embracing the Baroque or the Enlightenment thought, the Pardo brothers represented themselves in the social milieu with Christian surnames, as the inventors of Moor and Christian theatrical events, as the imitators of their monarch's devotion to the Immaculate Virgin, as enlightened individuals aware of the festive atmosphere of New Spain, as vecinos, as humble but religious Pardos who honored their ancestors, and as poor but with a legal consciousness.

Archival documents cannot attest to what happened later with the Pardos' cofradía. Perhaps the weight of the turbulent following years ended it but, before that happened, they obtained something valuable. As Martin proposes, in New Spain religious holidays could go beyond religious and civil solemnity. In most instances, the viceroyalty apparatus used ritual and allowed parody to provide its subjects with an "escape valve" from their problems and frustrations. It also allowed a "symbolic inversion." Martin follows the idea of Natalie Davis, who expresses that in rituals, individuals have an opportunity to conceive, even for a moment, an alternative social reality: the chance to represent "decent people" and wield fictitious power for a few hours. These are also perspectives that partakers can carry with them once the celebration is over.[54] This book makes the case that the Pardos not only represented themselves as decent Christian people but also gave life to the infidel Moor, perhaps the image that attracted the public during their representations and the one that allowed them to be, even for a few hours, the center of attention in the community, the one they took to their jacales (small adobe house) or the tavern in La Calle de Los Ladrones to make a toast for their successes once the feasts were over.

CAPELLANÍAS

SPIRITUALIZED LIVES IN A SILVER
HOUSE OF MIRRORS

It was a Saturday in 1735 when the bells of the church of San Joseph del Parral called the parishioners to join the Requiem Mass for the rest of the soul of Doña Catalina de Olarte. Her compadre, the patrón of her capellanía, had already lit the lamp she donated to the church as a pious work, just as she had stipulated in the testamentary clause. He was a member of the Cofradía del Santísimo Sacramento. The rest of his brothers had strategically positioned lilies and the image of Our Lady, acquired thanks to the income Doña Catalina's capellanía generated, which the woman had secured before her death and which, due to their administration skills, provided the cofrades with means to organize a celebration for their Marian advocation after the Requiem Mass.

Wearing a black cassock not long enough to hide his old and frayed shoes, the capellán received the faithful at the entrance. As adults and children of all races and calidades entered the Holy Precinct, their fearful gaze stopped at the altar, located at the back, from where Sacrificed Christ saw all of them. Four lighted candelabra adorned the space with wax candles on the table, covered with white tablecloths. The Chalice, the Sacred Vessel (made of silver), was ready to bow to Christ's sacrifice, when more than one commented that they felt a tremor in the floor, and with good reason, since Doña Catalina was buried there, on the left side of the church pantheon. Then Christ and his Father emanated from the pious objects, especially from Doña Catalina's lighted lamp, as some people were crossing themselves and their children. After celebrating the Eucharist and having helped the faithful deceased woman to pass through purgatory faster and with less hardship, the faithful left the church to continue celebrating life and death in other ways.

At the plaza mayor, while women and men were in their stalls selling their merchandise, some people (mostly women) made a line to get information about how to get a church credit to fund a capellanía and, hopefully, to buy some new clothes if the loan was enough. Others did not bother to line up since they were seriously considering moving to San Felipe El Real de Chihuahua, "el nuevo milagro minero" (the new mining miracle). While some members of the Cofradía del Santísimo Sacramento were acting in la plaza mayor, some old women grouped under a tree were complaining about the smell of change coming from the south, and young people were leaving. Why? Because, comparing them to the Pardo brothers, all were bad actors.

Wandering around the parish were Manuel Negro, Gaspar Negro, Juan Mulato, Francisco Ramón Mulato, Antonia Mulata, and Gertrudis Mulata, who some years before were the talk of the town: everyone wanted to know if they were the king of Spain's property or not. Nobody paid attention to them anymore, so they sat behind the church in a circle and prayed for the souls of their parents, grandparents, great-grandparents, and all their ancestors, asking them for guidance at the end of the ritual.

As represented in this pliego suelto, expressions of splendor and drama that characterized Baroque Catholicism were not exclusive to open settings. In fact, Spanish Baroque thought unearthed a more intimate and welcoming space: the spirit. The idea and sentiment of "living well to die better" were sheltered in capellanías, institutions through which women and men manifested and perpetuated the ambiguous relationship between life and death. The ritual of the Mass not only benefited the life of everyone who called himself a good Christian but also helped those already dead. Prayed Masses were special ceremonies dedicated to the souls of the deceased, and the holy precinct required precise ornaments, such as lilies and several candelabra. Generally, the capellanes, in the process of being ordained priests, officiated those Masses. The presence of the ornaments and the capellán had a cost, which the proceeds of the property income from which the capellanía would survive usually covered. The patrón received the money, since he was the administrator whom the deceased designated in the testamentary clause.

The institution of the capellanía has its origins in Iberia before the ninth century and was led by Christian warriors. To fight against the infidel, the most powerful weapon was not the sword but religion, which was used in various ways and forms. These powerful men decided to defeat the devil in hell itself through the institution of pious works and capellanías. They had decided to follow the path of St. Augustine, considering "Our Lord Jesus Christ" in their inheritances. Already from the laws of the Justinian Code, in passages of Gregory IX that deal with testaments and last wills, a theory of pious causes focused on the last will was formed with a perpetual character. A person left an amount of money or property to the Church so that after the death of the individual, it would be responsible for administering the sum. With the proceeds, the church paid a priest to give a certain number of Masses dedicated to the soul of the deceased. These Masses would be prayed indefinitely, for it was the way in which the deceased could save his soul from the devil in purgatory.[1]

Prayers were essential to facing the fearsome God of the Baroque Catholicism. Usually, the faithful lived in fear and died in hope. They believed that at the end of earthly life, God would require them to enter purgatory to suffer for their sins, and then they would face the final judgment of the Almighty in the Heavenly Court.

Pamela Voekel states that since the twelfth century, Catholics added individual judgment to the moment of death, hoping to have a collective judgment at the return of Christ. Once in the celestial tribunal, God scrutinized the biography of people. The holy attorneys (Saints) interceded in each case with the divine trial.[2] For this reason, the deceased depended on the suffrages (prayers and Masses) the living made for them since those prayers and rituals endowed "blessings" on the holy attorneys that each Christian had from the day of their birth. These, in turn, would appease the divine abhorrence of the sinful nature when the souls reached Heaven. It was unknown how long the souls would be detained in purgatory and when those would face God's final judgment. And it was precisely because of this uncertainty that the capellanías of prayed Masses were established, with the intention to last "forever and ever."

The promise of the eternal permanence of the capellanías was the factor that shaped a complicated apparatus to administer them. The product of the property income the testators left supported the perpetual duration of each capellanía. The one in charge of managing the rents and keeping the property in profitable condition was the patrón. At his death, or if when in life he, for whatever cause, could no longer fulfill his function, he had to assign his role to another individual in advance, or there would be no financial means to cover the expenses for prayed Masses.[3]

All this drama depended on the complicated network of participants who organized, maintained, and fostered it. Capellanías de misas rezadas (of prayed Masses) unified the idea of a peaceful life next to God after death. At the same time, these were opportunities to obtain pragmatic benefits. Thus, all social classes, whether they wanted to or not, were directly or indirectly related. Acting as capellanías' capellán, patrón, or cofradía brother implied a social role that bestowed a certain prestige. Above all, these were vehicles to construct a social-Christian image. With it, the faithful could have a good life "here" and in the hereafter.[4] Therefore, for all those involved to benefit from the capellanía, the role of the patrón was crucial.

This chapter addresses both the spiritual and the profane aspect of the capellanías in San Joseph del Parral during the second half of the seventeenth and throughout the eighteenth century. In the baroque ideological space, capellanías privileged the soul, but earthly life was vital as it could provide mortals with material means to keep them "alive" in death. In this town, the funders of capellanías de misas rezadas were mostly elite women and men, who were able to assume this responsibility by maintaining prosperous social and economic lives, although people of lower social status also funded those religious institutions. In fact, within the Spanish Baroque thought that permeated San Joseph del Parral's experience, from the mulato to the king, all people were somehow involved in matters related to capellanías that, as we will see, on several occasions were true dramas.

This chapter analyzes the mining town's inhabitants' involvement in the (not so) intimate Catholic ritual of capellanías. Perhaps because of its nature, it reinforced the Spanish Baroque ideology and practices as no other religious institution did. The analysis of capellanías best exemplifies how the ritual served Spanish women to express their thoughts and feelings about themselves and the world they lived in, and how some of them could, up to a certain point, oversee their destinies, not so much in life but after death. The documents inform about petitions, foundations, lawsuits, claims, and litigations presented before the Juzgado de Capellanías y Obras Pías (Court of Capellanías and Pious Works). This religious institution was the administrator of the capellanías' economic capital, thus ensuring that the faithful had a reliable means of obtaining income and guaranteeing goods under the concept of "spiritualized." The direct or indirect partaking in the complex scenario that constituted capellanías consisted of expressing individual needs and obtaining both spiritual and mundane benefits. This chapter will reflect how in San Joseph del Parral the Catholic Baroque discourse was very attached to the geographical reality and the natural wealth of Northern New Spain. We will see how distance, mining, local Indigenous rebellions, and enslaved African people played a role in the local reconfiguration of this universal institution and its ritual.

A document with a soldier's discourse—a letter the soldier issued sometime between 1648 and 1800—suggests that in the northern "war zone," death was always on the prowl. It also implies that individuals were always concerned for their souls' future. The file is not dated, nor does it include the protagonist's name. In his baroque manner of speech, the narrator projects himself as a man who lived in fear and wanted to die hopefully. He said, "Because of the lack of security in life that we have, mostly me, with a prison and border under my charge, frequent occurrences with barbarian Indians who invade it can take my life." As such, the document authorized the Corte Eclesiástica (Ecclesiastical Judge) of San Joseph del Parral to withdraw 6,000 pesos from his assets and establish a capellanía for prayed Masses. That was his last will, "in case I died (may God save me)," because the man had not made any legal testamentary provision to date and did not want to die intestate.[5]

This soldier's statement agrees with what this book has been addressing, that in San Joseph del Parral and throughout Northern New Spain, an atmosphere of constant threat developed because of people's and institutions' perceptions of Indigenous groups as "enemies and barbarian." As this man implies, death was the inseparable companion among those who defended the frontier. With the letter, he conveys the idea that death was a permanent reality, and its main protagonists were those Indigenous peoples. At the same time, this soldier's discourse discloses how individuals constructed or reconstructed the Spanish Baroque thought according to the circumstances of this remote place.

The soldier's desire was that he, as a testator, could designate a religious authority of the regular clergy to manage his capellanía.

In that way, the disposition of its assets would go directly to the Court of Capellanías and Pious Works. This institution administered the money or goods with which people funded capellanías or pious works (charities). For example, the founders' capital, or the income of other goods, was part of the Crédito Eclesiástico (Ecclesiastical Credit) of the Court of Capellanías. This institution provided wealth to all the regular clergy with that capital. This court itself had enough wealth to invest because it offered its capital as loans. In other words, this court was the primary source of credit in all New Spain.[6]

As Gisela von Wobeser explains, all economic activities during the viceroyalty era depended on credit or financing. For example, agriculture, livestock, mining, commerce, transportation, and crafts work were credit investments. Furthermore, dowries to enter convents or marriage, as well as home repairs and clergy education, including the founding of some capellanías, were handled on credit.[7] She believes that the material demands of high-ranking people influenced the use of credit for clothing, accommodation, transportation, participation in festivities, and endowment of pious works, among other goods or entertainment. Some miners and merchants, in addition to clergymen, landowners, women, public officials, the military, professionals, and artisans, received more than one loan from the Court of Capellanías.[8]

In New Spain, there were two significant sources of financing: merchants, who provided short-term loans, and ecclesiastical institutions. These, along with the occasional income charities and donations from the faithful provided, sought fixed income that would ensure they met spiritual objectives. In this way those entities sustained themselves without consuming the capital they possessed. Ecclesiastical Credit was one of this kind.[9] The institution approved a loan if people gave a guarantee in exchange, whether a house, accessories, orchards, bathhouses, workhouses, inns, factories, or other valuable goods. Individuals were usually assessed an annual interest rate of 5 percent—and yes, civil and ecclesiastical legislation condemned usury, but Ecclesiastical Credit always sought and found ways to justify it.[10]

There were productive investments with this money in agriculture, real estate, and urban goods. The finances went through the Consignment Census, as it was one of the most effective justifications for the Court of Capellanías to camouflage its role as a lender.[11] The Consignment Census worked in the following way: let's say that the applicants for a loan offered their profits from a rented house as an endorsement. At that moment, the candidates became "donors" through the Consignment Census, and the home and money from the rent became a capellanía. Those donors would not deposit their contribution (the capellanía/the house and the money from the rented house) in the administering institution, but rather the institution would "invest" those profits. That is, the Court of Capellanías granted credit (a loan) to the donors for an amount equal to their donation—the value of their houses or haciendas, for example—and invested in them. By carrying out the transaction in this way, there was no money involved between the institution-lender and the donors-debtors, so there was no usury.[12]

A Consignment Census case occurred in San Joseph del Parral sometime around 1680. It turns out that Don Pedro Martínez de Quiroga and Doña María de Quiroga had two haciendas of melting metal (silver), Santa Rosa and Espíritu Santo, which they wanted to use as collateral to get a loan. However, these properties were on the verge of being seized. The Quirogas asked to borrow money, putting those estates up as a "donation." However, at some point in the past, Doña María had gone to the Court of Capellanías to "establish a capellanía" (in reality, to ask for a loan) with the value of her estates.[13]

Given that the haciendas already had a mortgage, authorities estimated their value was not much. But the Quirogas' primary purpose in getting the loan was to prevent the properties from being auctioned after their deaths. That was why they wanted to establish a capellanía. With it, the payment of interest would not be the responsibility of their heirs but of those who bought or rented the properties.[14]

When Doña María died, she bequeathed the haciendas to her children. Then, the Court of Capellanías rented the estates to her husband, Don Pedro Martínez de Quiroga. From there, he was responsible for overseeing payment of the interest on the mortgage on the haciendas that, by then, were already owned by his children (the ones he had with his wife Doña María). Likewise, the Court of Capellanías appointed Don Alfonso Martínez de Artalejo, priest and sacristan of the parochial church, as the patrón of the capellanía Doña María established while she was still alive. Therefore, Artalejo was responsible for collecting the rent's estates from Quiroga.[15]

On June 15, 1684, Doña María's husband, Martínez de Quiroga, received a visit from Diego Machado, priest and fiscal promoter of the court. With him was Captain Nicolás Rojo de Soria, bailiff of the town. The fiscal promoter required Martínez de Quiroga to hand over 1,233 pesos and a tomín he owed Don Alfonso Martínez de Artalejo. Unfortunately, Martínez de Quiroga said that, at present, he did not have that amount. Artalejo learned of Quiroga's response that same day and immediately presented an idea to the promoter and bailiff: to obtain the money Quiroga owed him from the interest on the mortgage on the haciendas, and because he had not committed in any way to pay him, Artalejo asked to seize some assets of one of Martínez de Quiroga's haciendas. Thus, he could force the release of a few pesos, even if it was from time to time, until Quiroga could cover the entire amount owed.[16]

The goods Artalejo was referring to were ten piles of raw metal and seven enslaved Black people. Regarding the latter, Artalejo said they were "of mulato features." Then he gave their names and ages: Manuel Negro, 25; Gaspar Negro, 30; Juan Mulato, 10; Francisco Ramón Mulato, 10; Antonia Mulata, 12; and Gertrudis Mulata, 8. The Ecclesiastical Judge of the Kingdom of Nueva Vizcaya, Joseph de Morón, deemed Artalejo's idea to be of merit and immediately ordered the assets for auction. The order also called for Martínez de Quiroga to remain confined to his home under penalty of ex-communication.[17]

Hence, on June 21 of the same year, the town crier gave the first proclamation to auction the seven enslaved people. When Quiroga learned about it, he alleged that the auction was against the law and His Majesty's Pragmatic Cédulas, which ordered that no property belonging to the Ministry of the Treasury for the benefit of obtaining money should be dissipated or sold. Martínez de Quiroga asked for the auction proclamations to cease. Nobody paid attention to his request. The second proclamation occurred on June 24, and Martínez de Quiroga and Artalejo continued to argue. The former insisted on enforcing the King's Pragmatic Cédulas, and the latter repeated that those applied only to the property of profane estates but not to ecclesiastical property and the fruits of capellanías that, by law, were spiritual assets. While these two men continued contending, the town crier announced the third auction on the 27th of the same month.[18]

The auction of the enslaved African people did not stop until Captain Don Agustín Navarrete del Camino, Royal Official Judge and Administrator of the Azogues Reales, appeared before the authorities. He had the intention to resolve the case of Martínez de Quiroga and the haciendas of melting metal. Navarrete said that "in observance of the force of the Law, His Majesty prohibits, in similar estates . . . that in no case the flow of such important benefits to the public good be impeded." In short, Navarrete supported Martínez de Quiroga's claim about not taking His Majesty's assets: the enslaved African people. He argued that those were part of the mining industry. Then he told all those involved in the issue that the hacienda was in debt to His Majesty. In fact, they owed the king 5,496 pesos and his take in silver, the product of the quicksilver he had received for his benefit. Therefore, on behalf of His Majesty,

Navarrete commissioned the vicar to return the goods (the enslaved African people) to the hacienda (of which Martínez de Quiroga was patrón). He added that from that day on, the property had a new owner: Don Diego de Landavazos. Navarrete clarified that Landavazos needed to put the hacienda to work as soon as possible to cover the debt to His Majesty. As expected, the allegations continued, but in short, all those involved did what the Administrator of the Azogues ordered.[19]

At the end of this drama, Doña María's getting the Consignment Census appeal from the Court of Capellanías and Pious Works had no use. The truth was that the king of Spain deprived her heirs. Meanwhile, the Court of Capellanías saw two earnings escaping from its hands: those the previous haciendas' mortgage generated and the income the capellanía provided. Perhaps because it was the product of a Consignment Census, no one was concerned about Doña María de Quiroga's soul being eternally detained in purgatory.

Regarding Artalejo's statement on profane properties and estates of ecclesiastical goods and fruits of capellanías, which by law were spiritual goods, it is questionable whether the enslaved people were considered spiritualized or royal goods. The concept of spiritualized goods comes from the phenomenon Kathryn Burns identifies as "spiritual economy," where the spiritual and economical, the material and the sacred, merge into single management that consists of "businesses or exchanges where the spiritual and the economic could not disassociate." She suggests that during those times, spiritual values and practices permeated economic aspects to reduce their profane weight in an economy that occurred, first, in the religious realm.[20]

Additionally, the monetary goods capellanías generated were spiritualized products, so they were not profane. Hence, Artalejo probably believed that the enslaved people were spiritualized assets because they were possessions of the hacienda on which Doña María de Quiroga had founded her capellanía, despite it being under the Consignment Census. Perhaps because the profane value of these enslaved people dropped, authorities could auction them as spiritualized goods without the sale being a profit. But as Martínez de Quiroga and Navarrete indicated, those enslaved people who worked in the mining industry were, first and foremost, property of the haciendas to extract silver, a sector that, as has been observed, had received significant consideration from the Spanish Crown. The Habsburg kingdom's economic prosperity in the peninsula and America depended greatly on mining. In the end, in determining the spiritual or treasury value of the enslaved individuals, the crown's power prevailed over that of the Church. This is an example of the complex relationship between these two entities that, as indicated, became more intricate as the years passed. Either way, the Catholic Church and the crown assigned two new "price quotes" to enslaved Black people within capellanías and mines in Northern New Spain by including a debate on their spiritual vs. their production value.

It is necessary to highlight that negros and mulatos, unlike the enslaved Indigenous people acquired in Guerras Justas, had a commercial value in buying and selling markets during the seventeenth and eighteenth centuries. A relevant question is if their surplus value mirrored the metal richness of the northern soil. There were other testaments that included African-descent people as property to be inherited, although not all those wills included capellanías' clauses.[21] Indeed, there were more cases like the above, perhaps even more complicated. whether their surplus value, coupled with the Spanish medieval idea that they

For example, in 1724, the Court of Capellanías and Pious Works issued ordinances to control and order the people involved with the capellanías. Some included a penalty of ex-communication to all persons who made transfers and to buyers who made divisions of goods (as in the Quirogas' case). Moreover, if people discovered these irregularities, they had to expose them to the ecclesiastical judges. In case of ex-communication, the Court of Capellanías would get the entire product (goods). This court also recommended that capellanes officiate prayed Masses at the appointed time and place and to present the titles of the capellanías to the priests of their jurisdictions. Finally, it ordered the mandate to be disseminated with a proclamation on a public holiday so there would be no doubt among inhabitants.[22]

Spanish-Elite Women: A Tale of Life and Death

In San Joseph del Parral, material and spiritual demands did not leave women out. On the contrary, in the capellanías' realm, Spanish women's involvement stands out, especially during the second half of the seventeenth century. That is when most archival documents relate their participation in this religious institution. By "Spanish," this book refers to all those women and their descendants who arrived from the Spanish peninsula immediately after the town's establishment. As observed in chapter 3, although individuals and authorities could manipulate people's calidad in the social sphere, this research considers the qualifier of "Doña" to identify peninsular or "criollo" women. However, the trait is not entirely reliable. While New Spain society reserved "Don" and "Doña" titles for Spaniards, as we learned, those could also be mestizos or those from other races if their physiognomy favored their supposed European ancestors, from which they took social prestige. In Northern New Spain, the social status of "Doñas" could vacillate depending on both physical appearance and occupation. In 1649, for example, the local authority of San Joseph del Parral demanded that Doña Francisca depart from the town at least fifty leagues for her "scandalous" behavior.[23] Another example is Juana de Cobos, a baker-merchant who lived in the town of San Felipe El Real de Chihuahua for almost the entire eighteenth century. Official documents described her variously as mestiza, Spanish, or mulata, but at no time as "Doña." But, since she had a prominent economic and social presence in the town, some inhabitants awarded her the title of Doña.[24]

In the municipal and parochial archives, women who founded capellanías in San Joseph del Parral were wives of oligarchy men, usually miners, encomenderos, or even adelantados who retained privileges for having been part of the entradas (entrances) to the northern zone. To accurately provide the number of women present in the town during that time is practically impossible. As observed, in population censuses, registered vecinos had populated houses with women, children, or servants (Indigenous, negro, or mulato) not included in the survey. Furthermore, as Pilar Gonzalbo Aizpuru points out, it is difficult to find documents that report on an entire life trajectory of women: "The isolated references of one and the other suggest many possibilities of understanding the complex reality in which they unfolded."[25]

Margarita Iglesias Saldaña indicates that, as happened in the Western European medieval period, New Spain women played a leading role in public and private ceremonies. They even were, to a large extent, the holders of capellanías, through which they had multiple opportunities to be heads of lineage, a role that allowed them to strengthen family strategies and preserve family memory, along with assets, powers, and surnames.[26] Spanish women in San Joseph del Parral manifested those opportunities and roles. Apart from being heads of lineage and preservers of family memories, assets, powers, and surnames, they also had the opportunity to express individual wishes and wills not limited to the family sphere. Indeed, their wishes included their concern for the future of the people that surrounded them, deciding and controlling their own lives after death, and knowing how to exercise their legal rights in a highly patriarchal society. This chapter examines the cases of three Spanish elite women embodying the unique pious-baroque discourse in a town where the oligarchy formed and defined itself mainly based on geographical location and natural resources.

We begin with Doña Ana de Biezma. She was a vecina and a miner, the sister of the town's founder, Juan Rangel de Biezma, and the widow of Captain Bartolomé de Urbaneja, her first husband.

In 1645, Ana decided to establish a capellanía for prayed Masses. At that time, her second husband was Sebastián García de Rosi. In the testamentary clause dedicated to her capellanía, she named her husband patrón, and states that she does so willingly, being mentally sane, and:

> . . . so that our Lord God may be served . . . [I entrust] my soul and that of my parents, and that of my husband [the first one] and the rest of the deceased to receive benefit and suffrages . . . I founded a capellanía of prayed Masses to be said [for the souls all of them], from the day of the date of this letter onwards forever and ever.[27]

Ana indicated that her capellanía should be of fifty prayed Masses each year for the souls of the people she mentioned, including her own, when she died. So, Ana left the amount of 2,000 pesos as the principal, a house, and a ranch called La Ciénega, which belonged to her first husband, Captain de Urbaneja (he received it as a grant by the mercy of the lord governors of the New Vizcaya Kingdom).[28] As a perpetual capellán, for all the days of his life once he was ordained a priest, Ana appointed Bartolomé de Arriaga y Montenegro.[29]

Likewise, it was her will that the capellanía would extend to her brother, Juan Rangel de Biezma, to her sister-in-law, Doña Andrea Calderia, and their children who wished to be clerics, preferring the eldest to the youngest. If none of the children considered the priestly career, the capellanía would then encompass all the relatives she had up to the fourth degree. If among these were more than two who wished to be priests, the poorest and most virtuous would have preference. If no one resulted from Ana's relatives, her capellanía would consider San Joseph del Parral Indians who wished to be clerics, electing the most virtuous first and then the poorest. Finally, Ana granted a pious/charity work to the mayordomos of La Santa

Iglesia Parroquial del Real de San Joseph del Parral, her devotee and saint advocate, which consisted of renting and collecting the rents of the house mentioned before. She further declared that her husband did not force her to fund the capellanía. She ended the clause with a due oath.

Ana's capellanía reflects the family strategies carried out by some Spanish women in New Spain, like that of preserving family memory, assets, powers, and surnames. It is also the reflection of the idea or concept of family the Spaniards brought to New Spain, which emphasized the structure of an extensive kinship that included parents, children, siblings, uncles and aunts, cousins, nephews and nieces, and others. That type of family relationship recognized women as members. However, in New Spain, and the rest of America, this extended family could include the powers and material goods of the first Spanish individuals, in this case in Northern New Spain, that could have been rebuilt and perpetuated, such as those of Ana's first husband and her brother.

As previously observed, when adelantados secured official positions in Northern New Spain, they also forged fortunes to build extensive kinship ties with "surnames." They had the privilege of getting encomiendas and/or repartimientos: Indigenous labor for agriculture, mining, transportation, and commerce, among other means. And if business diversification was part of this enterprise, the encomendero could build lasting family fortunes.[30] The amount of wealth the Urbaneja and Biezma families had is unknown. However, Ana, having been the sole heir to her first husband, demonstrates those extensive kinship ties. At that time, these families only endured through access to great fortunes and accumulated achievements such as honor, purity of blood, and longevity. That is precisely one of Ana's perceived intentions in her capellanía: to extend kinship through honor, achievements, and material goods.

Ana also appears to have been a woman of her time. She was raised and trained under a legislation that established the limitations imposed on single and married women. They had to be submissive, at least formally, to their respective parents, brothers, husbands, or guardians. In the letter, mentioning her father, brother, capellán, and other male relatives can support this assertion. However, at the same time, it is observed that she had the opportunity to inherit, marry a second time, and to be owner of land and mines. In this regard, Gonzalbo Aizpuru indicates that in New Spain's mid-sixteenth century, Spanish women from the Iberian Peninsula (still few) had various opportunities to maintain and improve their social status. They could guide their destiny by choosing a husband, having access to the property, and establishing small businesses such as sawmills and workshops, among others. Those privileges allowed them to exercise control of family assets.[31] San Joseph del Parral witnessed a similar occurrence, but not until the middle of the seventeenth century, when the mining town was formed. The cases of Ana and other peninsular or Spanish-descent women demonstrate they had opportunities to be mining, land, and capellanías owners beyond the sixteenth century.

In fact, since 1524, Hernán Cortés demanded married adelantados or encomenderos to bring their wives to have a family life. They were part of the colonizing strategy in which women served as emissaries of Spanish cultural and religious models, a key piece in the defense policy and of promoting family coexistence. At the same time, the law allowed women to carry out commercial operations and launch lawsuits to claim property, money, and inheritances, among other matters. One hundred years later, these same situations occurred in Northern New Spain when the encomenderos were also required to bring their Spanish wives to engage in marital and family life.[32] Therefore, in Mexico City's sixteenth century, the first women of peninsular or Spanish descent had already established themselves. However, in San Joseph del Parral's seventeenth century, very few were choosing husbands, becoming landowners, or acquiring the viceroyalty's most privileged enterprise: mining.

The archival documents thus include women like Ana, who had a more direct "Spanish" family tie to adelantados, encomenderos, and oligarchs of the mining town.

In the testamentary clause, Ana conceived of herself as a miner and vecina who had the power and means to look after her family. At the same time, she manifested her interest in the town's religious future. In her capellanía, she appointed San Joseph as her holy advocate, the patron saint of both the mine and the town. Likewise, Ana left a pious work for the cofradía with that saint's name. Moreover, if her relatives did not want to pursue a priestly career, Ana wished to extend her capellanía to the most virtuous Indigenous men of the town. This woman thus transformed capellanías' universal pious discourse: by representing herself as part of the mining elite, selecting San Joseph as her advocate, and including the Indigenous men in her will and desires, although she did not clarify which Indigenous people she was referring to.

Doña Agustina de Grados's capellanía is the second case in this chapter. She was born in El Valle de San Bartolomé. She was the legitimate daughter of Francisco Hernández, a resident of Mexico City, and Isabel de Grados, a vecina of El Valle de San Bartolomé. One day on September 26, 1673, Agustina instituted a capellanía that reads:

> . . . being as I am, sick in bed; healthy of the understanding, memory, judgment, and will, of such which God . . . was served to give me. I believe in the Mystery of the Holy Trinity, God the Father, God the Son, and God of the Holy Spirit, in the Holy Mother Roman Catholic Church, in whose faith I must live and die, putting the sovereign Queen of Angels, Mary Most Holy Lady, as my intercessor advocate, so that in the Court of Divine Clemency may intercede for me with the Divine, forgive my faults and sins, and protect me at the time of my death, so that my soul

may be saved. I want to order my testament and last will in the following way: first, I entrust my soul to Our God, his precious blood and body, in the land from which it was formed. I ask him to take me, that my body be buried in the parish church of this town, in front of the altar of Souls.[33]

Agustina's pious language included what Baroque Catholicism considered the ideal death: expected after a long-suffered illness, such as the one Agustina might have experienced in her bed. It included the belief that illness was a great teacher because it fostered patience and serenity so that the dying person would dispatch earthly affairs and prepare her/himself to receive the last rites with dignity, the sacrament with which an individual would achieve the grace of a good death.[34] Baroque death was a whole dramatic process. First, the dying person had to come face to face with the devil. He appeared in one's weakest moments: during the agony. At that time, Satan offered the dying individual various temptations, including the hope of eternal life and the company of loved ones.[35] But this was a "diabolical" lie. If the sick person did not succumb to the devil's temptation, he would go to Heaven as a soldier of God, but not without first going through purgatory.

Agustina chose the sovereign Queen of the Angels as an intercessory attorney when facing the Final Judgment upon her death. Voekel explains that at the time of drawing up a will, the notary and testator's minds had the conception of Divine Glory as a Heavenly Court setting.[36] Thus, when Agustina says that she is ill and bedridden, it is most likely that the notary was at her home, in her room, writing the pious speech of the dying woman. Even more, in baroque death, the ideal place for the agony of the sick person's unction was the interior of the bedroom of the dying person. The individual was supposed to be before the gaze of relatives, friends, and community people. The scene aimed to remind them of life's finite nature and the omnipresence of death. Therefore, they needed to prepare themselves to await its arrival with a soul free of guilt.[37] It is impossible to know if Agustina fashioned her capellanía in front of family or friends, apart from the required witnesses. However, Voekel's description helps to complete an image that occurred in more than a one-bed chamber in New Spain. Thus, capellanías became part of Baroque Catholicism: the religion of showing and the ritual of observing.[38]

Nevertheless, like Ana de Biezma, Agustina was concerned with the practical things of life, for these were the means to achieve eternal life. When she passed away, she wanted her executors to impose a capellanía of prayed Masses on her house. With the fruit of its rental income, twelve prayed Masses a year would be given for her soul and the soul of Captain Galindo, her husband. Six of the prayed Masses would be for the Blessed Sacrament. Besides that, she appointed Pedro de Chavarría as patrón and capellán. He would ensure that those prayed Masses were given "forever and ever" and take charge of any repairs the rental housing would need. Likewise, she appointed Agustín García, her compadre, and Juan Hernández, her brother, as executors and asset holders.[39]

In a practical sense, the cases of the capellanías of Agustina and Ana are similar, especially when they granted deference to the men of the family, which was expected in a patriarchal society where the father, husband, brother, or uncle directed and supervised the behavior of all the members of his family. However, the man of the house observed women's behavior more closely since the idiosyncrasy of that time judged them as weak beings in almost every way. In the absence of a father or husband, the figure of the patriarch could fall to a grandfather, brother, uncle, or any other man from the close or extended family. Women used the role models patriarchal societies imposed to their advantage, but not openly. Usually, most of them acted in a subordinate position to which the law and custom relegated them. However, women who belonged to the elite could, on some occasions, retain family privileges.[40]

In comparing Ana's and Agustina's capellanías' founding deeds, it is possible to observe specific differences. Agustina indicated her desire to be buried in the cemetery, which was attached to the parish church, just in front of the altar of souls. According to baroque thought and per New Spain's death practices, Spanish or Indigenous elite's wills requested burials in church cemeteries. The custom dates to the eleventh century, during the reign of Alfonso El Sabio X, who communicated the idea that souls would be closer to God and holy figures if the deceased were buried within the church grounds. The cemeteries outside the churches' parameters were undesirable because demons lived there. Therefore, graves within church land would remind relatives and inhabitants who attended Mass that they had to pray for the repose of the souls of their relatives and neighbors who were, practically, under their feet. Burial in church cemeteries also implied making social class distinctions. For example, elite families expected to have crypts in which to bury all their offspring. Likewise, church cemeteries sectioned their spaces, and prices varied according to the place closest or farthest from the enclosure. Agustina, for example, chose to be buried in front of the altar of souls. Usually, these altars were no further than the middle of the cemetery, which meant that Agustina chose the most expensive one.[41]

However, because Agustina was part of the Spanish-mining elite and had sufficient financial resources, it is striking that she did not have a family crypt. As the sergeant indicated at the beginning of this chapter, the members of the military corps, who in San Joseph del Parral usually belonged to the mining elite, could lose their lives from one moment to the next at the hands of the "enemy Indigenous peoples." Along with the constant migration in the mining centers and the epidemics that occurred in different years during the seventeenth century, the situation could have contributed to San Joseph del Parral's lacking durable family chains to establish "ancestry" crypts in the parish church's cemetery, although there could be exceptions.

The truth is that in her testamentary clause, Agustina gives the impression of not having been part of a large family. Unlike Ana, Agustina did not remarry after her widowhood. At least, she did not have a husband at the time of establishing her capellanía. In her will, Agustina named her brother, Juan Hernández, and her compadre, Agustín García, as executors of the will and property holders. As universal heirs, she named María García, her goddaughter, who was the legitimate daughter of Agustín García, Agustina's compadre, and María Camacho, Agustín's wife. She also named another goddaughter, María Galindo, whom she raised at home, and about whom she did not give further information. These dispositions may indicate that Agustina had no children of her own. In sum, Agustina joined the pious-baroque discourse and its mortuary ritual by starring in a scene of agony before the arrival of death. At the same time, she expressed her will and desire for how her soul would exist in the "beyond." Her social class and economic means allowed her to fulfill her wish: that her body and soul were closer to God, the holy figures, and the town's people. Perhaps her requests resulted from the lack of a network of immediate relatives of a woman whose life was somehow structured as the local actuality dictated.

The third capellanía case is under the name of Doña Catalina de Olarte. This is one that appears indirectly in an archival document dating from 1739. On it, Don Joseph Ochoa, Ecclesiastical Judge of San Joseph del Parral, said that the hacienda San Lorenzo in El Valle de San Bartolomé had a capellanía of prayed Masses, and Doña Catalina de Olarte was the founder. The document indicates that authorities could not find the founding deed. They speculated that someone drew it up in 1715. Ochoa said that Catalina's capellanía had the intention that every Saturday of the year, the capellán must burn a lamp on the altar of Nuestra Virgen de la Soledad in the parish church that bore the same name. The clause indicated that the capellán had to perform this action every time the town celebrated the holy sacrifice of the Mass. However, in the document, Ochoa stated that nobody had lit the lamp for almost four years.[42]

On this occasion, the protagonist of the capellanía was not so much the holder as the object and its mission: the lamp, which was a gift for Nuestra Virgen de la Soledad, who in turn was the arbiter of Catalina's soul when at her death she would go before the Celestial Court. In capellanías, it was usual for the founders to dedicate objects such as lamps, jewels, or other ornaments of monetary and spiritual value to honor God and the saints. By adorning a sacred place like the church, the donor helped enhance the liturgical rites. However, individuals gave gifts to parishes for other motives. When the believer wanted to show his devotion, for example, an object of value dignified worship in the churches. That was also a gesture that came from groups or communities. The objects seemed to offer splendor and drama to the sacred place and ritual. Those also impressed the faithful, who, during Mass, could derive a sacred experience from those ornaments. Thus, through the objects and the Mass ritual, the believer could experience God, in the very moment the sign and its meaning united.[43]

In addition, it was probable that Ochoa was concerned with the spiritual value of Catalina's lamp but also about the fact that none lit it. The concern was that the deceased could not achieve her will; in other words, Catalina's soul was detained in purgatory. Given that designated religious objects demanded care and devotion, how much more so a lamp that could not light itself. Catholic Baroque ritual included the belief that the sacred emanated from the light with the power to penetrate the physical. Then, during the Eucharist, God and saints manifested.[44] Therefore, if none lit the lamp, Catalina's soul would not receive the intervention that La Virgen de la Soledad was expected to give her during Saturday's prayed Mass: when the Virgin and God were supposed to show up in the object's light.

It is essential to consider that the Masses had a redemptive power. They took that power from the Council of Trent (Catholic

Reformation), which was how the creation of capellanías became universal. Mortals could achieve the soul's salvation through good works, but the redemptive power of the Mass was of utmost importance. The offering of the Mass was the legitimate tradition of the Apostles to erase sins and sorrows and to give satisfaction and other needs to the faithful, either alive or dead. The doctrine of the Mass consisted of giving thanks to God, plus the true and proper sacrifice instituted in Jesus Christ. During Mass, God was appeased and benign, and this was when He offered gifts of grace and penance and forgave sins, hence the need for the Mass for the deceased. Through it, people could make intercessions for the souls detained in purgatory, and in this way those souls could leave that horrible place sooner.[45]

However, for Ochoa, the point was that the people who had that obligation did not light the lamp. Who were these people? According to Ochoa, these were the capellán and mayordomos of the Archicofradía del Santísimo Sacramento, whom Catalina had left as beneficiaries of the income from the San Lorenzo hacienda. The capellán, who offered a prayed Mass on Saturdays, and the mayordomos in charge were supposed to divide the revenue among them in exchange for the pious work they received from Catalina. They had to ensure that a priest conducted the ritual and that someone lit the lamp. Ochoa asked for explanations, first, from the capellán who, in 1739, oversaw Catalina's capellanía. He asked that person to do what his predecessor capellanes carefully did: to collect the revenues from the capellanía so he could carry out the deceased's will. But when asked, the capellanes of the cofradía replied that none oversaw collecting these revenues.[46]

At Ochoa's declaration and request, the Ecclesiastical Judge of the Court of Capellanías and Pious Works ordered an investigation for the hacienda of melting silver not to be lost. The current patrones of Catalina's capellanía had to disclose if they had received the revenue from the hacienda. The judge also required to know if the inheritance deeds contained the handover of the property.[47] Subsequently, Don Pedro Domingo de Lugo emerged to say that he had owned the San Lorenzo hacienda so that the lamp on the altar de la Soledad would burn with the revenues he obtained from it. He had acquired the farm through his wife, Doña María de Orrantia, who received the hacienda from her paternal grandmother, María Teresa de Montelongo. The tax on the capellanía was 7,000 pesos. Six thousand were part of three capellanías of 2,000 pesos each, which Catalina had supposedly left, and the 1,000 remaining were added so that, from their revenues, the lamp could burn.[48]

Domingo de Lugo said he had paid the rent for the hacienda for sixteen consecutive years to Don Manuel de Herrera, Don Bonifacio de Arriaga, and Don Ignacio Joseph Romano. They were the ones who supervised individuals who had to light the lamp during those years. After that, Domingo de Lugo transferred the hacienda to Don Manuel de San Juan de la Santa Cruz of the Orden de Santiago, a neighbor of the mining town of San Felipe El Real de Chihuahua. In 1739, he owned the hacienda and was owed five years in rent because none collected it since the founding deed of Catalina's capellanía did not appear. However, the Capellanías Court located Catalina's will, which informed that she indeed had left a capellanía deed. Then, the court ordered the collection of those five years' rent from Santa Cruz. Likewise, it required the current mayordomos of the Archicofradía del Santísimo Sacramento that, from then on, they would run with the collection of the revenues and use them in their destination: to light Catalina's lamp every Saturday during Mass.[49]

Catalina's lamp reveals more openly how the spiritual economy of the capellanías worked. On the one hand, the importance of the patrones and capellanes stands out since they supervised "starting" and maintaining the machinery that would give the coins to officiate the prayed Masses, decorate the temples, and, in this case, light the lamp. On the other hand, with the passing of the years, the capellanías involved more and more people: the buyer of a property, the person in charge of renting it and delivering the profits to the patrón, the capellán or the mayordomos of cofradías who, in turn, had an obligation to watch over the prayed Masses. Through this complex chain of obligations, the capellanía could run as the proprietors desired, "forever and ever." However, some of the capellanías did not last even for fifteen or twenty years. In all these scenarios, it is essential to consider that Ana, Agustina, and Catalina founded their capellanías to die confident since this institution would ensure them a less painful passage through purgatory. However, because of the complications in which some capellanías were involved, the passage through that horrible place was delayed or detained forever and ever, as in Catalina's case.

A similar situation occurred with Ana's capellanía founded in 1645. Thirty-three years later, in 1678, Don Domingo de Apresa Falcón appeared before the Court of Capellanías. He said that he had bought from Francisco Fernández de la Vega the metal that was on the ranch called La Ciénega and in some houses. All were Ana de Biezma's properties; those were the assets she used to acquire her capellanía of fifty prayers. In 1678, the patrones of her capellanía were the mayordomos of La Iglesia de San José, and the capellán was Nicolás de Pastrana. The issue was that Apresa Falcón wanted these people to receive the houses and the ranch so that they could rent them and get the profits since he declined the right to rent them. The mayordomos and the capellán appeared before the Capellanías Court and said there was no place for Apresa Falcón's petition. According to them, the houses were in deplorable condition, and no one was interested in renting the hacienda because of the threatening invasions of the enemy Indians. They did not want to get the properties because, since they would not be able to rent them, they would fail in their obligation, and the capellanía would be affected, "letting down the souls for whom it was imposed."[50]

Another capellanía duty, usually of the patrón but sometimes also of the capellán, was to keep the properties in good condition.

In fact, as Agustina did, most of the possessors indicated in the capellanía's deed that the patrón had to oversee keeping the properties in good condition as they aged. This pledge was rarely kept, unfortunately. As a document dating from 1803 informs, besides the capellanía's lamp, Catalina de Olarte founded another capellanía in 1695 with her hacienda of melting silver. However, the letter indicates that by the early nineteenth century, the hacienda "had already fallen."[51] The idea of "forever and ever" that capellanías intended to reach was far from being achieved, as it was in the hands of people who traveled, moved, got sick, and inevitably died. Likewise, the situation the Provincia de Santa Bárbara was experiencing in the economy and labor spheres, and the supposed "enemy Indian attacks," affected the entire chain of obligations the capellanías required.

It is essential to remember that the document on Catalina's lamp shows that San Joseph del Parral's inhabitants shared and believed in the Catholic Baroque discourse/ideology. In addition, when rendering accounts to the ecclesiastical authorities, the spiritual had economic and social value that the Court of Capellanías supported and justified. The endowment of goods to establish capellanías reflected the religious-baroque mentality of the time. By donating these goods, the founder believed he or she was performing a supreme act of religious piety, which charged itself with a dense redemptive significance. This act had only one objective: the eternal salvation of the donor's soul. Then, this aim became an act of expiation (amendment/ penalty) by restoring assets sometimes unfairly acquired or whose lawful possession was in doubt at the end of life.[52] In this regard, it is worth questioning whether the capellanías funded in San Joseph del Parral included assets that were mostly mining estates and if their origin was in doubt, were those automatically spiritualized because they were an act of atonement?

Apparently, they were or had the potential to be because this kind of conversion, almost magical, from the profane to the spiritual, allowed the holders of capellanías to feel relieved and die in holy peace. At the same time, the spiritualized goods allowed the patrons, capellanes, and mayordomos to carry out material and economic transactions the Capellanía Court protected. This religious institution was the engine that made the capellanías and pious works run, thus allowing faithful Catholics to have a reliable means of obtaining income and guaranteeing goods under the concept of "spiritualized."[53]

However, the Court of Capellanías did not always have the right conditions to grow its wealth. Sometimes it had to deal with an inefficient collection system due to investment insecurity and poor administration despite having a good number of specialized employees like the ordinary judge, the testament inspector, the defense attorney (for the court), the tax defender, the treasurer, the income collector, and the property administrator, among others. All these employees had to travel long distances to attend to the affairs and business of the court, and they did not always arrive at the right time to supervise investments, collect revenues, manage capellanías, and invest, monitor, and comply with the capellanía and other tasks. Almost all capellanías' buildings were in debt, and bankruptcies and auctions were common. In many cases, no notice was given about the death of the capellán, and that meant stagnation in the production of income and profits for the court.[54] Despite these blunders, people continued to give money to found capellanías, and men and women continued to borrow because the Church was the only institution that was considered honest, permanent, and perpetual.[55]

Women in Capellanías' Claims

As expressed previously, the capellanías did not only include the deceased's world and their souls. These religious institutions involved a complicated network of actors who somehow marked the drama of daily life in San Joseph del Parral. The death of a capellán, the transfer of property, and sometimes the lack of precision in the testamentary clauses on which the capellanías were based were occasions for legal claims or lawsuits. Women were part of this process on some occasions, not always as founders but also as individuals who deserved rights the law protected. In San Joseph del Parral, individuals attained capellanías mainly through housing properties or mining estates, whose owners often belonged to the oligarchy. These were captains, sergeants, merchants, mayors, mine owners, and wives, widows, and daughters of these powerful men. For the latter, capellanías were opportunities to seek social and economic well-being in the "here and now" of life.

That was what Ana and Teresa de Barrios, sisters, did in 1659 when they appeared before the court to claim the benefits of the capellanía their grandfather, Juan de Barrios, had founded on a hacienda that benefited from obtaining money. This property, which included residential houses for labor gangs, the grandfather bequeathed to Ana and Teresa's father, Captain Sebastián de Barrios, who had died by that time. On behalf of their brothers, these two women requested an account of the present state in which ". . . the capellanía that was imposed on the assets that remained of Captain Juan de Barrios [the grandfather] . . . in the profit of the hacienda, from the end of December 1653, which Don Toribio Díaz de Quintanilla served [rented] it, until 1654." From 1653 to 1655, Juan Fernández de Carrión, the town's mayor whose discourse was analyzed in chapter 4, had been renting it. However, in 1656, authorities seized the property because he did not deliver the rental payment. Then, the Court of Capellanías collected the money resulting from the embargo from Ana and Teresa. They stated that "we do not owe, nor are we obliged to pay, the expenses of the capellanía [since] we were caused many cuts while we were trying to find someone to rent it."[56]

The document does not disclose whether the court considered Ana and Teresa's claims. They were determined, as evidenced in their speech, not to pay their grandfather's capellanía debt. By expressing their intention not to conform, the sisters were ensuring the family's financial well-being. Moreover, they did not hold back in doing so. However, their statement put Fernández de Carrión in the foreground. They presented him as the person responsible for the seizure of their property and its economic shortcomings. Ana and Teresa's case stands out because they did not use a legal representative, as was common in those days for men and women when appearing before civil or ecclesiastical authorities. Neither the patriarch of the family, nor any man, accompanied them, which was unusual in a patriarchal society.

Doña Feliciana de Urquiza did go with her husband, Juan Aguirre, to file a claim with the court regarding a capellanía. It was May 1678, and the husband spoke for her once before the ecclesiastical authority. He said, "The Doña is the legitimate daughter and heir of Captain Don Pedro de Urquiza and Doña María de Laxan, vecinos from Minas Nuevas." Aguirre went on to say that Don Pedro, Doña Feliciana's father, had been the patrón of a capellanía that consisted of offering twelve prayed Masses per year, which gave the patrón the amount of thirty pesos, the product of the rent of the house that guaranteed that capellanía. Therefore, since Doña Feliciana's father had already died, she was heir to all her father's rights and actions since he neglected to name a person to relieve him of his position before he died.[57]

According to Juan Aguirre, Doña Feliciana had to replace her father as patrón, appoint a capellán to continue the prayed Masses, and receive the thirty pesos, the house's income. Aguirre added that he and his wife had already named Ambrosio Quijada as capellán. From that day on, this individual had to request and obtain the deed of the capellanía Feliciana's father previously administered. Finally, Aguirre and Doña Feliciana swore with the sign of the Holy Cross before God Our Lord that "there had been neither a gift nor bribery nor corruption . . . [that] the Doña has not been forced by her husband's saying, not someone else." However, it seemed that Aguirre's statement was not enough for the Court of Capellanías because in July of the same year, Doña Feliciana had to appear alone to give her statement. During this appearance, she said, "With the license that my husband gives me, that I am the heir to the Captain of Urquiza, my late father . . . I have the right of patronage that is refuted."[58] As can be seen, regardless of whether these women used representatives in their claims, the law allowed them to claim their assets, mainly when the well-being of the family depended on them. Ana and Teresa, like Feliciana, knew how to take advantage of capellanías' law mechanisms in their favor. Both institutions protected them from possible societal judgments: Ana and Teresa could not be viewed as women interested in profane aspects since the hacienda and the house they claimed were spiritualized goods.

As is evident, in San Joseph del Parral capellanías served as more than supporting the clergy and preserving family assets; they reflect the equal importance of spirituality and materiality in that society. The feminine world integrated pious language to represent itself, whether as good Christian sisters or wives, dying patients, miners, or donors of valuable objects to enhance the experience of the Mass. These images-roles loaded with a "pious" meaning allowed them to obtain the spiritual and profane ends they sought. Spanish elite women founded capellanías, and with those, some of them preserved family memory, property, and surnames. However, they also had the opportunity to decide for themselves in the earthly life and the "afterlife." And they likely continued to do so throughout the eighteenth century, even with the arrival of the Bourbon reforms. The crown was ambiguous about the Catholic Church's role in the renovation plan for the viceroyalty. It delayed limiting and eliminating the Church's control over spiritualized goods and ecclesiastical credit. While that situation was defined, the news of the Enlightenment spread, especially among the wealthy social classes. As history has shown, women also became moved by the idea of "personal happiness," which led them to continue seeking their well-being.

Retelling the Value of Spiritualized Lives in a House of Mirrors

As observed, capellanías of prayed Masses were at the heart of the baroque drama in San Joseph del Parral as those complex institutions reveal how life and death had almost the same significance for all the town's inhabitants. Soldiers' concerns about directing their souls to Heaven, men of wealth inheriting goods to their souls, and decisions as to whether or not enslaved Africans were spiritualized goods or the king's assets generated scenarios in which most members of society participated. The loans the Capellanías Court provided under the Consignment Census were perhaps the most apparent sign that inhabitants performed various social, economic, religious, and political theatricalities in the mining community due to all the mechanisms implied to erase the profane side of Church transactions.

Regarding the value of enslaved Africans in the intricate case of Martínez de Quiroga, for example, the year in which the dispute took place and the years in which these individuals arrived at the town must be considered. The lawsuit between Quiroga and Artalejo occurred in 1684, while the sale of enslaved Black people occurred between 1632 and 1657. Supposing those individuals arrived during the years of their commercialization when the degree of mestizaje was not yet significant, it is highly probable that by 1684 Manuel Negro, Gaspar Negro, Juan Mulato, Francisco Ramón Mulato, Antonia Mulata, and Gertrudis Mulata still conserved "mulato features," as Artalejo said. It is also probable that they were a family. This detail may indicate that forced labor in the mines and haciendas may have limited mestizaje and fostered family unions between enslaved Africans. However, it could have helped to strengthen the idea that this kind of "family gang" belonged to the hacienda of melting silver. Then, their value was that of production.

The ambiguity about the value of property in the capellanías adds to the presence of supposed "enemy Indians." In the documents, various individuals mentioned how Indigenous attacks affected the lives of the people and the entire Provincia de Santa Bárbara. However, it is also probable that some capellanes or patrones, unable to fulfill their obligations in the capellanías, used the town's cultural memory about the incursions of the "barbarians" to justify their lack of compromise. Therefore, enslaved negros and mulatos, and the image of the enemy Indians, appeared in a scene revealing the role that the geographic location and the wealth of natural resources of Northern New Spain played in creating a history for Northern New Spain. On the other hand, this chapter reveals how economic and family situations were multifaceted for Spanish-elite women. Some of them were miners, widows with wealth but without direct family, or sisters and daughters of captains or sergeants, all protected by the law and by the ambiguous capellanías' ideology about spiritualized goods. With their assets, those women could freely express wishes, make claims, and seek the good of their relatives. Among them, Doña Ana de Biezma stands out for showing concern for her descendants and the town's future. In her capellanía, she also included, albeit last, Indigenous men of the town who would be supported to follow a priestly education, given that they were virtuous. Moreover, people constantly confronted capellanías' ideal with reality. Houses deteriorated and lamps went unlit due to the lack of attention from the patrones and capellanes. Haciendas stopped producing profits because of the supposed incursions of "enemy Indians." The truth was that a whole baroque life dedicated entirely to preparing to receive a good death and secure a place in the church cemetery could be easily truncated, and souls detained in purgatory for eternity.

Another certainty was that as Catholic institutions, capellanías did not last either. On December 26, 1804, the Bourbon government finally struck a heavy blow against the Catholic Church's power. La Real Cédula Sobre Enajenación de Bienes Raíces y Cobro de Capitales de Capellanías y Obras Pías para la Consolidación de Vales Reales (the Royal Decree on the Disposal of Real estate and Collection of Capital from Capellanías and Obras Pías for the Consolidation of Royal Vouchers) had a new policy: to shake the economic base on which the Church relied, both in the peninsula and in America. Nonetheless, apparently, the regime did not consider that the economic base of the Church in the New World was different from that of Spain. The latter, for example, based its economy mainly on real estate, while the former based its value on the capital available from capellanías and pious works. The Church in New Spain did not invest as much in properties. Still, The Church in New Spain was the financial capital of thousands of farmers, miners, and businesspeople, among others, received in the form of loans in exchange for a mortgage pledge and as payment of revenues. This Bourbon Cédula caused severe damage to the composition of the New Hispanic financial system, which led to a deeper division between the Church and the State. Despite the shift, some capellanías managed to last a little beyond the nineteenth century, but they disappeared definitively with the Nationalization of Ecclesiastical Property during the War of the Reform, 1857–1860.[59] Martín suggests that more research is needed on the effect of the Bourbon reforms' social, political, and economic innovations in Mexico during the later period of the colony.[60] The situation of the capellanías, from the last half of the eighteenth century to the first half of the nineteenth century, would surely be a subject of historical richness to analyze since it is evident that the capellanías reflect the effort of the Catholic Church to avoid the Bourbon reforms and prevail beyond the nineteenth century.[61]

DRAMA'S DÉNOUEMENT

In *El Parral de mis recuerdos* (*Memories of Parral*), Salvador Prieto Quimper builds a cultural memory of the current city of Hidalgo del Parral. His mid-twentieth-century memoir evokes the arrival of the Spaniards—men who, according to the author, were "courageous Christian knights who left a legacy in the mining town through the inheritance of blood." Regarding their descent, he adds, "Their heirs are prominent men of the city, as long as they are capable of demonstrating a direct link with the Spaniards." Among the prominent men of Parral, he mentions Dr. Francisco Perches and Don Trinidad Villaverde, whom the author describes as men "with unmistakable Basque surnames," who, according to him, are like "the knights of the Order of Calatrava, 'sin tacha y sin mancha' (without mark and stain), descendants of the oldest regional families." In short, Prieto Quimper describes these individuals as "honest men, in the fairest sense of the word."[1] The author suggests that the proof of those men's morality manifests through surnames loaded, by the force of inheritance, with a medieval "honor" the peninsular ancestors brought to the mining town around 1632. Now, they are the guardians of a selective medieval memory that ignores men and women who live in silence in the municipal and parochial archives.

However, this cultural history book exhibited how in San Joseph del Parral, all segments of the population—from the absent King of Spain to the dispossessed (people of African descent, Indigenous, mixed, and women)—participated in the Catholic ritual from 1632 to the end of the 1800s, using negotiation tools that led them to craft something new: a local culture and identity out of a universal one. Geography, natural resources, migratory Indigenous groups, and the European arrival counted for creating a highly diverse, unstable, violent, patriarchal, racialized, hierarchical, and ambiguous society. Throughout this time in La Nueva Vizcaya converged pre-Hispanic, medieval, modern, humanistic, Renaissance, and Enlightenment ideologies that Spanish Baroque thought, highly theatrical and immersed in Catholic ritual, brought together, proving to be a cohesive element to produce a functioning culture in the mining town.

The compilation of this cultural history research with scarce documentation and with the main contributors living (or dying) in the obscurantism of the archives was a task that required various methodological and theoretical devices this book borrowed from some post-structuralists and sociocultural theorists. That was how we comprehend the multiple meanings of words in Alcalde Fernández de Carrión's 1649 discourse and how convenient it was for him to create a "vicious but necessary" opposite group to consolidate his hegemony. The scarcity of information about La Cofradía de Nuestra Señora de La Candelaria de Los Naturales and the Indigenous Mexicanos allowed us to appreciate how a cultural memory in the form of a legend claims both a local and "Spanish-Medieval" history with the miracle of La Virgen del Rayo.

This book also reveals how, in contrast to historian Nicole von Germeten's assertion, La Cofradía de La Inmaculada Concepción de Los Pardos proved successful rather than otherwise, not only during the end of the seventeenth century but throughout the eighteenth century, during the Bourbon reforms. While negotiating their involvement in Catholic rituals, the Pardos' discourse proved to have a baroque touch, as they could represent themselves in the social scenario even as better Christians than the Spanish using an acculturated discourse. However, perhaps the most valuable element the Pardos revealed was the possibility of African culture transference and the creation or recreation of a diasporic frontier identity as far as Northern New Spain.

Lastly, capellanías exhibited the true meaning of the Catholic Baroque mentality: to live a good life to die even better. We can appreciate most people in New Spain valued death perhaps more than life, so they were willing to borrow money to fund capellanías. The Catholic Church created a complex apparatus that revealed its "spiritual economy" idea about monetary transactions and merchandise constituting spiritual goods without any connotation of the profane. This baroque institution welcomed women's immersion with open arms in economic-spiritual transactions, perhaps because women desired and knew how to manage their families' economic futures and negotiate their wills using a highly baroque discourse.

Overall, this book's best friend was historical imagination. Inspired by Saidiya Hartman's cultural history and critical fabulation, historical narratives evinced through pliegos sueltos were one part of the methodological tools employed to give voice to people who lived in silence in the archives. Although yet more individuals are "detained in the archives' purgatory," this book's pliegos sueltos act as scenarios for all those without surnames who were waiting there to be liberated and be part of the history they also created. As John Thornton proposes, from an anthropological view, culture is a total lifeway for society, including, among other things, kinship, language and literature, art, music, dance, and religion, elements that are not equally fixed and are, as Don Quijote de la Mancha used to say, "como la guerra, sujetas a continua mudanza" (as in war, subject to continuous change).[2] Then, this book closes with a last question: When, in its constant cultural transformation, would Northern Mexico's cultural memory be a more inclusive one?

NOTES

Introduction

1. Pliegos sueltos were popular theatrical narratives in Spain during the sixteenth and seventeenth centuries. Derived from scholar Saidiya Hartman's historical speculation approach and adapted from primary and secondary sources, this book uses pliego suelto as a research method and will be elaborated on in the methodology and theory section in this introduction.

2. The ethnic category of "Indian" is a construction used to identify the Latin American Native groups. It was and still is a derogatory term that has been replaced in contemporary times by "Indígenas" (Indigenous). Although this book prefers to use "Indigenous," it also utilizes "Indian" and "Naturales" when contextualizing or reconstructing events contained in the archival material. This book will shorten the two brotherhoods' official names as follows: La Cofradía de Los Pardos and La Cofradía de Los Naturales. This book will use "Pardo brothers" and "Naturales brothers" for members of the two confraternities it analyzes. When "Pardo" and "Naturales" words are capitalized, those refer to members of the two religious congregations. It will also contextualize racial categorizations for people of African descent: "negro/a," for example, literally means "black," but in a town with individuals identified as "mulatos," "criollos," or "pardos," the term "negro/a" was meant to indicate "born in Africa."

3. Lisa Voigt, *Spectacular Wealth: The Festivals of Colonial South American Mining Towns* (Austin: University of Texas Press, 2016), 14, ProQuest Ebook Central, accessed March 5, 2023.

4. Hereafter, Provincia de Santa Bárbara will be designated "provincia" to avoid its being confused with the mining and agricultural town Santa Bárbara.

5. Cheryl E. Martin, *Governance and Society in Colonial Mexico: Chihuahua in the Eighteenth Century* (Stanford: Stanford

University Press, 1996), 118.

6.   Chantal Cramaussel, *Poblar la frontera: la provincia de Santa Bárbara en Nueva Vizcaya durante los siglos XVI y XVII* (Zamora: Colegio de Michoacán, 2006).

7.   Robert C. West, *La comunidad minera en el norte de la Nueva España: El distrito minero de Parral*, trans. Ricardo Cabrera Figueroa (Chihuahua: Talleres Gráficos del Gobierno del Estado, 2002).

8.   Susan M. Deeds, *Defiance and Deference in Mexico's Colonial North: Indians Under Spanish Rule in Nueva Vizcaya* (Austin: University of Texas Press, 2003). Encomienda and repartimiento were labor systems the Spanish crown developed in the New World toward the right to use Indigenous people as a workforce. The two systems will be addressed in chapter 1.

9.   Juan Pedro Viqueira Albán, ¿Relajados o Reprimidos?: Diversiones públicas y vida social en la Ciudad de México durante el Siglo de las Luces (México, D.F: Fondo de Cultura Económica, 1987); Linda Ann Curcio-Nagy, *The Great Festivals of Colonial Mexico City: Performing Power and Identity* (Albuquerque: University of New Mexico Press, 2004); Carolyn Dean, *Inka Bodies and the Body of Christ: Corpus Christi in Colonial Cuzco, Peru* (Durham, NC: Duke University Press, 1999); Voigt, *Spectacular Wealth*.

10.   Viqueira Albán, ¿Relajados o Reprimidos?, 282.

11.   "Viceroyalty" refers to kingdoms (conformed with provinces/governances). The Hapsburg Crown did not mention "colonies" but rather viceroyalties. By that time, there were seven viceroyalties in Europe: Aragón, Cataluña, Valencia, Navarra, Cerdeña, Silicia, and Nápoles. The term "colonia" appeared in 1748, with the foundation of "Colonia del Nuevo Santander." Alfredo Jiménez Nuñez, *El Gran Norte de México: una frontera imperial en la Nueva España (1540–1820)* (Tebar: Madrid, 2006), 41–42, 47, 304.

12.   Anne J. Cruz and Mary Elizabeth Perry, "Introduction: Culture and Control in Counter-Reformation Spain," in *Culture and Control in Counter-Reformation Spain*, ed. Anne J. Cruz and Mary Elizabeth Perry (Minneapolis: University of Minnesota Press, 1992), ix–xxiv.

13. Curcio-Nagy, *The Great Festivals*, 11.
14. Gisela Von Wobeser, *Vida eterna y preocupaciones terrenales: las capellanías de misas en La Nueva España, 1660–1821* (México, D.F: Universidad Autónoma de México, 2005), 8.
15. Hereafter, I will use Spanish Baroque or simply "baroque."
16. José Antonio Marvall, *Culture of the Baroque: Analysis of a Historical Structure*, trans. Terry Cochran (Minneapolis: University of Minnesota Press, 1986), 2–8.
17. Antonio Rivera García, "Espíritu y poder en el barroco español," in *Barroco*, ed. Pedro Aullón de Haro (Madrid: Verbum Editorial, 2004), 567–96, 569–70.
18. Mateo Casini, "Some Thoughts on the Social and Political Culture of Baroque Venice," in *Braudel Revisited: The Mediterranean World, 1600–1800*, eds. Gabriel Piterberg, Teófilo F. Ruiz, and Geoffry Symcox (Toronto: University of Toronto Press, 2010), 179.
19. Antonio Rubial García, *El paraíso de los elegidos: una lectura de la historia cultural de Nueva España (1521–1804)* (México, D.F.: Fondo de Cultura Económica, Universidad Nacional Autónoma de México, Facultad de Filosofía y Letras, 2010), 37.
20. Mario Martínez Sánchez-Barba, *La época dorada de América: pensamiento, política, mentalidades* (Madrid: Biblioteca Nueva, 2008), 39–44.
21. Pamela Voekel, *Alone Before God: The Religious Origins of Modernity in Mexico* (Durham, NC: Duke University Press, 2002), 4.
22. Kristiaan Aercke, *Gods of Play: Baroque Festive Performances as Rhetorical Discourse* (New York: New York State University Press, 1994), 58–59, 77.
23. Martínez Sánchez-Barba, *La época dorada de América*, 39–44.
24. Eva Botella-Ordinas, "'Exempt from Time and from Its Fatal Change': Spanish Imperial Ideology, 1450–1700," *Renaissance Studies* 26, no. 4 (2012): 580–604; Paul E. Hoffman, "Diplomacy and the Papal Donation 1493–1585," *The Americas* 30, no. 2 (1973): 151–83, accessed July 5, 2021, doi:10.2307/980555.
25. Henry Kamen, *Brevísima historia de España* (México, D.F.: Grupo Planeta, 2014), 550.

26. Michael Mullett, *The Catholic Reformation* (London: Taylor & Francis Group, 1999), 205, accessed March 2, 2023, ProQuest Ebook Central.

27. Rubial García, *El paraíso de los elegidos*, 180, 192.

28. Voekel, *Alone Before God*, 2–8.

29. Ralph Baver and José Antonio Mazzotti, eds., *Creole Subjects in Colonial America: Empires, Texts, Identities* (Chapel Hill: University of North Carolina Press, 2009), 40.

30. Voekel, *Alone Before God*, 125. Spanish Baroque manifestation in New Spain will be covered later.

31. This book uses "ritual" in the singular as a category of analysis. In the plural, "rituals" refer to various religious events.

32. J. P. Hoffman, "Introduction: Improving Our Understanding of Religious Ritual," in *Understanding Religious Ritual: Theoretical Approaches and Innovations*, ed. J. P. Hoffman (New York: Routledge, 2012), 1–4. Hoffman offers an extensive list of ritual's functions, among which are teaches, socializes, generates beliefs, separates, creates boundaries, transforms social status, performs, and encourages and creates memories and narratives.

    Up to 1960, scholars studying the religious ritual's formality are Robertson Smith, Emilie Durkheim, Marcel Mauss, and Claude Lévi-Strauss, among others. After that date, ritual specialists include Mary Douglas, Victor Turner, and Robert Wuthnow. More recent experts on the history of religion and religious studies are Jonathan Z. Smith and Catherine Bell, followed by Timothy Nelson, Douglas A. Marshall, and Géraldine Mossière, among others.

33. Michael B. Aune and Valerie M. Demarinis, "Introduction," in *Religious and Social Ritual: Interdisciplinary Explorations*, eds. Michael B. Aune and Valerie M. Demarinis (New York: State University of New York, 1996), 3; Hoffman, "Introduction," 3.

    Some scholars have proposed the creating of memories and identities through religious rituals since the early twentieth century: E. Durkheim, *The Elementary Forms of Religious Life*, trans. K. E. Fields (New York: Free Press, 1912); V. Turner, *The Ritual Process: Structure and Antistructure* (Chicago: Aldine, 1969); C. Bell, *Ritual Theory, Ritual Practice* (New York: Oxford University Press, 1992); P. Collins, "Thirteen Ways of Looking

at a 'Ritual,'" *Journal of Contemporary Religion* 20, no. 3 (2005);
R. A. Rappaport, *Ritual and Religion in Making a Humanity*
(Cambridge: Cambridge University Press, 1999); Robert M.
McCauley and E. Thomas Lawson, *Bringing Ritual to Mind*
(New York: Cambridge University Press, 2002); Adam Sutcliffe,
Anna Maerker, and Simon Sleight, "Introduction: Memory,
Public Life and the Work of the Historian," in *History, Memory,
and Public Life: The Past in the Present*, eds. Adam Sutcliffe, Anna
Maerker, and Simon Sleight (New York: Routledge, 2018); John
Czapucka and Jan Assmann, "Collective Memory and Cultural
Identity," *New German Critique*, no. 65 (1995): 125–26.

34. Peter Burke, *What Is Cultural History?* (Cambridge: Polity Press,
2029); Anna Green, *Cultural History* (Basingstoke, UK: Palgrave
Macmillan), 2008.

35. The Archivo Municipal and the Archivo Parroquial exist as
microfilms in the University of Texas at El Paso (UTEP)
Library. The former has a guide, "Archivo Municipal del
Hidalgo del Parral, Chihuahua, México, 1631–1821," edited by
Robert McCaa, Carolyn Roy, and Rosa María Arroyo Duarte.
However, this archive is now called Archivo Histórico del
Municipio de Parral-Fondo Colonial (AHMP.FC). This book
used the two versions (AMHP-UTEP and AHMP.FC) to
examine documents related to Government and Administration,
Justice, Church, Treasury, and Notaries.

Some of the historians who have utilized one of the
two versions of the archive are Florence Barkin, *Black Slave
Trade in the Seventeenth Century Real of San Joseph del Parral
from 1631–1645* (Tempe: Arizona State University-Center for
Latin American Studies), 1977; Vincent Villanueva Mayer,
"The Black Slave on New Spain's Northern Frontier: San Jose
de Parral 1632–1676" (PhD diss., University of Utah, 1975);
West, *La comunidad minera*; Cramaussel, *Poblar la frontera*
and *La provincia de Santa Bárbara 1563–1631* (Chihuahua:
Secretaría de Educación y Cultura, 1990); and Deeds, *Defiance
and Deference*. Martin only mentions them in *Governance and
Society*. Last, Nicole von Germeten used the archives to inves-
tigate La Cofradía de la Inmaculada Concepción de los Pardos
in *Black Blood Brothers: Confraternities and Social Mobility for*

Afro-Mexicans (Gainesville: University Press of Florida, 2006).

36. I agree with historian Germeten: "Although the Archivo Municipal de Hidalgo del Parral's records are well indexed, numeric references to documents are erratic." Germeten, chap. 6, note 6.

37. Some historians and scholars that have proposed or applied "against the grain" in their research are Daniel K. Richter, *Facing East from Indian Country: A Native History of Early America* (Cambridge, MA: Harvard University Press, 2001); Camila Townsend, *Malintzin's Choices: An Indian Woman in the Conquest of Mexico* (Albuquerque: University of New Mexico Press, 2006); Nupur Chaudhuri, Sherry J. Katz, and Mary Elizabeth Perry, eds. *Contesting Archives: Finding Women in the Sources* (Urbana: University of Illinois Press, 2010).

38. To explore colonial semiosis further, see Walter Mignolo, "Afterword: From Colonial Discourse to Colonial Semiosis," *Dipositio* 14, nos. 36/38 (1989): 333–37.

39. Among the post-structuralist thinkers who address the poly-semic character of language are Jean-Francoise Lyotard, Roland Barthes, Jacques Derrida, Giles Deleuze, Felix Guttari, Michel Foucault, and Richard Rorty, as proposed by Patricia Seed, "Review: Colonial and Postcolonial Discourse," *Latin American Association* 26, no. 3 (1991), 181–200.

40. Mikhail Bakhtin, *Rabelais and His World* (Bloomington: Indiana University Press, 2009); Benjamin Bailey, "Heteroglossia and Boundaries: Processes of Linguistic and Social Distinction," in *Bilingualism: A Social Approach*, ed. Monica Heller (UK: Palgrave Macmillan, 2007); Juan Villegas, *Historia multicultural del teatro y las teatralidades en América Latina* (Buenos Aires: Galerna, 2005).

41. Dean, *Inka Bodies*, 2–3.

42. Cheryl S. McWatters, "Speculation, History, Speculative History," *Accounting History Review* 26, no. 1 (February 2016): 1–4.

43. Paul E. Bolin, "Imagination and Speculation as Historical Impulse: Engaging Uncertainties within Art Education History and Historiography," *Studies in Art Education* 50, no. 2 (2009): 110–23, 110–11, 120, http://www.jstor.org/stable/25475894.

Other works on historical speculation/imagination are J. L. Gaddis, *The Landscape of History: How Historians Map the Past* (New York: Oxford University Press, 2002); J. H. Plumb, *The Death of the Past* (Boston: Houghton Mifflin Company, 1971); J. Richardson, "What If? Alternative Histories and Their Future Implications," *Foresight* 9 (2): 36–45; T. Walch and M. Harding, "American Mysteries, Riddles, and Controversies!" *Prologue* 39, no. 2 (Summer 2007): 6–10; Richter, *Facing East from Indian Country*; Townsend, *Malintzin's Choices*; David J. Staley, *Historical Imagination* (New York: Routledge, 2020).

44. Saidiya Hartman's main areas of study in cultural history are the Atlantic slave trade and the discipline of history. The scholar addresses the fábula (fable) as a narrative of events/transitions from one state to another caused and experienced by actors/agents that perform actions. Critical fabulation method allows the scholar "to jeopardize the status of events, to displace the received or authorized account, and to imagine what might have happened, might been said, or might have been done." That is how Hartman exploits "the transparency of sources" as fiction of history. Saidiya Hartman, "Venus in Two Acts," *Small Axe* 12, no. 2 (2008): 1–14, 11–12, muse.jhu.edu/article/241115. The development of Hartman's critical fabulation method can be appreciated in her three books: *Scenes of Subjection: Terror, Slavery, and Self-Making in Nineteenth Century America* (New York: Oxford University Press), 1997; *Lose Your Mother: A Journey Along the Atlantic Slave Route* (New York, Farrar, Straus & Giroux, 2008); and *Wayward Lives, Beautiful Experiments: Intimate Histories of Social Upheaval* (New York: W. W. Norton & Company, 2019).

45. Pliego suelto is addressed in John Beverley, "Going Baroque?" *Boundary* 2, nos. 15/16 (1988): 27–39, 30, https://doi.org/10.2307/303244.

46. Marvall, *Culture of the Baroque*, 6–10.

47. When I create the pliego suelto using specific primary or secondary sources, I cite the sources.

48. Villegas, *Historia multicultural del teatro*, 18.

49. Kathryn Burns, *Colonial Habits: Convents and the Spiritual Economy of Cuzco, Peru* (Durham, NC: Duke University

Press, 1999).

50. The word "bárbaro" is of Nahuatl origin and was used to distinguish the barbarian people from the Toltecs. In New Spain, the nomads on the other side of the northern border were called "Chichimecas," and the area "La Gran Chichimeca" was called "Mundo Bárbaro." Jiménez Nuñez, *El Gran Norte de México*, 71.

51. West, *La comunidad minera*; D. A. Brading, *Mineros y comerciantes en el México borbónico (1763–1810)* (México, D.F.: Fondo de Cultura Económica, 1971); P. J. Bakewell, *Minería y sociedad en México colonial: Zacatecas 1546–1700* (México, D.F.: Fondo de Cultura Económica, 1976); Oscar Alatriste, *Desarrollo de la industria y la comunidad minera de Hidalgo del Parral durante la segunda mitad del siglo XVIII (1765–1810)* (México, D.F.: Universidad Nacional Autónoma de México, 1983); Deeds, *Defiance and Deference*; Cramaussel, *La provincia de Santa Bárbara* and *Poblar la frontera*; Martin, *Governance and Society*.

52. Ignacio Martínez, *The Intimate Frontier: Friendship and Civil Society in Northern New Spain* (Tucson: University of Arizona Press, 2019).

53. George Wolfskill and Stanley Palmer, eds., *Essays on Frontiers in World History* (College Station: Texas A&M University Press, 1983); Donna Guy and Tom Sheridan, eds., *Contested Ground: Comparative Frontiers on the Northern and Southern Edges of the Spanish Empire* (Tucson: Arizona University Press, 1998); Paul Redman, Cynthia Radding, and Chad Bryant, eds., *Borderlands in World History, 1700–1914* (London: Palgrave Macmillan, 2014).

54. Ana María Alonso, *Thread of Blood: Colonialism, Revolution, and Gender on Mexico's Northern Frontier* (Tucson: University of Arizona Press, 1995); James Brooks, *Captive and Cousins: Slavery, Kinship, and Community in the Southwest Borderlands* (Chapel Hill: University of North Carolina Press, 2002); Pekka Hämäläinen, *The Comanche Empire* (New Haven, CT: Yale University Press, 2008).

55. James Sweet, *Recreating Africa: Culture, Kinship, and Religion in the African-Portuguese World, 1441–1770* (Chapel Hill: University of North Carolina Press, 2003); John K. Thornton, "Central Africa in the Era of the Slave Trade," in *Slaves, Subjects, and*

Subversives: Blacks in Colonial Latin America, eds. Jane G. Landers and Barry M. Robinson (Albuquerque: University of New Mexico Press, 2006), 83–110; Walter Hawthorne, *From Africa to Brazil: Culture, Identity, and an Atlantic Slave Trade, 1600–1830* (New York: Cambridge University Press, 2020); and Frank T. Proctor III, *Damned Notions of Liberty: Slavery, Culture, and Power in Colonial Mexico, 1640–1749* (Albuquerque: University of New Mexico Press, 2010).

56.   Barkin, *Black Slave Trade*; Villanueva Mayer, "The Black Slave."
57.   Germeten, *Black Blood Brothers*.

Chapter 1

1.   In the archival documents, racial and job categories ("naborío," for example, refers to "agricultural worker") follow some people's names, e.g., Juan Francisco Indio naborío. All the primary source translations from Spanish to English are mine. AMHP-UTEP. 1632. 12. _7 ff. G-7. ff 1–7. Gregorio Francisco Indio Mexicano; AMHP-UTEP. 1634-B. 661. 631. _3 ff. D-102. ff 1–3.1665. Francisco Indio; AMHP-UTEP. 1665-A. 1997. 725. _10 ff. G-7. ff 1–5. Miguel Franco Indio; AMHP-UTEP. 1665-A. 1999. 785. _ 12 ff. G-22ª. ff 1–6. Juan Francisco Indio Naborío; AMHP-UTEP. 1673-B. 2413. 543. _15 ff. D-116. ff 1–4. Juan Diego Indio.
2.   Historian Chantal Cramaussel highlights the agricultural development in the Provincia de Santa Bárbara. Cramaussel, *Poblar la frontera*.
3.   Kamen, *Brevísima historia de España*, 81, 90.
4.   Rubial García, *El paraíso de los elegidos*, 20–21.
5.   Al-Andalus referred to Spanish territory during the Arab occupation from 711 to 1942. Juan Joseu Castanera, *Sobre la venida del apóstol Santiago a España: Discurso leído en la Universidad Central* (Madrid: Imprenta de Don Pedro Montero, 1857), 5, 7.
6.   Rubial García, *El paraíso de los elegidos*, 22–24.
7.   José Manuel Nieto Sotia, *La época medieval: iglesia y cultura* (Madrid: AKAL, 2002), 210.
8.   Kamen, *Brevísima Historia de España*, 555.
9.   Ibid., 617, 713–15.
10.   Sara Gottardi, "Visigothic Division and Muslim Preservers of Order," *Hispanófila*, no. 178 (2016): 230. https://www.jstor.org/

stable/90012376.

11. Kamen, *Brevísima Historia de España*, 617, 713–15.

12. Rubial García, *El paraíso de los elegidos*, 22–24, 169.

13. Matthew Carr, *Blood and Faith: The Purging of Muslim Spain* (New York: The New Press, 2009), 386.

14. Charles G. Nauert Jr., *Culture of Renaissance Europe: New Approaches to European History* (Cambridge: University of Cambridge Press, 1995), 96.

15. James Amelang, "The Myth: Perceptions of Sociability," in *Mediterranean Urban Culture 1400–1700*, ed. Alexander Cowan (Exeter: University of Exeter Press, 2000), 15–16.

16. Ibid., 17–18.

17. Benjamín Arbel, "The Port Towns of the Levant in Sixteenth-Century Travel Literature," in *Mediterranean Urban Culture 1400–1700*, ed. Alexander Cowan (Exeter: University of Exeter Press, 2000), 151–64, 152–53.

18. José Sánchez, *Hispanic Heroes of Discovery and Conquest of Spanish America in European Drama* (Barcelona: Editorial Castalia, 1978), 21.

19. Nauert Jr., *Culture of Renaissance Europe*, 122, 171, 189.

20. Javier García Gibert, *La <<humanitas>> Hispana: sobre el humanismo literario en los siglos de oro* (Salamanca: Ediciones Universidad de Salamanca, 2010), 24–27.

21. Ibid., 28–29.

22. Martínez Sánchez-Barba, *La época dorada de América*, 29–33.

23. Nauert Jr., *Culture of Renaissance Europe*, 178.

24. García Gibert, *La <<humanitas>>*, 24.

25. Maureen Ihrie and Salvador Oropeza, eds., *World Literature in Spanish: An Encyclopedia* (Santa Bárbara: ABC-CLIO, 2011), 68.

26. David J. Weber, *La frontera española en América del norte* (México, D.F.: Fondo de Cultura Económica, 2000), 43.

27. Pedro Bossio, "Exploring the Roots of Chronic Underdevelopment: The Colonial *Encomienda* and *Resguardo* and Their Legacy to Modern Colombia," (thesis, City University of New York, 2018), 5–6.

28. David Piñera Ramírez y Catalina Velázquez Morales, "Consideraciones generales," in *Visión histórica de la frontera norte de México, Tomo II: de los aborígenes al septentrion novohispano*,

ed. David Piñera Ramírez (Universidad Autónoma de Baja California-Centro de Investigaciones Históricas: Editorial Kino/El Mexicano, 1994), 255–59.

29. Piñera Ramírez y Velázquez Morales, "Consideraciones generales," 255.

30. Jiménez Núñez, *El Gran Norte de México*, 84, 109, 255.

31. Carroll L. Riley and Howard D. Winters, "The Prehistoric Tepehuan of Northern Mexico," *Southwestern Journal of Anthropology* 19, no. 2 (1963): 177–85, 80–82.

32. Cramaussel, *Poblar la frontera*, 72.

33. Jiménez Núñez, *El Gran Norte de México*, 84, 109, 255.

34. Santa Bárbara was not its political/formal name until later when it was part of the kingdom of La Nueva Vizcaya.

35. William B. Griffen, *Indian Assimilation in the Franciscan Area of Nueva Vizcaya* (Tucson: University of Arizona Press, 1979), open-access edition by University of Arizona Press, 2022, "Introduction."

36. Jiménez Núñez, *El Gran Norte de México*, 75–76, 84, 255.

37. West, *La comunidad minera*, 36.

38. Jiménez Núñez, *El Gran Norte de México*, 75–76, 109–10.

39. Ibid., 75–76, 109–10.

40. Bakewell, *Minería y sociedad en México colonial*, 176.

41. Brading, *Mineros y comerciantes en el México borbónico*, 139.

42. Ibid., 106–7.

43. Elías Amador, *Bosquejo histórico de Zacatecas, Volumen I* (Zacatecas: Escuela de Artes y Oficios en Guadalupe, 1892), 370, 422, 521.

44. Amador, *Bosquejo histórico de Zacatecas*, 297.

45. Bakewell, *Minería y Sociedad en México colonial*, 22–41.

46. Riley and Winters, "The Prehistoric Tepehuan of Northern Mexico," 80–82, 85, 177, 180–82, 185.

47. Cramaussel, *Poblar la frontera*, 37–38. The most straightforward meaning of the term "vecino" is neighbor, a person who lives in a particular neighborhood, but back then, the term had other connotations on which I will elaborate later.

48. There are no archival records of the early contact between the Spaniards and the Indigenous population in the Provincia de Santa Bárbara. Griffen, *Indian Assimilation*, "Introduction."

49. Tamar Herzog, *Defining Nations: Immigrants and Citizens in Early Modern Spain and Spanish America* (New Haven, CT: Yale University Press, 2003), 6.
50. Griffen, *Indian Assimilation*, "Introduction."
51. West, *La comunidad minera*, 18.
52. Debra Blumenthal, *Enemies and Familiars: Slavery and Mastery in Fifteenth Century Valencia* (Ithaca, NY: Cornell University Press, 2009), 14–16. Among those offenses were adultery and robbery.
53. Brígida Von Mentz, "Esclavitud y semi esclavitud en el México antiguo y en la Nueva España (con énfasis en el siglo XVI)," *Studia Historica: Historia Antigua* [En línea] 25 (2007), 553, http://revistas.usal.es/index.php/0213-2052/article/view/1203.
54. Ibid.
55. Cramaussel, *Poblar la frontera*, 186–87, 226–27.
56. Von Mentz, "Esclavitud y semiesclavitud," 553.
57. Cramaussel, *Poblar la frontera*, 187.
58. Ibid., 96.
59. Chantal Cramaussel, "Encomiendas, repartimientos y conquista de Nueva Vizcaya," *Historias, INAH*, no. 25 (1991): 73–91, 75. "Hacienda" could refer to a smelter estate or agricultural farm.
60. West, *La comunidad minera*, 47.
61. Mats Lundahl, "Spain and the Conquest of America: Profits, Religion, and Forced Labour in the Fifteenth and Sixteenth Centuries," in *Trade, Growth, and Development: The Role of Politics and Institutions*, ed. Göte Hansson (New York: Routledge, 1993), 54.
62. Cramaussel, "Encomiendas, repartimientos y conquista," 73.
63. Cramaussel, *La provincia de Santa Bárbara*, 12–13.
64. Cramaussel, *Poblar la frontera*, 47, 236.
65. Ibid., 47, 236. Another use of the term "naborío" is "hacienda worker," and an Indigenous person working as such was called "Indio naborío," like the Indigenous Mexicanos and Otomíes who occupied the current states of Mexico and Hidalgo. The word means "laborer," and it referred to people who earned a "wage" and served for certain months on the haciendas. Yolanda Lastra de Suárez, *Los otomíes: su lengua y su historia* (México, D.F.: Universidad Autónoma de México, 2006), 148.

66. Cramaussel, *Poblar la frontera*, 234.

67. West, *La comunidad minera*, 136.

68. Cramaussel, *Poblar la frontera*, 234.

69. Cramaussel, *La provincia de Santa Bárbara*, 12–13.

70. Jiménez Núñez, *El Gran Norte de México*, 124, 125.

71. Zacarías Márquez Terrazas y Libertad Villarreal, *Pueblos mineros de Chihuahua* (Chihuahua: Gobierno del Estado, 1995), 20–21, 27.

72. Jiménez Núñez, *El Gran Norte de México*, 124, 125.

73. At the Jesucristo Northern mission field, Franciscans established Parras Mission in 1598, Tepehuanes Mission in 1608, San Pablo Balleza Mission in 1611, and La Alta Tarahumara Mission in 1680. Griffen, *Indian Assimilation*, "Introduction."

74. West, *La comunidad minera*, 136.

75. Griffen, *Indian Assimilation*, "Introduction."

76. AMHP-UTEP. 1632. 6. 209. _7 ff. D-103. ff 1–7. AMHP-UTEP. 1632. 11. 370. _1+ ff. G-3. ff 1–5.

77. Cramaussel, *Poblar la frontera*, 236.

78. AMHP-UTEP. 1632. 12. _7 ff. G-7. ff 1–7. Gregorio Francisco Indio Mexicano; AMHP-UTEP. 1634-B. 661. 631. _3 ff. D-102. ff 1–3.1665. Francisco Indio; AMHP-UTEP. 1665-A. 1997. 725. _10 ff. G-7. ff 1–5. Miguel Franco Indio; AMHP-UTEP. 1665-A. 1999. 785. _12 ff. G-22ª. ff 1–6. Juan Francisco Indio Naborío; AMHP-UTEP. 1673-B. 2413. 543. _15 ff. D-116. ff 1–4. Juan Diego Indio.

79. AMHP-UTEP. 1633-C. 106. 1597. _11 ff. G-49. ff 1–3.

80. Cramaussel, *Poblar la frontera*, 236.

81. Griffen, *Indian Assimilation*, "Introduction."

82. Ibid.

83. Márquez Terrazas and Villarreal, *Pueblos mineros de Chihuahua*, 20–21, 27.

84. Cramaussel, *La provincia de Santa Bárbara*, 96.

85. Ibid., 49, 57, 59, 138–40. Since 1570, some enslaved people worked in the Provincia de Santa Bárbara, most of whom were from the same zone. Likewise, captive Indigenous people from the lower Río Conchos arrived, proof of the slave market that was carried out in the area. Cramaussel, *Poblar la frontera*, 188. By 1581, the Provincia de Santa Bárbara came to be classified

as a place of "slave market." Cramaussel, *La provincia de Santa Bárbara*, 57, 59.

86. Ibid., 49, 57, 59, 118–19, 138–40.
87. Cramaussel, *Poblar la frontera*, 59.
88. Cramaussel, *La provincia de Santa Bárbara*, 83.
89. Ibid., 139.
90. Ibid., 49, 57, 59, 96, 138–40.
91. West, *La comunidad minera*, 18.
92. Cramaussel, *Poblar la frontera*, 148–49, 155.

Chapter 2

1. AMHP-UTEP. 1642-A. 580. 471. _19 ff. 1638–1642. G-56. ff 1–19, Beatriz Negra Criolla; AMHP-UTEP.1640-B. 440. 1109. _ 33 ff. G-. ff 1–13, Diego Esclavo Criollo; AMHP-UTEP.1642-B. 607. 1152. _ 6 ff. G-66. ff 1–6, Domingo Esclavo Criollo and Pedro Esclavo; AMHP-UTEP. 1644-B. 737. 778. _ 5 ff. G-16. ff 1–5, Ángela Esclava de la Nación Angola; AMHP-UTEP.1658-B. 1666. 722. _ 16 ff. G-23. ff 1–16, María de Tierra Angola and her three children. AHMP.FC. F03.001.001. ff 1–12 provides information about the music played in the town during religious celebrations. Information about the jobs of people of African descent is from Robert McCaa, "Calidad, Clase, and Marriage in Colonial Mexico: The Case of Parral 1788–1790," *The Hispanic American Historical Review* 64, no. 3 (1984), 477–78. Information about the architecture of San Joseph del Parral is from Cramaussel, *Poblar la frontera*, 110, 124. Information about Corpus Christi celebrations in Mexico City is from Curcio-Nagy, *The Great Festivals*, 28. Information about demons in parades is from Voekel, *Alone Before God*, 4.

2. Colin A. Palmer, *Slaves of the White God: Blacks in Mexico, 1570–1650* (Cambridge, MA: Harvard University Press, 1976), 6–7.

3. John Thornton, *Africa and Africans in the Making of the Atlantic World, 1400–1800* (Cambridge: Cambridge University Press, 1998), 43.

4. Sweet, *Recreating Africa*, 191.

5. Palmer, *Slaves of the White God*, 6–7.

6. Nehemia Levtzion and Randall L. Pouwels, eds., *The History of Islam in Africa* (Athens: Ohio University Press, 2000), 2–3.

7. Thornton, *Africa and Africans*, 13, 23, 28–29, 35.
8. Lynne Guitar, "Boiling It Down: Slavery on the First Commercial Sugarcane Ingenios in the Americas (Hispaniola, 1530–45)," in *Blacks in Colonial Latin America*, Jane G. Landers and Marry M. Robinson, eds. (Albuquerque: University of New Mexico Press, 2006), 39–41.
9. Ibid., 39–82, 41–43, 49–53.
10. Ibid., 42.
11. Palmer, *Slaves of the White God*, 7.
12. Guitar, "Boiling It Down," 57–59.
13. Matthew Restall, "Black Conquistadors: Armed Africans in Early Spanish America," *The Americas* 57, no. 2 (2000): 171–205, http://www.jstor.org/stable/1008202. In Spanish and Portuguese America, enslaved Africans accompanied the earliest settlers as military allies, more often in colonies with hostile Native American groups. Thornton, *Africa and Africans*, 149.
14. Cramaussel, *Poblar la frontera*, 201.
15. Palmer, *Slaves of the White God*, 22, 31.
16. Herman L. Bennett, *Africans in Colonial Mexico: Absolutism, Christianity, and Afro-Creole Consciousness, 1570–1640* (Bloomington: Indiana University Press, 2003), 21, 23–27.
17. Palmer, *Slaves of the White God*, 20.
18. Bennett, *Africans in Colonial Mexico*, 21, 23–27.
19. Palmer, *Slaves of the White God*, 20.
20. Frank Proctor III, "African Diasporic Ethnicity in Mexico City to 1650," in *Africans to Spanish America: Expanding the Diaspora*, eds. Sherwin K. Bryan, Rachel Sarah O'Toole, and Ben Vinson III (Urbana: University of Illinois Press: 2012), 51.
21. Bennett, *Africans in Colonial Mexico*, 23–28.
22. Palmer, *Slaves of the White God*, 78–79.
23. Ibid., 80.
24. Villanueva Mayer, "The Black Slave," 12.
25. Palmer, *Slaves of the White God*, 80.
26. Cramaussel, *Poblar la frontera*, 202.
27. Proctor, "African Diasporic Ethnicity," 51. This fact invites the question as to whether the continuation of the practice was an exception for Northern New Spain due to the lack of labor force, as happened with the enslavement of Indigenous peoples in the

Provincia de Santa Bárbara.
28. Cramaussel, *Poblar la frontera*, 203.
29. Ibid., 202.
30. Villanueva Mayer, "The Black Slave," 24–26.
31. Cramaussel, *Poblar la frontera*, 147.
32. AMHP-UTEP. 1642-A. 580. 471. _19ff. 1638-1642 G-56.
33. AMHP-UTEP. 1640-B. 440. 1109._ 33ff. G-2.
34. AMHP-UTEP. 1658-B. 1666.722. _ 16ff. G23.

Chapter 3
1. West, *La comunidad minera*, 15–16, 42.
2. Cramaussel, *Poblar la frontera*, 108–12, 135, 145.
3. Ibid., 145. Besides the lack of accuracy in population numbers, the parish records are incomplete or nonexistent. There is no list of tributaries, as the taxation of the Indians in Nueva Vizcaya was not regulated. During the first half of the seventeenth century, most Natives were still considered gentiles, so there is no trace of them in the parish archives since the Catholic Church did not administer the sacraments to them. With this panorama, tracing their genealogy has been impossible because most did not have surnames in the archival documents. Ibid., 108–12.
4. Cramaussel, *Poblar la frontera*, 108–12, 135, 145.
5. Ibid., 35–36.
6. Martin, *Governance and Society*, 149, 151.
7. Cramaussel, *Poblar la frontera*, 35–36.
8. María Elena Martínez, *Genealogical Fictions: Limpieza de Sangre, Religion, and Gender in Colonial Mexico* (Stanford: Stanford University Press, 2008), 142, 166.
9. Pilar Gonzalbo Aizpuru, "La trampa de las castas," in Solange Alberro and Pilar Gonzalbo Aizpuru, eds., *La sociedad novo-hispana: Estereotipos y realidades* (México, D.F.: El Colegio de México, 2013).
10. McCaa, "Calidad, Clase, and Marriage," 477–78.
11. Martin, *Governance and Society*, 6, 156.
12. Cramaussel, *Poblar la frontera*, 253–57.
13. Ibid., 247, 249.
14. Villanueva Mayer, "The Black Slave," 12.
15. Cramaussel, *Poblar la frontera*, 247, 249.
16. AMHP-UTEP. 1670-B. 2280. 760. 3 ff. G-2. ff 1–3.

17. AMHP-UTEP. 1633-C. 111. 1639. 8 ff. G-42. ff 1–8.
18. AMHP-UTEP.1676-D. 2605. 2379. 29 ff. G-56. ff 1–12.
    AMHP and APSJP contain essential data about raptos (kidnapping) and rape of women, usually mulatas, Indigenous, mestizas, and more mixed women that Spanish, mulato, Indigenous, mestizo, and more mixed men perpetrated.
19. AMHP-UTEP.1641-C. 536. 1936. 14 ff. G-48. ff 1–14.
20. AMHP-UTEP. 1661-C. 1820. 1960. 58 ff. G-4. ff 1–6.
    AMHP-UTEP. 1667-B. 2124. 1318. 9 ff. G-69. ff 1–9.
21. AMHP-UTEP. 1649-D. 1045. 2213. 10 ff. G-89. ff 1–10.
    AMHP and APSJP contain substantial records of cases of adultery.
22. AMHP-UTEP.1642-B. 622. 1337. 10 ff. G-8. ff 1–10.
23. AMHP-UTEP.1654-C. 1424. 1490. 30 ff. G-44ᵃ. ff 1–5.
24. Cramaussel, *Poblar la frontera*, 258–59, 262.
25. AMHP-UTEP. C10. 6416.372._5ff. 1705-AMHP-UTEP. 1718-C. 3900.2467. _65ff. G-35.
26. AMHP-UTEP. 1652- A. 1238. _1 ff. Véase no. 7070 (I9.4). D-100. f 1: war provisions against Salinero Indians; AMHP-UTEP. 1652-B. 1258. 301. _129 ff. Véase no. 7067 (I9.1). G-75. ff 1–30: war provisions against Toboso Indians; AMHP-UTEP. 1653-C. 1366 .1880. _ 32 ff. D-104.ff 1–32: petitions about possible Babanes and Salinero rebellions; AMHP-UTEP. 1655-A. 1448. 231. _ 24ff. G5: war provisions against the Real Crown enemy Indians because of their frequent abuses; AMHP-UTEP. 1655-A. 1449. 330. _ ff. D-102: war provisions against rebel Indians; AMHP-UTEP. 1656-A. 1506. 40. _ 62 ff. G-3. ff 1–62: war provisions against Tarahumara Indians, enemies of the Royal Crown; AMHP-UTEP. 1657-A. 1593. 25. _ 7 ff. D-101. ff 1–7: war provisions against rebel Indians; AMHP-UTEP. 1658-A. 1648. 160. _ 36 ff. G-6. ff 1–36: war provisions against Indios alzados due to the war they waged against the Royal Crown in Rio Conchos, Santa Catalina, and San Juan del Río regions (Tobosos, Nonoxes, and Acoclames lands).
27. AMHP-UTEP.1667-A. 2056. 69. _ 8 ff. G-4. ff 1–8. This file contains information about motives San Joseph del Parral authorities had to make war "a sangre y fuego" (with blood

and fire) against Indios rebeldes (rebels) fighting against the Royal Crown.

AMHP-UTEP.1667-B. 2129. 1366. _6 ff. G-74. ff 1–6. This file deals with demands against enemy Tobosos, Salineros, and other Indian nations due to robbery, killings, and other violence throughout La Nueva Vizcaya.

28. AMHP-UTEP.1649-D. 1019. 1798. _ 5 ff. G-62. ff 1–5. Doña Isabel de Urdiñola. Pesos en reales: unit of silver currency eight-real Spanish peso (dollar).

29. AMHP-UTEP.1649-A. 966. 89. _ 4 ff. Véase no. 7061 (I7.20). G-10. ff 1–4. This file includes names of donors from the Indé town; AMHP-UTEP.1651-A. 1152. 5. _ 9 ff. Véase no. 7043 (I7.2). G-49. ff 1–9. This file informs about authorities asking neighbors for monetary donations to finance war against the enemy Indians.

30. AHMP.FC. A16.001.019.

31. AHMP.FC. A02.001.005.

32. AMHP-UTEP. 1649 D. 1041. 2145. _ 27 ff. G-85. f 3–5.

33. AMHP-UTEP.1653-A. 1329. 221._ 4 ff. G-43. ff 1–4.

34. AHMP.FC. D12.014.347.

35. AMHP-UTEP. 1655-A. 1440. 102. _ 3 ff. G-35.

36. AMHP-UTEP.1633-C. 100. 1509. _ 48 ff. G-60b. ff 1–22.

37. AMHP-UTEP. 1679. 2686. 24. _1+ ff. D-106. ff 1–2: Capitán Juan Leal asks for encomienda of Indios; AMHP-UTEP. 1699. 3292. 42. _6 ff. D-104. ff 1–6: Don José Neyra y Quiroga representing Diego Álvarez Salgado asking for fifteen Indios of Nación Concha to work in his hacienda; AMHP-UTEP. 1707. 3520. 4. _ 14 ff. G-. ff 1–14: Hacienda de los Molinos asks for Indians; AMHP-UTEP. 1720-A. _ 9 ff. D-147. ff 1–9. 3954. 576: Gobernador del Parral, Don Martin de Alday, inquires with Virrey Márquez de Balero about the repartimiento of Indios for Parral, Chihuahua, and Cusihuiriachi. It is important to note that even when in 1671, the Audiencia of Guadalajara abolished the repartimiento system in La Nueva Vizcaya through a royal certificate, the towns did not apply it since forced labor on farms and mines prevailed until the eighteenth century. West, *La comunidad minera*, 136–38.

38. AMHP-UTEP. 1725-C. 4321. 1843. _ 6 ff. D-125d. ff 1–6.

39. AMHP-UTEP.1710. 3639. 67. _3 ff. G-7. ff 1–3: Durango; AMHP-UTEP.1718-A. 3868. 152. _13 ff. G-4. ff 1–13: donations to make war against the Indian enemies of the crown; AMHP-UTEP.1725-C. 4309. 1705. _ver 1725C- D123n. 16 ff. D-123h. ff 1–16: San Juan del Río Papasquiaro e Indé; AMHP-UTEP.1755. 4832. 3. _5 ff. G-5. ff 1–5. _ 5 ff. G-5. ff 1–5: San Felipe el Real.

40. AMHP-UTEP.1704-A. 3435. 217. 18 ff. D-104; AMHP-UTEP.1708. 3565. 77. 8 ff. G-5; AMHP-UTEP.1727-A. 4348. 162. 45 ff. G-6.

41. AMHP-UTEP.1712. 3706. 530. 1+ ff. G-10.

42. AMHP-UTEP.1716-A. 3792. 4. 37 ff. D-101; AMHP-UTEP.1718-A. 3878. 573. 2 ff. G-12.

43. Cramaussel, *La provincia de Santa Bárbara*, 49.

44. AHMP.FC. A02.001.025.

45. AMHP-UTEP. 1633-B. 60. 960. _ 6 ff. G-67. ff 1–6: Andrés Gónzalez de Obregón against Gregorio Carbajal; AMHP-UTEP. 1640-B. 427. 919. _ 5 ff. G-35. ff 1–5: Martín de Carbajal against Francisco Lobato; AMHP-UTEP. 1640-B. 440. 1109. _ 33 ff. G-2. ff 1–11: Juan Martínez and María Rodríguez against Sebastián de Montenegro.

46. AMHP-UTEP. 1634. 143. 416. _ 4 ff. G-3. ff 1–4.

47. AMHP-UTEP. 1648. 953. 860. _12 ff. D-108. ff 1–12.

48. AHMP.FC. D34.006.152.

49. AMHP-UTEP. 1635. 188. 828. _ 3 ff. G-34. ff 1–3.

50. AMHP-UTEP. 1635. 193. 904. _10 ff. G-5. ff 1–10.

51. AHMP.FC. D48.002.042.

52. AHMP.FC. D48.002.048.

53. AMHP-UTEP. C 16.1769. 6511. 649. [Incomplete.] _1+ ff. R-202. ff 1–7.

54. AMHP-UTEP. 1771. 5054. 22. _ 3 ff. G-1d. ff 1–3.

55. AHMP.FC. D12.035.672.

56. AHMP.FC. D01.003.043.

57. AMHP-UTEP. 1641-C. 526. 1827. _ 7 ff. G-53. ff 1–7.

58. AMHP-UTEP. 1649-D. 1023. 1828. _ 42 ff. G-67. ff 1–15: Juan Echeverría looking for his servant, Antonio Esclavo.

59. AMHP-UTEP. 1654-B. 1415. 1345. _32 ff. G-35. ff 1–11: Juan de Los Reyes inherited Antonia Esclava and her four children;

AMHP-UTEP. 1657-A. 1623. 676. _ [see no. 1617]. 4 ff. G-10. ff 1–4: Doña Micaela de Heradillo inherited Nicolasa Esclava and her two children; AMHP-UTEP. 1660-B. 1731. 1168. _7 ff. G-35. ff 1–7: Juana Carrera inherited Nicolás Esclavo.

60. AMHP-UTEP.1743. 4770. 80. _6 ff. G-7. ff 1–6: Mengoreta Esclavo and Francisco Esclavo; AMHP-UTEP. 1642-B. 618 .1299. _3 ff. G-12. ff 1–3: Francisco Mulato.

61. Cramaussel, *Poblar la frontera*, 201.

62. Villanueva Mayer, "The Black Slave," 49.

63. Juana Patricia Pérez Munguía, "Derecho indiano para esclavos, negros y castas. Integración, control y estructura estamental," *Memoria y Sociedad* 7 (2003): 198, 200, 205.

64. West, *La comunidad minera*, 60n16.

65. AMHP-UTEP.1648. 952. 854. _ 5 ff. D-107. ff 1–5.

66. Martínez, *Genealogical Fictions*, 166.

67. Louis Moreri, *El gran diccionario histórico, o miscelánea curiosa de la historia sagrada y profana* (Paris: Hermanos de Tournes, 1753), 769–70.

68. Martin, *Governance and Society*, 37.

69. AHMP.FC. D47.004.042.

70. Cramaussel, *Poblar la frontera*, 202.

71. AMHP-UTEP. 1642-B. 618. 1299. _3ff. G12.

72. AMHP-UTEP. 1743. 4770. 80. _6ff. G-7.

73. AMHP-UTEP. 1717. 3854. _17ff. Véase no. 6463 (C13.568). Rescatado. G-40.

74. AMHP-UTEP. 1708. 3596. 743._ 4 ff. G-32. ff 1–4.

75. AMHP-UTEP. 1633-C. 115. 1710. _G-37. ff 1–3: A lawsuit against Juan de Santa Anna and Mulata Francisca for cohabitation; AMHP-UTEP. 1633-C. 121.1934. _5 ff. D-105. ff 1–5: A lawsuit against Ambrosio Sáez and Francisca de la Cruz, Mulata, for cohabitation; AMHP-UTEP. 1635. 191 873. _10 ff. G-2. ff 1–5: A lawsuit against Juan Núñez Matos and Ana de Castañeda, Mulata, for cohabitation; AMHP-UTEP. 1640-C. 450. 1405. _7 ff. G-18. ff 1–7: A lawsuit against Francisco Lovato, merchant married in Mexico City, and Juana, Mulata, for cohabitation; AMHP-UTEP. 1640-C. 448. 1380. _4 ff. G-20. ff 1–4: A lawsuit against Capitán Juan de Heredia and Beatriz Macías Mulata for more than fifteen years

of cohabitation; AMHP-UTEP. 1650. 1096. 6. _G-18. ff 1–6:
A lawsuit against Salvador Mulato and an Indigenous man
named Constantino for kidnapping María Orejón, a mulato
woman married to a Spanish man; AMHP-UTEP. 1651-B.
1233. 1410. _2 ff. D-128. ff 1–2: A lawsuit against Cristóbal
de Ontiveros and Josefa de Ribera, free mulata, for cohabitation; AMHP-UTEP. 1725-C. 4294. 1582._ 4 ff. D-121e. ff
1–4: A lawsuit against Antonio Santos, married to María de la
Encarnación and Petrona, mulata, for cohabitation.

76. AMHP-UTEP. 1634. 148. 516. _21 ff. G-12. ff 1–7.
77. AMHP-UTEP. 1716-B. 3816. 1128. _5 ff. D-117. ff 1–5.
78. AMHP-UTEP. 1667-B. 2117. 1220. _23 ff. G-62. ff 1–10.
79. AMHP-UTEP. 1641-B. 502. 1465. _25 ff. G-52. ff 1–7.
80. AMHP-UTEP. 1720-A. 3947. 498. _19 ff. D-116. ff 1–7.
81. AMHP-UTEP.1642-B. 617. 1254. _43 ff. G-13. ff 1–15: A lawsuit against Francisco Brito, Black slave of Capitán Galiano, and
against Juan de la Cruz, Negro criollo slave of Capitán Galiano,
for entering the house of Gobernador Don Melchor de Valdez;
AMHP-UTEP.1642-B. 607. 1152. _ 6 ff. G-66. ff 1–6: Lawsuit
against Domingo Negro Criollo Esclavo of Francisca Barrios,
widow, and against Pedro Negro Esclavo of Francisco Romo,
merchant, for robbery; AMHP-UTEP. 1640-C. 459. 1542.
_4 ff. G-90. ff 1–4: Lawsuit against María Gerónima of Pardo
Color for robbery; AMHP-UTEP. 1637-B. 281. 1139._18 ff.
G-19. ff 1–6: Lawsuit against Juana, free mulata, for robbery.
82. El Archivo General de la Nación (AGN). The Santa Inquisición
court has records of some cases of mulato and Indigenous people
accused of witchcraft. These two are the most striking: AGN/
Instituciones Coloniales/ Inquisición (61) / Volumen 525/
Título: Expediente 48. Fecha (s): AÑO 1691. Nivel de descripción: Unidad documental compuesta (Expediente). Volumen
y soporte: Fojas: 20. Productores: (Pendiente). Alcance y con-
tenido: El Sr. Fiscal del Santo Oficio sobre una denuncia que se
hizo en contra de Antonia de Soto, mulata, esclava de Francisco
de Noriega, vecino de la Ciudad de Durango, de diferentes
hechos, con pacto con el demonio. Parral. AGN/ Instituciones
Coloniales/ Inquisición/ Inquisición (61) / Volumen 661/Título:
Expediente 22. Fecha(s): AÑO 1685. Nivel de descripción:

Unidad documental compuesta (Expediente). Volumen y
soporte: Fojas: 25. Productores: (Pendiente) Alcance y con-
tenido: El Sr. Fiscal del Santo Oficio contra un Mulato llamado
Bernabé, y por mal nombre Barrabás, por hechicero. Parral.

83. West, *La comunidad minera*, 109.
84. AMHP-UTEP. 1642-B. 615. 1244. _3 ff. G-19. ff 1–3.
85. AMHP-UTEP. 1651-B. 1219. 1246. _7 ff. G-51. ff 1–7.
86. AMHP-UTEP. 1669-A. 2250. 948. _4 ff. G-48. ff 1–4.
87. AMHP-UTEP. 1699. 3314. 789. _11 ff. D-123. ff 1–6: To clarify whether Nicolás Mulato de Castañeda was or was not guilty
for being among enemy Indians; AMHP-UTEP. 1644-C. 761.
1378. _3 ff. G-50. ff 1–3: A lawsuit against the slave Diego for
hurting Mulato Diego Germán, servant of Capitán Gregorio de
Carbajal, during a revolt that involved Indios, mestizos, negros,
and mulatos.
88. AMHP-UTEP. 1674-B. 2525. 2069. _7 ff. D-165. ff 1–7:
Testimony for the case against Felipe de Salas Mulato Indio
who injured an individual; AMHP-UTEP. 1688-C. 304.9
1659. _4 ff. D-135. ff 1–4: Lawsuit against José de Magallanes
for injuries to and bad treatment of Andrés de Rivera Mulato
Indian; AMHP-UTEP. 1693-B. 3162. 1347. _10 ff. D-130.
ff 1–5: Lawsuit against an Esclavo Mulato Indio for robbery;
AMHP-UTEP. 1651-B. 1218. 1238. _6 ff. G-52. ff 1–6:
Lawsuit against an Indio de Nación Concho, or mulato, or mestizo, for robbery.
89. Martínez, *Genealogical Fictions*, 162–66.
90. Ibid.
91. AMHP-UTEP. 165-D. 1320.2009. _3ff. D-112.
92. AMHP-UTEP. 1672-B 2391 1359. _6 ff. G-39.
93. AMHP-UTEP. 1673-D 2458 2153. _18 ff. D-150.
94. AMHP-UTEP. 1709. 3625 638. _14 ff. D-124.
95. AMHP-UTEP. 1720-B. 1344. _6 ff. D-113e.
96. AMHP-UTEP. 1736. 4698 437. _2 ff. G-15.
97. AMHP-UTEP. 1724-D. 4236 2612. _24 ff. D-166.
98. AMHP-UTEP. 1771. 5053. 17. _3 ff. G-1c.

Chapter 4

1. Mexico City's celebration, as described, was taken from
Curcio-Nagy, *The Great Festivals*, 28. Valencia's celebration, as

described, was taken from Teófilo Ruíz, *Spanish Society, 1400–1600* (New York: Pearson, 2001), 154.

2. Cramaussel, *Poblar la frontera*, 110, 124.
3. Martin, *Governance and Society*, 102.
4. Teófilo F. Ruíz, *A King Travels: Festive Traditions in Late Medieval and Early Modern Spain* (Princeton, NJ: Princeton University Press, 2012), 249.
5. Ibid., 284.
6. Patricia Lopes Don, "La construcción del orden colonial: carnavales, triunfos y dioses de la lluvia en el nuevo mundo: una fiesta cívica en México-Tenochtitlán en 1539," *Relaciones* 76, no. 19 (1998): 57–59.
7. Kamen, *Brevísima historia de España*, 2611, 2620.
8. Peter Burke, *Popular Culture in Early Modern Europe* (New York: New York University Press, 1978), 207–8.
9. Ruíz, *Spanish Society*, 129, 131–33, 136.
10. Autos-da-fé were part of the Spanish Inquisition ceremony. They announced the secular authorities performing the execution of a sentence of a condemned heretic. Francisco Bethencourt, "The Auto da Fé: Ritual and Imagery," *Journal of the Warburg and Courtauld Institutes* 55 (1992): 155–56.
11. AHMP.FC. A16.001.008. f 1.
12. Lourdes Amigo Vázquez, *Toros y toreros en Valladolid durante los siglos XVII y XVIII* (Valladolid: Real Academia de Bellas Artes de la Purísima Concepción, 2012), 20–21.
13. Nicolás Rangel, *Historia de toreo en México: época colonial 1(529–1821)* (Ciudad de México: Imprenta Manuel León Sánchez, 1924), 8.
14. Ibid., 142.
15. Yanna Yannakakis, *The Art of Being In-between: Native Intermediaries, Indian Identity, and Local Rule in Colonial Oaxaca* (Durham, NC: Duke University Press, 2008), 116.
16. Ibid., 115, 117.
17. Francisco Javier Guillamón Álvarez, "Algunas reflexiones sobre el cabildo colonial como institución," *Anales de Historia Contemporánea* 8 (1990–1992): 151–54.
18. Ibid., 151–54.
19. María del Valle Borrero Silva, "La administración de la

Provincia de Sonora: los alcaldes mayores en la primera mitad del siglo XVIII," *Temas Americanistas*, no. 21 (2008): 55–57.

20. Villanueva Mayer, "The Black Slave," 56.

21. Cramaussel, *Poblar la frontera*, 407–8.

22. AHMP.FC. A16.001.008. f 1.

23. Martin, *Government and Society*, 100.

24. As Martin indicates, public celebrations in Northern New Spain were an opportunity to attract mine workers since many residents from nearby areas attended. Martin, *Governance and Society*, 116.

25. Voekel, *Alone Before God*, 4.

26. Hans Belting, *Imagen y culto: una historia de la imagen anterior a la era del arte* (México, D.F.: Ediciones AKAL, 2010), 230.

27. Cheryl E. Martin addresses the festive ritual in colonial Chihuahua in *Governance and Society*, chapters 4 and 5.

28. Martínez Sánchez-Barba, *La época dorada de América*, 39–44.

29. Curcio-Nagy, *The Great Festivals*, 28.

30. Voekel, *Alone Before God*, 4.

31. Sergi Doménech García, "Función y discurso de la imagen de devoción en Nueva España. Los 'verdaderos retratos' marianos como imágenes de sustitución afectiva," *Tiempos de América: Revista de historia, cultura y territorio*, no. 18 (2011): 88.

32. This is anthropologist Clifford Geertz's idea. Brian Larkin, *The Very Nature of God: Baroque Catholicism and Religious Reform in Bourbon Mexico City* (Albuquerque: University of New Mexico Press, 2010), 8–10.

33. Larkin, *The Very Nature of God*, 6.

34. Martínez Sánchez-Barba, *La época dorada de América*, 39–44.

35. Curcio-Nagy, *The Great Festivals*, 1–2, 7.

36. AHMP.FC. A16.001.008. f 5.

37. Jiménez Núñez, *El Gran Norte de México*, 124, 125.

38. Ibid., 126.

39. AHMP.FC. A16.001.008. f 1.

40. This paragraph summarizes the data gathered from the AMHP-UTEP documents used throughout chapter 2.

41. Bakhtin, *Rabelais and His World*.

42. Gonzalo Soto Posada, *Filosofía Medieval* (Bogotá: Editorial San Pablo, 2007), 64.

43. Curcio-Nagy, *The Great Festivals*, 6.
44. In her book, the author examines different periods in which people of African descent and Indigenous groups participated in rebellions. Natalia Silva Prada, *La política de una rebelión: los indígenas frente al Tumulto de 1692 en la Ciudad de México* (México, D.F.: Colegio de México, 2007).
45. AHMP.FC. A16.001.008. f-1.
46. William Taylor, *Drinking, Homicide and Rebellion in Colonial Mexican Villages* (Stanford: Stanford University Press, 1979), 41–43.
47. Ibid., 28, 33.
48. Jiménez Núñez, *El Gran Norte de México*, 86.
49. Alfonso Paredes y Fructuoso Irigoyen-Rascón, "Jikuri, the Tarahumara Peyote Cult: An Interpretation," in *The Mosaic of Contemporary Psychiatry in Perspective*, eds. Anthony Kales and Chester M. Pierce (New York: Springer, 1992), 123.
50. Deeds, *Defiance and Deference*, 28.
51. Ruíz, *A King Travels*, 246.
52. Irving Albert Leonard, *Baroque Times in Old Mexico: Seventeenth Century Persons, Places, and Practices* (Ann Arbor: University of Michigan Press, 1966), 34.
53. Ibid., 37.
54. Cheryl E. Martin, "Public Celebrations, Popular Culture and Labor Discipline in Eighteenth-Century Chihuahua," in *Rituals of Rule, Rituals of Resistance: Public Celebrations and Popular Culture in México*, eds. William H. Beezley, Cheryl E. Martin, and William E. French (Wilmington, DE: Scholarly Resources Press, 1994), 99.
55. Curcio-Nagy, *The Great Festivals*, 74.

Chapter 5
1. AHMP. 1669-A. 2206. 177. 1+ ff. D-100. f 3.
2. Ibid.
3. Márquez Terrazas and Villarreal, *Pueblos mineros de Chihuahua*, 38.
4. María Dolores Palomo Infante, *Juntos y congregados: historia de las cofradías en los pueblos de indios tzotziles y tzeltales de Chiapas (siglos XVI al XIX)* (México, D.F.: Centro de Investigaciones y Estudios Superiores de Antropología Social, 2009), 18–19.

5.   Francisco Javier Fernández Conde, *La religiosidad medieval en España: plena Edad Media (ss. XI–XII)* (Oviedo: Universidad de Oviedo, 2000), 317–20.
6.   Ibid., 480.
7.   Miguel Ángel Núñez Beltrán, *La oratoria sagrada de la época del barroco: doctrina, cultura y actitud ante la vida desde los sermones sevillanos del siglo XVII* (Sevilla: Universidad de Sevilla, 2000), 199–229.
8.   Rubial García, *El paraíso de los elegidos*, 22–24.
9.   Palomo Infante, *Juntos y congregados*, 18–19.
10. Asunción Lavrín, "Cofradías novohispanas: economía material y espiritual," en *Cofradías, Capellanías y obras pías en la América Colonial*, eds. María del Pilar Martínez López-Cano, Gisela von Wobeser, and Juan Guillermo Muñoz Correa (México, D.F.: Universidad Autónoma de México, 1998), 52–53.
11. Laura Dierksmeier, "Religious Autonomy and Local Religion Among Indigenous Confraternities in Colonial Mexico, Sixteenth-Seventeenth century," in *Indigenous and Black Confraternities in Colonial Latin America: Negotiating Status Through Religious Practices*, eds. Javiera Jaque Hidalgo and Miguel Valerio (Bronx: Amsterdam University Press, 2022), 38, 50, 51, accessed March 28, 2023, ProQuest Ebook Central.
12. María Isabel Monroy Castillo, ed., *Constructores de la nación: la migración tlaxcalteca en el norte de la Nueva España* (San Luis Potosí: El Colegio de San Luis, Gobierno del Estado de Tlaxcala, 1999), 20, 24, 28.
13. AMHP-UTEP. 1632. 12. _7 ff. G-7. ff 1–7, Gregorio Francisco Indio Mexicano; AMHP-UTEP. 1634-B. 661. 631. _3 ff. D-102. ff 1–3.1665, Francisco Indio; AMHP-UTEP. 1665-A. 1997. 725. _10 ff. G-7. ff 1–5, Miguel Franco Indio; AMHP-UTEP. 1665-A. 1999. 785. _12 ff. G-22ª. ff 1–6, Juan Francisco Indio Naborío; AMHP-UTEP. 1673-B. 2413. 543. _15 ff. D-116. ff 1–4, Juan Diego Indio.
14. Márquez Terrazas's footnote in West's book is number 15. West, *La comunidad minera*, 59–63. Now called Huejotitán, the town is located 44 miles east of Hidalgo del Parral.
15. Cramaussel, *La provincia de Santa Bárbara*, 47, 236.
16. Márquez Terrazas's footnote in West's book is number 15. West,

La comunidad minera, 59–63.

17. He uses naborío instead of laborío.
18. Márquez Terrazas and Villareal, *Pueblos mineros de Chihuahua*, 9, 34.
19. Ibid., 35–36.
20. Ibid., 36.
21. Ibid.
22. APSJP-UTEP. Rollo 4. Capellanías, Cofradías. 691. 4:4. 1636–1815. Cofradía de la Candelaria. ff 692–700.
23. AMHP-UTEP.1642-B. 614. 1239. _ 3 ff. G-20. ff 1–3.
24. APSJP-UTEP. Rollo 4. Capellanías, Cofradías. 691. 4:4. 1636–1815. Cofradía de la Candelaria. f 694. Tomín: silver coin (1.79 grams of silver). Three tomines equaled a peso in silver.
25. APSJP-UTEP. Rollo 4. Capellanías, Cofradías. 691. 4:4 1636–1815. Cofradía de la Candelaria. f 698.
26. APSJP-UTEP. Rollo 4. 691. Capellanías, Cofradías. 4:4. 1636–1815. Cofradía de la Candelaria. f 724.
27. AMHP-UTEP. 1669 A. 2206. 177. _ f 1–3. 1+ ff. D-100. f 1–3.
28. AMHP-UTEP. 1704-A. 3437. 253. _10 ff. D-136. Ff 1–10.
29. Sara Sánchez de Olmo, "Imagen mariana y construcción de la identidad socio-religiosa en el Michoacán colonial," *Dimensión Antropológica* 55 (2012): 71–73, http://www.dimensionantropo-logica.inah.gob.mx/?p=8129
30. Palomo Infante, *Juntos y congregados*, 14–15.
31. Joan C. Bristol, *Christians, Blasphemers, and Witches* (Albuquerque: University of New Mexico Press, 2007), 95, 97.
32. Marialba Pastor, *Cuerpos sociales, cuerpos sacrificiales* (México, D.F.: Universidad Autónoma de México, 2004), 133.
33. Sweet, *Recreating Africa*, 206.
34. Palmer, *Slaves of the White God*, 7.
35. Joan C. Bristol, "Afro-Mexican Saintly Devotion in a Mexico City Alley," in *Africans to Spanish America: Expanding the Diaspora*, eds. Sherwin K. Bryant, Rachel Sarah O'Toole, and Ben Vinson III (Urbana: University of Illinois Press, 2012), 116, ProQuest Ebook Central, https://ebookcentral.proquest.com/lib/msmc-ebooks/detail.action?docID=3414198.
36. Palmer, *Slaves of the White God*, 55.
37. Cristina Verónica Masferrer León, "Confraternities of People

of African Descent in Seventeenth-Century Mexico City," in *Indigenous and Black Confraternities in Colonial Latin America: Negotiating Status Through Religious Practices*, eds. Javiera Jaque Hidalgo and Miguel Valerio (Bronx: Amsterdam University Press, 2022), 65, accessed March 28, 2023, ProQuest Ebook Central.

38. Bristol, "Afro-Mexican Saintly Devotion," 123. For a more detailed analysis of 1612 Black confraternity conspiracies, see Miguel A. Valerio, "Cultura afrobarroca mexicana: soberanía negra en las calles de la Ciudad de México, 1610," *Latin American Research Review* (2023): 1–18, doi:10.1017/lar.2023.13.

39. Palmer, *Slaves of the White God*, 54.

40. Ibid., 52.

41. Krystle Farman Sweda, "'Of All Type of *Calidad* or Color': Black Confraternities in a Multiethnic Mexican Parish, 1640–1750," in *Indigenous and Black Confraternities in Colonial Latin America: Negotiating Status Through Religious Practices*, eds. Javiera Jaque Hidalgo and Miguel Valerio (Bronx: Amsterdam University Press, 2022), 95, accessed March 28, 2023, ProQuest Ebook Central.

42. Valerio, "Cultura afrobarroca mexicana."

43. Germeten, *Black Blood Brothers*.

44. Ibid., 156–67.

45. Ibid., 166. I sought information in this regard. I found that the Cofradía de La Santa Veracruz Nueva (1638–1719) included mulatos and mestizos but not Indigenous people, even though all these groups worked together in construction works in Nueva Veracruz. Rosa Elena Rojas, "Esclavos de Obraje: Consuelo en la Devoción. La Cofradía de la Santa Veracruz Nueva fundada por Mulatos, Mestizos y Negros. Coyoacán, siglo XVII," *Nuevo Mundo/ Mundos Nuevos: Debates 2012*, Coord. Rafael Castañeda García, 18/11/2012, https://nuevomundo.revues.org/64339?lang=en.

46. Dierksmeier, "Religious Autonomy," 54.

47. Mancuso, *Cofradías mineras*, 110–11.

48. Danielle Terrazas Williams, "Capitalizing Subjects: Free African-Descended Women of Means in Xalapa, Veracruz during the Long Seventeenth Century" (PhD diss., Duke

University, 2013), 60.

49. Pat Carroll, "Black Aliens and Black Natives in New Spain's Indigenous Communities," in *Black Mexico: Race in Society from Colonial to Modern Times*, ed. Ben Vinson (Albuquerque: University of New Mexico Press, 2009), 86.
50. Mancuso, *Cofradías mineras*, 20–21.
51. Palmer, *Slaves of the White God*, 39.
52. Cramaussel, *Poblar la frontera*, 203.
53. Germeten, *Black Blood Brothers*, 169.
54. Ibid., 169.
55. AMHP-UTEP. 1650. 1142. _6. 1+ ff. See no. 6350 (C7.715). Rescued. R-215. ff 1–3.
56. Ibid., 174, 183.
57. AMHP-UTEP. 1660C. 1752. 1398. _4ff. G1. 1–4 ff.
58. AHMP.FC. D16.001.002. ff 1–12. Germeten identifies Juan de Dios Vargas as mulato, but the archival documents identify him as mestizo. Germeten, *Black Blood Brothers*, 167n26.
59. APSJP-UTEP. Rollo 4. Capellanías, Cofradías. 001.4:1. 1648–1829. Capellanías. ff 109–110. This archive has documents that do not follow a theme or category. The guide indicates that this roll has records about capellanías but contains texts about various cofradías.
60. AMHP-UTEP. 1712. 3704. 484._ 6 ff. G-5f.
61. APSJP-UTEP. Rollo 4. Capellanías, Cofradías. 629. 4:2. 1671–1714. Cofradía de la Inmaculada Concepción. ff 640–641.
62. APSJP-UTEP. Rollo 4. Capellanías, Cofradías. 629. 4:2. 1671–1714. Cofradía de la Inmaculada Concepción. ff 642–45.
63. APSJP-UTEP. Rollo 4. Capellanías, Cofradías. 629. 4:2. 1671–1714. Cofradía de la Inmaculada Concepción. f 681.
64. APSJP-UTEP. Rollo 4. Capellanías, Cofradías. 629. 4:2. 1671–1714. Cofradía de la Inmaculada Concepción. ff 670–75.
65. Philip Terry, *Terry's Guide to Mexico* (Boston: Houghton Mifflin Co., 1935), 365.
66. Germeten, *Black Blood Brothers*, 159, 166.
67. Herman L. Bennett, *Colonial Blackness: A History of Afro-Mexico* (Bloomington: Indiana University Press, 2010), 6–7. Reference to Germeten is on p. 16n11.

Chapter 6

1. Antonio Domínguez Ortíz, *España, tres milenios de historia* (Madrid: Marcial Pons, 2007), 233–35.
2. Martin, *Governance and Society*, 104.
3. Domínguez Ortíz, *España, tres milenios de historia*, 233–35.
4. Martin, *Governance and Society*, 102, 119.
5. Curcio-Nagy, *The Great Festivals*, 110.
6. Susan Deans-Smith, "The Working Poor and Eighteenth-Century Colonial State: Gender, Public Order, and Work Discipline," in *Rituals of Rule, Rituals of Resistance: Public Celebrations and Popular Culture in México*, eds. William H. Beezley, Cheryl E. Martin, and William E. French (Wilmington, DE: Scholarly Resources Press, 1994), 48.
7. Curcio-Nagy, *The Great Festivals*, 101–4.
8. AMHP-UTEP. 1788 B. 5624. 857. _1+ ff. G-12f, G-12g, G-12h. ff 1–2.
9. David Carbajal López, "La reforma de las cofradías novo-hispanas en el Consejo de Indias, 1767–1820," *Revista Complutense de Historia de América*, no. 38 (2012): 83.
10. The tithe was a kind of tax that the faithful paid to the Church and comprised ten percent of their income. Manuel Ceballos Ramírez, "Iglesia Católica, Estado y sociedad en México: tres etapas de estudios de investigación," *Frontera Norte* 15, no. 8 (1996): 92.
11. Ceballos Ramírez, "Iglesia Católica, Estado y sociedad," 92.
12. AHMP.FC. A16.004.106. ff 34–36.
13. AHMP.FC. A16.004.106. ff 36–38.
14. AHMP.FC. A16.004.106. ff 44–55.
15. This was when the city council decided to change the date of the celebration of the Immaculate Virgin from January to May due to bad storms registered in the winter season. AHMP.FC. A16.004.106. ff 73–76.
16. AHMP.FC. A16.004.106. ff 59-63, 77–96.
17. AMHP-UTEP. 1788 B. 5620. 821. _1+ ff. G-12d. ff 3–4.
18. AMHP-UTEP. 1788 B. 5620. 821. _1+ ff. G-12d. ff 4–6.

Chapter 7

1. In this historical narrative, I recreated a primary source: AMHP-UTEP. 1764. 4930. 201. _5 ff. G-21. f 1–5.

2. In this historical narrative, I recreated the following sources: AMHP-UTEP. 1764. 4930. 201. _5 ff. G-21. f 1–5. AHMP. FC. A20.003.059. ff 1–4. Ysla Campbell, "En torno a la historia de la literatura en Nueva Vizcaya (oralidad, visualización y textos)," *Estado actual de los estudios sobre el Siglo de Oro: Actas del II Congreso Internacional de Hispanistas del Siglo de Oro* 1 (1993), 214–16.
3. In this sense, it is important to note that the figures given in percentages, or the number of inhabitants, are approximations. As expressed in previous chapters, there was a high degree of racial manipulation in the provincia. Germeten, *Black Blood Brothers*, 162.
4. Ibid., 162–63.
5. Martin, *Governance and Society*, 1.
6. Alatriste, *Desarrollo de la industria*, 26.
7. Ibid., 28, 29.
8. Ibid., 31.
9. AHMP.FC. A20.003.059. ff 1–4.
10. Clara Bargellini, "El arte de las misiones del norte de la Nueva España," *história, histórias. Brasilia* 1, no. 2 (2013), 153–55.
11. AMHP-UTEP. 1794. 5822. 596._ G-20. f 1–3.
12. Campbell, "El teatro de la Nueva Vizcaya," 58.
13. Ibid., 61–62.
14. Campbell, "En torno a la historia de la literatura en Nueva Vizcaya," 214–16.
15. Curcio-Nagy, *The Great Festivals*, 123–24.
16. Ibid., 129.
17. AHMP.FC.A.03.002.031. ff 1–5.
18. AHMP.FC. A.03.002.031. ff 1–5.
19. AHMP.FC. A.03.002.031. ff 1–5.
20. AHAD-10. Folder No. 2. 0314 - 1665. AHAD-10. Folder No. 2. 0421-1669.
21. AHAD-173. 0143 - 1790.
22. AHAD-192. 0818 - 1799.
23. Patricia Fogelman, "Coordenadas marianas: tiempos y espacios de devoción a la Virgen a través de las cofradías porteñas coloniales," *Trabajos y Comunicaciones* [En línea], no. 30–31(2004–2005), 126, http://www.fuentesmemoria.fahce.unlp.edu.ar/

artrevistas/pr.312/pr.312.pdf.

24. AHMP FC. A07.001.004. f 1–3.
25. AHMP.FC. A07.001.004. ff 1–3.

Chapter 8

1. AHMP.FC. D52.004.082. ff 1–13.
2. Curcio-Nagy, *The Great Festivals*, 6.
3. Germeten, *Black Blood Brothers*, 179.
4. Villanueva Mayer, "The Black Slave," 77.
5. AHMP.FC. A07.001.001. ff 1–2.
6. Villegas, *Historia multicultural*, 18.
7. AMHP-UTEP. 1687-B. 3012. 899. [Also in 1688A.619 D-137, no. 3027.] 5ff. ff 1–5.
8. AMHP-UTEP. 1724-A. 4210. 2062. _6 ff. D-156. ff 1–6.
9. AMHP-UTEP. 1725-C. 4303. 1704. _ 5 ff. D-123b. ff 1–5; AMHP-UTEP. 1727-C. 4389. 1685. _ Extraviado el legajo original. 5 ff. G-27k. ff 1–5; AMHP-UTEP. 1727-C. 4396. 2025. _ 92 ff. G-31. ff 1–10.
10. AHMP.FC. A07.001.001. ff 1–2.
11. AHMP.FC. A16.004.106. ff 1–6.
12. AMHP-UTEP. 1731 B. 4621.1028. _ 2 ff. G- 55. ff 1–2.
13. AHMP.FC. A16.004.106. ff 3–4.
14. Joanna Kozinska Frybes, "La representación encarnada: una reflexión sobre el teatro evangelizador en la Nueva España," in *Foro hispánico: discurso colonial hispanoamericano* 4, ed. Sonia Rose de Fuggle (Amsterdam: Rodopi B.V., 1992), 111.
15. Max Harris, *Aztecs, Moors, and Christians: Festivals of Reconquest in Mexico and Spain* (Austin: University of Texas Press, 2000).
16. Kozinska Frybes, "La representación encarnada," 103.
17. Karoline Cook, "Forbidden Crossings: Morisco Migration to Spanish America," (PhD diss., Princeton University, 2008), 85–105.
18. AHMP.FC. A16.004.106. ff 9–10.
19. Bailey, "Heteroglossia and Boundaries," 257–58.
20. Perhaps he was right, because I found no information about other cofradías organizing the Battle between Moors and Christians in the files I consulted.
21. José María Ruano de la Haza, "The World as a Stage: Politics, Imperialism and Spain's Seventeenth Century Theatre," in *A*

History of Theatre in Spain, eds. María M. Delgado and David T. Gies (Cambridge: Cambridge University Press, 2012), 57–63.

22. Palmer, *Slaves of the White God*, 6–7.
23. AHMP.FC. A16.004.106. ff 10–12.
24. Deeds, *Defiance and Deference*, 125.
25. AHMP.FC. A16.004.106. f 13.
26. AHMP.FC. A16.004.106. f 15.
27. In population censuses, for example, "vecino" was used to identify the registered "vecinos" (neighbors) who had populated houses: with women, children, or servants (Indigenous, black, or mulato) although none of them were included in the census. Pilar Gonzalbo Aizpuru, "Las mujeres novohispanas y las contradicciones de una sociedad patriarcal," in *Las mujeres en la construcción de las sociedades Iberoamericanas*, eds. Pilar Gonzalbo Aizpuru and Berta Ares Queija (México, D.F.: Colegio de México, 2004), 121.
28. Cramaussel, *La provincia de Santa Bárbara*, 40.
29. Jacob Olupona, "The Spirituality of Africa," interview by Anthony Chiorazzi, *The Harvard Gazette*, October 6, 2015, https://news.harvard.edu/gazette/story/2015/10/the-spirituality-of-africa/.
30. Sweet, *Recreating Africa*, 6, 103, 116.
31. Thornton, *Africa and Africans*, 199, 204, 206, 217–18.
32. Bennett, *Africans in Colonial Mexico*, 84, 89.
33. Proctor, "African Diasporic Ethnicity," 62.
34. Bennett, *Africans in Colonial Mexico*, 84, 89.
35. Palmer, *Slaves of the White God*, 146.
36. Bristol, "Afro-Mexican Saintly Devotion," 116.
37. AHMP.FC. A16.004.106. f 15.
38. Manuel García Castellón, "La crónica mestiza de Poma de Ayala: Grito contra la alineación física y espiritual de los andinos," *Proyecto Ensayo Hispánico*, ed. José Luis Gómez-Martínez. http://www.ensayistas.org/filosofos/peru/guaman/introd.htm.
39. AHMP.FC. A16.004.106. f 16.
40. Martin, *Governance and Society*, 105.
41. AHMP.FC. A16.004.106. ff 17–18.
42. Thornton, *Africa and Africans*, 235–36.
43. AHMP.FC. A16.004.106. f 18.

44. AHMP.FC. A07.001.003. ff 1–4.
45. AHMP.FC. A07.001.003. f 6.
46. Ibid.
47. Bennett, *Africans in Colonial Mexico*, 3.
48. AHMP.FC. A07.001.003. ff 7–8.
49. AHMP.FC. A16.004.106. ff 20–22.
50. AHMP.FC. A16.004.106. f 26.
51. AHMP.FC. A16.004.106. ff 31–33.
52. Martin, *Governance and Society*, 116.
53. Sara Ortelli, "Las reformas borbónicas vistas desde la frontera. La élite neovizcaína frente a la injerencia estatal en la segunda mitad del siglo XVIII," *Boletín del Instituto de Historia Argentina y Americana "Dr. Emilio Ravignani"* 3, no. 28, (2005), 19–20, 24. Redalyc, https://www.redalyc.org/articulo.oa?id=379444922001.
54. Martin, *Governance and Society*, 114–16.

Chapter 9

1. *Homenaje al profesor Juan Torres Fontes* (Murcia: Universidad de Murcia y Academia Alfonso X el Sabio, 1987), 139–40.
2. Voekel, *Alone Before God*, 28.
3. The Church divided itself between the regular and secular clergy in New Spain. The former were religious orders with convents, seminaries, sponsored schools, hospitals, and charities. The secular clergy organized itself in various dioceses: Mexico, Puebla, Oaxaca, Guadalajara, Michoacán, Sonora, Durango, Yucatán, and Chiapas. A bishop or archbishop governed them. In the most important dioceses, it was an ecclesiastical council. Each diocese's territory was divided into parishes. The Inquisition, charities, asylums, schools, and the Court of Capellanías and Pious Works were also part of the secular clergy. Each of these institutions had to raise funds and manage them. This situation created a massive economic inequality among the different institutions. Gisela von Wobeser, *El crédito eclesiástico en la Nueva España, Siglo XVIII* (México, D.F.: Universidad Autónoma de México, 1994), 9–13.
4. Marcela Rocío García Hernández, "Las capellanías de misas en la Nueva España," in *La Iglesia en Nueva España: problemas y perspectivas de investigación*, ed. María del Pilar Martínez López-Cano (México, D.F.: Universidad Autónoma de México,

2010), 268.

5.   APSJP-UTEP. Rollo 4. Capellanías, Cofradías. 001. 4:1.
     1648–1829. Capellanías. ff 581–90.

6.   Von Wobeser, *El crédito eclesiástico en la Nueva España*,
     308, 72, 25.

7.   Ibid., 303.

8.   Ibid., 9, 72, 74.

9.   Ibid., 309, 313.

10. María del Pilar Martínez-López Cano, "La iglesia y el crédito
     en Nueva España: entre los viejos presupuestos y nuevos retos de
     investigación," in *La iglesia en Nueva España: problemas y perspec-
     tivas de investigación*, ed. María del Pilar Martínez-López Cano
     (México, D.F.: Universidad Autónoma de México, 2010), 313.

11. Von Wobeser, *El crédito eclesiástico en la Nueva España*, 35–36.

12. The Consignment Census includes applying for a loan to estab-
     lish a capellanía. Gisela von Wobeser, "El uso del censo consig-
     nativo para realizar transacciones crediticias en la Nueva España.
     Siglos XVI al XVIII," in *Memoria del IV congreso de Historia del
     Derecho Mexicano*, ed. Beatriz Bernal (México, D.F: Instituto
     de Investigaciones Jurídicas, Universidad Autónoma de México,
     1988), 1167.

13. APSJP-UTEP. Rollo 4. Capellanías y Cofradías. 001: 4:1.
     1648–1829. Capellanías. ff 280–284.

14. Von Wobeser, *El crédito eclesiástico en la Nueva España*, 29, 33.

15. APSJP-UTEP. Rollo 4. Capellanías y Cofradías. 001: 4:1.
     1648–1829. Capellanías. ff 280–284.

16. Ibid., ff 284–85.

17. Ibid., ff 286–87.

18. Ibid., ff 287–23.

19. Ibid., ff 324–30.

20. Burns, *Colonial Habits*, 2–3.

21. AHMP.FC. D47.003.027. In 1657, Sebastián González,
     Micaela de Herradillo's husband, claimed a group of enslaved
     people that Micaela's aunt, Catalina Félix, had bequeathed.
     AHMP.FC. D48.006.113. In 1723, Juan de Zaragoza and José
     de Zaragoza claimed "three pieces of slaves" that Cristóbal Arias
     bequeathed.

22. APSJP-UTEP. Rollo 4. Capellanías, Cofradías. 001: 4:1.

1648–1829. Capellanías. ff 400–409.

23. AMHP-UTEP. 1649 B. 980. 547. _23 ff. G-19. ff 1–10.

24. Martin, *Governance and Society*, 171.

25. Gonzalbo Aizpuru, "Las mujeres novohispanas y las contradicciones," 121.

26. Margarita Iglesias Saldaña, "El deber ser de las mujeres y su rol en el establecimiento de los vínculos capellánicos en la pervivencia de los linajes coloniales. Imaginarios, representaciones y comportamientos," *Palimpsesto* 1, no. 2 (2004), 1–5.

27. APSJP-UTEP. Rollo 4. Capellanías, Cofradías. 001. 4:1. 1648–1829. Capellanías. ff 140–42. Ana de Biezma's capellanía foundation letter is in a page from 1670. It is priest Bartolomé de Arteaga's declaration to Sebastián García, Ana's second husband. At that time, de Arteaga was Ana's capellanía-capellán owner. In the letter, he informed of the delivery of the earnings, which were the product of Ana's assets contained in her capellanía.

28. In the letter, Ana de Biezma mentions that her first husband, de Urbaneja, received this award for his discovery and role as a settler of the New Vizcaya kingdom and says she was the sole heir to the deceased's property.

29. APSJP-UTEP. Rollo 4. Capellanías, Cofradías. 001. 4:1. 1648–1829. Capellanías. ff 143–45.

30. John E. Kicza, "El papel de la familia en la organización empresarial en la Nueva España," in *Familia y poder en la Nueva España: memoria del tercer simposio de historia de las mentalidades*, ed. Solange Alberro (México, D.F.: Instituto Nacional de Antropología e Historia, 1991), 76.

31. Gonzalbo Aizpuru, "Las mujeres novohispanas y las contradicciones," 124, 125.

32. María José Encontra y Vilalta, "Las mujeres españolas en la capital de la nueva España, durante el siglo XVI," *Contribuciones a las Ciencias Sociales* (2014). www.eumed.net/rev/cccss/29/mujeres-espanolas.html.

33. APSJP-UTEP. Rollo 4. Capellanías, Cofradías. 001. 4:1. 1648–1829. Capellanías. f 92.

34. María Concepción Lugo Olín, "Los sacramentos: un armamento para santificar el cuerpo y sanar el alma," in *Cuerpo y religión en*

el México barroco, eds. Antonio Rubial García and Doris Bieñko de Peralta (México, D.F.: Instituto Nacional de Antropología e Historia, 2011), 51.

35. Voekel, *Alone Before God*, 28.
36. Ibid., 34.
37. Lugo Olín, "Los sacramentos," 51.
38. Larkin, *The Very Nature of God*, 4.
39. APSJP-UTEP. Rollo 4. Capellanías, Cofradías. 001. 4:1. 1648–1829. Capellanías. ff 92–95.
40. Pilar Gonzalbo Aizpuru and Berta Ares Queija, eds., *Las mujeres en la construcción de las sociedades iberoamericanas* (México, D.F.: Colegio de México, 2004), 11.
41. Voekel, *Alone Before God*, 17, 39.
42. APSJP-UTEP. Rollo 4. Capellanías, Cofradías. 001. 4:1. 1648–1829. Capellanías. f 428.
43. Larkin, *The Very Nature of God*, 4–5.
44. Ibid., 4.
45. Von Wobeser, *El crédito eclesiástico en la Nueva España*, 274–75.
46. APSJP-UTEP. Rollo 4. Capellanías, Cofradías. 001. 4:1. 1648–1829. Capellanías. ff 428–41.
47. Catalina founded her capellanía in 1715. By 1739, the hacienda was sold and thereafter rented out.
48. APSJP-UTEP. Rollo 4. Capellanías, Cofradías. 001. 4:1. 1648–1829. Capellanías. ff 428–41.
49. Ibid.
50. APSJP. Rollo 4. Capellanías, Cofradías. 001. 4:1. 1648-1829. f 620.
51. Ibid.
52. Candelaria Castro Pérez, Mercedes Calvo Cruz, and Sonia Granado Suárez, "Las capellanías en los siglos XVII–XVIII a través del estudio de su escritura de fundación," *Anuario de Historia de la Iglesia*, no. 16 (2007), 336.
53. García Hernández, "Las capellanías de misas," 279–80.
54. Von Wobeser, *El crédito eclesiástico en la Nueva España*, 32, 69.
55. Michael P. Costeloe, *Church Wealth in Mexico: A Study of the Juzgado de Capellanías in the Archbishopric of Mexico 1800–1856* (Cambridge: Cambridge University Press, 1967), 66.
56. APSJP-UTEP. Rollo 4. Capellanías, Cofradías. 001. 4:1.

1648–1829. Capellanías. ff 53–54.

57. Ibid., ff 33–36.

58. Ibid.

59. Von Wobeser, *El crédito eclesiástico en la Nueva España*, 32.

60. Martin, *Governance and Society*, 197.

61. Gloria Delgado, *Historia de México* (New York: Pearson Education, 2006), 369.

Drama's Dénouement

1. Salvador Prieto Quimper, *El Parral de mis recuerdos: datos para la biografía de una noble ciudad de provincia* (México, D.F.: Editorial Jus, 1948), 71, 285.

2. Thornton, *Africa and Africans*, 206; Miguel de Cervantes Saavedra (1547–1616), *El ingenioso hidalgo Don Quijote de la Mancha* (Madrid: Espasa-Calpe, 1966), capítulo XVIII.

BIBLIOGRAPHY

Primary Sources

Archivo Municipal de Hidalgo del Parral (AMHP-UTEP) / Archivo
Histórico del Municipio de Parral. Fondo Colonial (AHMP.FC)
Archivo Parroquial de San José del Parral (APSJP-UTEP) / Archivo
Parroquial del Municipio de Parral (APMP)
Archivo Histórico del Arzobispado de Durango (AHAD)
Archivo General de la Nación (AGN)

Secondary Sources

Aercke, Kristiaan. *Gods of Play: Baroque Festive Performances as
Rhetorical Discourse*. New York: New York State University
Press, 1994.

Alatriste, Oscar. *Desarrollo de la industria y la comunidad minera de Hidalgo del Parral durante la segunda mitad del siglo XVIII
(1765–1810)*. México, D.F. Universidad Nacional Autónoma de
México, 1983.

Alonso, Ana María. *Thread of Blood: Colonialism, Revolution, and
Gender on Mexico's Northern Frontier*. Tucson: University of Arizona
Press, 1995.

Amador, Elias. *Bosquejo histórico de Zacatecas, Volumen I*. Zacatecas:
Escuela de Artes y Oficios en Guadalupe, 1892.

Amelang, James. "The Myth: Perceptions of Sociability." In
Mediterranean Urban Culture 1400–1700, edited by Alexander
Cowan, 15–30. Exeter: University of Exeter Press, 2000.

Amigo Vázquez, Lourdes. *Toros y toreros en Valladolid durante los siglos
XVII y XVIII*. Valladolid: Real Academia de Bellas Artes de la
Purísima Concepción, 2012.

Arbel, Benjamin. "The Port Towns of the Levant in Sixteenth-Century
Travel Literature." In *Mediterranean Urban Culture 1400–1700*,

edited by Alexander Cowan, 151–65. Exeter: University of Exeter Press, 2000.

Assmann, Jan, and John Czapucka. "Collective Memory and Cultural Identity." *New German Critique*, no. 65 (1995): 125–33. doi:10.2307/488538.

Aune, Michael B., and Valerie M. Demarinis. "Introduction." In *Religious and Social Ritual: Interdisciplinary Explorations*, edited by Michael B. Aune and Valerie M. Demarinis, 1–18. New York: State University of New York Press, 1996.

Bailey, Benjamin. "Heteroglossia and Boundaries: Processes of Linguistic and Social Distinction." In *Bilingualism: A Social Approach*, edited by Monica Heller, 257–77. UK: Palgrave, Macmillan, 2007.

Bailey Glasco, Sharon. *Constructing Mexico City: Colonial Conflicts Over Culture, Space, and Authority*. Basingstoke: Palgrave, Macmillan, 2010.

Bakewell, J. P. *Minería y sociedad en México colonial: Zacatecas 1546–1700*. México, D.F.: Fondo de Cultura Económica, 1976.

Bakhtin, Mikhail. *Rabelais and His World*. Bloomington: Indiana University Press, 2009.

Bargellini, Clara. "El arte de las misiones del norte de la Nueva España." *história, histórias* 1, no. 2 (2013): 123–66.

———. *Marcos de veneración: los retablos virreinales de Chihuahua*. Chihuahua: Programa Editorial Gobierno del Estado, Instituto Chihuahuense de la Cultura, 2011.

Barkin, Florence. *Black Slave Trade in the Seventeenth Century Real of San Joseph del Parral from 1631–1645*. Tempe: Arizona State University-Center for Latin American Studies, 1977.

Baver, Ralph, and José Antonio Mazzotti, eds. *Creole Subjects in Colonial America: Empires, Texts, Identities*. Chapel Hill: University of North Carolina Press, 2009.

Bell, C. *Ritual Theory, Ritual Practice*. New York: Oxford University Press, 1992.

Belting, Hans. *Imagen y culto: una historia de la imagen anterior a la era del Arte*. México, D.F.: Ediciones AKAL, 2010.

Bennett, Herman L. *Africans in Colonial Mexico: Absolutism, Christianity, and Afro-Creole Consciousness, 1570–1640*. Bloomington: Indiana University Press, 2003.

———. *Colonial Blackness: A History of Afro-Mexico.* Bloomington: Indiana University Press, 2010.

Bethencourt, Francisco. "The Autoda Fé: Ritual and Imagery." *Journal of the Warburg and Courtauld Institutes* 55 (1992): 155–68.

Beverley, John. "Going Baroque?" *Boundary* 2, nos. 15/16 (1988): 27–39. https://doi.org/10.2307/303244.

Blumenthal, Debra. *Enemies and Familiars: Slavery and Mastery in Fifteenth Century Valencia.* Ithaca, NY: Cornell University Press, 2009.

Bolin, Paul E. "Imagination and Speculation as Historical Impulse: Engaging Uncertainties within Art Education History and Historiography." *Studies in Art Education* 50, no. 2 (2009):110–23.

Bossio, Pedro. "Exploring the Roots of Chronic Underdevelopment: The Colonial *Encomienda* and *Resguardo* and Their Legacy to Modern Colombia." Thesis, City University of New York, 2018.

Botella-Ordinas, Eva. "'Exempt from Time and from Its Fatal Change': Spanish Imperial Ideology, 1450–1700." *Renaissance Studies* 26, no. 4 (2012): 580–604. http://www.jstor.org/stable/24420174.

Brading, D. A. *Mineros y comerciantes en el México borbónico (1763–1810).* México, D.F.: Fondo de Cultura Económica, 1971.

Bristol, Joan C. "Afro-Mexican Saintly Devotion in a Mexico City Alley." In *Africans to Spanish America: Expanding the Diaspora*, edited by Sherwin K. Bryant, Rachel Sarah O'Toole, and Ben Vinson III, 114–35. Urbana: University of Illinois Press, 2012. ProQuest Ebook Central. https://ebookcentral.proquest.com/lib/msmc-ebooks/detail.action?docID=3414198.

———. *Christians, Blasphemers, and Witches.* Albuquerque: University of New Mexico Press, 2007.

Brooks, James. *Captive and Cousins: Slavery, Kinship, and Community in the Southwest Borderlands.* Chapel Hill: University of North Carolina Press, 2002.

Burke, Peter. *Popular Culture in Early Modern Europe.* New York: New York University Press, 1978.

———. *What is Cultural History?* Cambridge: Polity Press, 2029.

Burns, Kathryn. *Colonial Habits: Convents and the Spiritual Economy of Cuzco, Peru.* Durham, NC: Duke University Press, 1999.

Campbell, Ysla. "El teatro de la Nueva Vizcaya." *Criticón* 1, no. 51 (1991): 57–63.

———. "En torno a la historia de la literatura en Nueva Vizcaya (oralidad, visualización y textos)." *Estado actual de los estudios sobre el Siglo de Oro: Actas del II Congreso Internacional de Hispanistas del Siglo de Oro* 1 (1993): 209–16.

Carbajal López, David. "La reforma de las cofradías novohispanas en el Consejo de Indias, 1767–1820." *Revista Complutense de Historia de América*, no. 38 (2012): 79–101.

Carr, Matthew. *Blood and Faith: The Purging of Muslim Spain.* New York: The New Press, 2009.

Carroll, Pat. "Black Aliens and Black Natives in New Spain's Indigenous Communities." In *Black Mexico: Race in Society from Colonial to Modern Times*, edited by Ben Vinson, 72–95. Albuquerque: University of New Mexico Press, 2009.

Casini, Mateo. "Some Thoughts on the Social and Political Culture of Baroque Venice." In *Braudel Revisited: The Mediterranean World, 1600–1800*, edited by Gabriel Piterberg, Teófilo F. Ruíz, and Geoffry Symcox, 177–206. Toronto: University of Toronto Press, 2010.

Castanera, Juan Joseu. *Sobre la venida del apóstol Santiago a España: Discurso leído en la Universidad Central.* Madrid: Imprenta de Don Pedro Montero, 1857.

Castro Pérez, Candelaria, Mercedes Calvo Cruz, and Sonia Granado Suárez. "Las capellanías en los siglos XVII–XVIII a través del estudio de su escritura de fundación." *Anuario de Historia de la Iglesia*, no. 16 (2007): 335–47.

Ceballos Ramírez, Manuel. "Iglesia Católica, Estado y sociedad en México: tres etapas de estudios de investigación." *Frontera Norte* 8, no. 15 (1996): 91–106.

Cervantes Saavedra, Miguel de (1547–1616). *El Ingenioso Hidalgo Don Quijote De La Mancha.* Madrid: Espasa-Calpe, 1966.

Chaudhuri, Nupur, Sherry J. Katz, and Mary Elizabeth Perry, eds. *Contesting Archives: Finding Women in the Sources.* Urbana: University of Illinois Press, 2010.

Coleman, David. *Creating Christian Granada: Society and Religious Culture in an Old-World Frontier City, 1492–1600.* Ithaca, NY: Cornell University Press, 2003.

Collins, P. "Thirteen Ways of Looking at a 'Ritual.'" *Journal of Contemporary Religion* 20, no. 3 (2005): 323–42.

Cook, Karoline. "Forbidden Crossings: Morisco Migration to Spanish America, 1492–1650." PhD diss., Princeton University, 2008.

Costeloe, Michael P. *Church Wealth in Mexico: A Study of the Juzgado de Capellanías in the Archbishopric of Mexico 1800–1856.* Cambridge: Cambridge University Press, 1967.

Cramaussel, Chantal. "Encomiendas, repartimientos y conquista de Nueva Vizcaya." *Historias. INAH,* no. 25 (1991): 73–91.

———. *Poblar la frontera: la provincia de Santa Bárbara en Nueva Vizcaya durante los siglos XVI y XVII.* Zamora: Colegio de Michoacán, 2006.

———. *La provincia de Santa Bárbara, 1563–1631.* Chihuahua: Secretaría de Educación y Cultura, 1990.

Cruz, Anne J., and Mary Elizabeth Perry. "Introduction: Culture and Control in Counter-Reformation Spain." In *Culture and Control in Counter-Reformation Spain,* edited by Anne J. Cruz and Mary Elizabeth Perry, ix–xxiii. Minneapolis: University of Minnesota Press, 1992. http://www.jstor.org/stable/10.5749/j.ctttv4gm.3.

Curcio-Nagy, Linda Ann. *The Great Festivals of Colonial Mexico City: Performing Power and Identity.* Albuquerque: University of New Mexico Press, 2004.

Dean, Carolyn. *Inka Bodies and the Body of Christ: Corpus Christi in Colonial Cuzco, Peru.* Durham, NC: Duke University Press, 1999.

Deans-Smith, Susan. "The Working Poor and Eighteenth-Century Colonial State: Gender, Public Order, and Work Discipline." In *Rituals of Rule, Rituals of Resistance: Public Celebrations and Popular Culture in México,* edited by William H. Beezley, Cheryl E. Martin, and William E. French, 47–75. Wilmington, DE: Scholarly Resources Press, 1994.

Deeds, Susan M. *Defiance and Deference in Mexico's Colonial North: Indians Under Spanish Rule in Nueva Vizcaya.* Austin: University of Texas Press, 2003.

Delgado, Gloria. *Historia de México.* New York: Pearson Education, 2006.

Del Valle Borrero Silva, María. "La administración de la Provincia de Sonora: los alcaldes mayores en la primera mitad del siglo XVIII." *Temas Americanistas,* no. 2 (2008): 48–65.

Dierksmeier, Laura. "Religious Autonomy and Local Religion Among Indigenous Confraternities in Colonial Mexico,

Sixteenth-Seventeenth century." In *Indigenous and Black Confraternities in Colonial Latin America: Negotiating Status Through Religious Practices*, edited by Javiera Jaque Hidalgo and Miguel Valerio, 37–62. Bronx: Amsterdam University Press, 2022. ProQuest Ebook Central.

Doménech García, Sergi. "Función y discurso de la imagen de devoción en Nueva España. Los 'verdaderos retratos' marianos como imágenes de sustitución afectiva." *Tiempos de América: Revista de historia, cultura y territorio*, no. 18 (2011): 77–94.

Domínguez Ortíz, Antonio. *España, tres milenios de historia.* Madrid: Marcial Pons, 2007.

Durkheim. E. *The Elementary Forms of Religious Life.* Translated by K. E. Fields. New York: Free Press, 1912.

Encontra y Vilalta, María José. "Las mujeres españolas en la capital de la nueva España, durante el siglo XVI." *Contribuciones a las Ciencias Sociales*, 2014. www.eumed.net/rev/cccss/29/mujeres-espanolas.html.

Fernández Conde, Francisco Javier. *La religiosidad medieval en España: plena Edad Media (ss. XI–XII).* Oviedo: Universidad de Oviedo, 2000.

Fogelman, Patricia. "Coordenadas marianas: tiempos y espacios de devoción a la Virgen a través de las cofradías porteñas coloniales." *Trabajos y Comunicaciones* [en línea] nos. 30–31 (2004–2005): 118–38. http://www.fuentesmemoria.fahce.unlp.edu.ar/artrevistas/pr.312/pr.312.pdf.

Gaddis, J. L. *The Landscape of History: How Historians Map the Past.* New York: Oxford University Press, 2002.

García Castellón, Manuel. "La crónica mestiza de Poma de Ayala: Grito contra la alineación física y espiritual de los andinos." *Proyecto Ensayo Hispánico*, edited by José Luis Gómez Martínez. http://www.ensayistas.org/filosofos/peru/guaman/introd.htm.

García Gibert, Javier. *La <<humanitas>> Hispana: sobre el humanismo literario en los siglos de oro.* Salamanca: Ediciones Universidad de Salamanca, 2010.

García Hernández, Marcela Rocío. "Las capellanías de misas en la Nueva España." In *La Iglesia en Nueva España: problemas y perspectivas de investigación*, edited by María del Pilar Martínez López-Cano, 267–303. México, D.F.: Universidad Autónoma de México, 2010.

Germeten, Nicole von. *Black Blood Brothers: Confraternities and Social Mobility for Afro-Mexicans*. Gainesville: University Press of Florida, 2006.

Gonzalbo Aizpuru, Pilar. "Las mujeres novohispanas y las contradicciones de una sociedad Patriarcal." In *Las mujeres en la construcción de las sociedades Iberoamericanas*, edited by Pilar Gonzalbo Aizpuru and Berta Ares Queija, 121–40. México, D.F.: Colegio de México, 2004.

———. "La trampa de las castas." In *La sociedad novohispana: Estereotipos y realidades*, edited by Solange Alberro and Pilar Gonzalbo Aizpuru, 17–22. México, D.F.: El Colegio de México, 2013.

Gonzalbo Aizpuru, Pilar, and Berta Ares Queija, eds. *Las mujeres en la construcción de las Sociedades Iberoamericanas*. México, D.F.: Colegio de México, 2004.

Gottardi, Sara. "Visigothic Division and Muslim Preservers of Order." *Hispanófila*, no. 178 (2016): 221–32. https://www.jstor.org/stable/90012376.

Green, Ann. *Cultural History*. Basingstoke, UK: Palgrave Macmillan, 2008.

Griffen, William B. *Indian Assimilation in the Franciscan Area of Nueva Vizcaya*. Tucson: University of Arizona Press, 1979. Open-access edition by Arizona Press, 2022. https://open.uapress.arizona.edu/projects/indian-assimilation-in-the-franciscan-area-of-nueva-vizcaya.

Guillamón Álvarez, Francisco Javier. "Algunas reflexiones sobre el cabildo colonial como Institución." *Anales de Historia Contemporánea* 8 (1990–1992): 151–61.

Guitar, Lynne. "Boiling It Down: Slavery on the First Commercial Sugarcane Ingenios in the Americas (Hispaniola, 1530–45)." In *Slaves, Subjects, and Subversives: Blacks in Colonial Latin America*, edited by Jane G. Landers and Barry M. Robinson, 39–82. Albuquerque: University of New Mexico Press, 2006.

Guy, Donna, and Tom Sheridan, eds. *Contested Ground: Comparative Frontiers on the Northernand Southern Edges of the Spanish Empire*. Tucson: University of Arizona Press, 1998.

Hämäläinen, Pekka. *The Comanche Empire*. New Haven, CT: Yale University Press, 2008.

Harris, Max. *Aztecs, Moors, and Christians: Festivals of Reconquest in*

Mexico and Spain. Austin: University of Texas Press, 2000.

Hartman, Saidiya. *Lose Your Mother: A Journey Along the Atlantic Slave Route.* New York, Farrar, Straus & Giroux, 2008.

———. *Scenes of Subjection: Terror, Slavery, and Self- Making in Nineteenth Century America.* New York: Oxford University Press, 1997.

———. "Venus in Two Acts." *Small Axe* 12, no. 2 (2008): 1–14. muse.jhu.edu/article/241115.

———. *Wayward Lives, Beautiful Experiments: Intimate Histories of Social Upheaval.* New York: W. W. Norton & Company, 2019.

Hawthorne, Walter. *From Africa to Brazil: Culture, Identity, and an Atlantic Slave Trade, 1600–1830.* New York: Cambridge University Press, 2020.

Herzog, Tamar. *Defining Nations: Immigrants and Citizens in Early Modern Spain and Spanish America.* New Haven, CT: Yale University Press, 2003.

Hoffman, J. P. "Introduction: Improving Our Understanding of Religious Ritual." In *Understanding Religious Ritual: Theoretical Approaches and Innovations*, edited by J. P. Hoffman, 1–8. New York: Routledge, 2012.

Hoffman, Paul E. "Diplomacy and the Papal Donation 1493–1585." *The Americas* 30, no. 2 (1973): 151–83. doi:10.2307/980555.

Homenaje al profesor Juan Torres Fontes. Murcia: Universidad de Murcia y Academia Alfonso X el Sabio, 1987.

Iglesias Saldaña, Margarita. "El deber ser de las mujeres y su rol en el establecimiento de los vínculos capellánicos en la pervivencia de los linajes coloniales. Imaginarios, representaciones y comportamientos." *Palimpsesto* 1, no. 2 (2004): 1–5.

Ihrie, Maureen, and Salvador Oropeza, eds. *World Literature in Spanish: An Encyclopedia.* Santa Bárbara: ABC-CLIO, 2011.

Leonard, Irving Albert. *Baroque Times in Old Mexico: Seventeenth Century Persons, Places, and Practices.* Ann Arbor: University of Michigan Press, 1966.

Jiménez Núñez, Alfredo. *El Gran Norte de México: una frontera imperial en la Nueva España (1540–1820).* Madrid: Tebar, 2006.

Kamen, Henry. *Brevísima historia de España.* México, D.F.: Grupo Planeta, 2014.

Kicza, John E. "El papel de la familia en la organización empresarial en la Nueva España." In *Familia y poder en la Nueva España: memoria del tercer simposio de historia de las mentalidades*, edited by Solange Alberro, 75–85. México, D.F.: Instituto Nacional de Antropología e Historia, 1991.

Kozinska Frybes, Joanna. "La representación encarnada: una reflexión sobre el teatro evangelizador en la Nueva España." In *Foro hispánico: discurso colonial hispanoamericano*, edited by d. Sonia Rose de Fuggle, 101–14. Amsterdam: Rodopi B.V., 1992.

Larkin, Brian. *The Very Nature of God: Baroque Catholicism and Religious Reform in Bourbon Mexico City*. Albuquerque: University of New Mexico Press, 2010.

Lastra de Suárez, Yolanda. *Los otomíes: su lengua y su historia*. México, D.F.: Universidad Autónoma de México, 2006.

Lavrín, Asunción. "Cofradías novohispanas: economía material y espiritual." In *Cofradías, Capellanías y obras pías en la América Colonial*, edited by María del Pilar Martínez López-Cano, Gisela Von Wobeser, and Juan Guillermo Muñoz, 49–64. México, D.F.: Universidad Autónoma de México, 1998.

Levtzion, Nehemia, and Randall L. Pouwels, eds. *The History of Islam in Africa*. Athens: Ohio University Press, 2000.

Lopes Don, Patricia. "La construcción del orden colonial: carnavales, triunfos y dioses de la lluvia en el nuevo mundo: una fiesta cívica en México-Tenochtitlán en 1539." *Relaciones* 76, no. 19 (1998): 52–89.

Lugo Olín, María Concepción. "Los sacramentos: un armamento para santificar el cuerpo y sanar el alma." In *Cuerpo y religión en el México barroco*, edited by Antonio Rubial García and Doris Bieñko de Peralta, 41–62. México, D.F.: Instituto Nacional de Antropología e Historia, 2011.

Lundahl, Mats. "Spain and the Conquest of America: Profits, Religion, and Forced Labour in the Fifteenth and Sixteenth Centuries." In *Trade, Growth, and Development: The Role of Politics and Institutions*, edited by Göte Hansson, 43–70. New York: Routledge, 1993.

McCauley, Robert N., and E. Thomas Lawson. *Bringing Ritual to Mind: Psychological Foundations of Cultural Forms*. New York: Cambridge University Press, 2002.

Mancuso, Laura. *Cofradías mineras: religiosidad popular en México y Brasil, siglo XVIII*. México, D.F.: El Colegio de México, Centro de Estudios Históricos, 2007.

Márquez Terrazas, Zacarías, and Libertad Villarreal. *Pueblos mineros de Chihuahua*. Chihuahua: Gobierno del Estado, 1995.

Martin, Cheryl E. *Governance and Society in Colonial Mexico: Chihuahua in the Eighteenth Century*. Stanford: Stanford University Press, 1996.

———. "Public Celebrations, Popular Culture and Labor Discipline in Eighteenth-Century Chihuahua." In *Rituals of Rule, Rituals of Resistance: Public Celebrations and Popular Culture in México*, edited by William H. Beezley, Cheryl E. Martin, and William E. French, 95–114. Wilmington, DE: Scholarly Resources Press, 1994.

Martínez, Ignacio. *The Intimate Frontier: Friendship and Civil Society in Northern New Spain* (Tucson: University of Arizona Press, 2019).

Martínez, María Elena. *Genealogical Fictions: Limpieza de Sangre, Religion, and Gender in Colonial Mexico*. Stanford: Stanford University Press, 2008.

Martínez-López Cano, María del Pilar. "La iglesia y el crédito en Nueva España: entre los viejos presupuestos y nuevos retos de investigación". In *La iglesia en Nueva España: problemas y perspectivas de investigación*, edited by María del Pilar Martínez López Cano, 311–52. México, D.F.: Universidad Autónoma de México, 2010.

Martínez Sánchez-Barba, Mario. *La época dorada de América: pensamiento, política, mentalidades*. Madrid: Biblioteca Nueva, 2008.

Martínez Sánchez-Barba, Mario. "Public Celebrations, Popular Culture and Labor Discipline in Eighteenth-Century Chihuahua." In *Rituals of Rule, Rituals of Resistance: Public Celebrations and Popular Culture in México*, edited by William H. Beezley, Cheryl E. Martin, and William E. French, 95–114. Wilmington, DE: Scholarly Resources Press, 1994.

Marvall, José Antonio. *Culture of the Baroque: Analysis of a Historical Structure*. Translated by Terry Cochran. Minneapolis: University of Minnesota Press, 1986.

Masferrer León, Cristina Verónica. "Confraternities of People of African Descent in Seventeenth-Century Mexico City." In *Indigenous and Black Confraternities in Colonial Latin America: Negotiating Status Through Religious Practices*, edited by Javiera Jaque Hidalgo and Miguel Valerio, 63–90. Bronx: Amsterdam University Press, 2022. ProQuest Ebook Central.

McCaa, Robert. "Calidad, Clase, and Marriage in Colonial Mexico: The Case of Parral 1788–1790." *The Hispanic American Historical*

Review 64, no. 3 (1984): 477–502.

McWatters, Cheryl S. "Speculation, History, Speculative History." *Accounting History Review* 26, no. 1 (February 2016).

Mignolo, Walter. "Afterword: From Colonial Discourse to Colonial Semiosis." *Dipositio* 14, nos. 36/38 (1989): 333–37.

Monroy Castillo, María Isabel, ed. *Constructores de la nación: la migración tlaxcalteca en el norte de la Nueva España.* San Luis Potosí: El Colegio de San Luis, Gobierno el Estado de Tlaxcala, 1999.

Moreri, Luis. *El gran diccionario histórico, o miscelánea curiosa de la historia sagrada y Profana.* Paris: Hermanos de Tournes, 1753.

Mullett, Michael. *The Catholic Reformation.* London: Taylor & Francis Group, 1999. ProQuest Ebook Central.

Nauert, Charles G., Jr. *Culture of Renaissance Europe: New Approaches to European History.* Cambridge: University of Cambridge Press, 1995.

Nieto Sotia, José Manuel. *La época medieval: iglesia y cultura.* Madrid: AKAL, 2002.

Núñez Beltrán, Miguel Ángel. *La oratoria sagrada de la época del barroco: doctrina, cultura y actitud ante la vida desde los sermones sevillanos del siglo XVII.* Sevilla: Universidad de Sevilla, 2000.

Olupona, Jacob. "The Spirituality of Africa." Interview by Anthony Chiorazzi. *The Harvard Gazette*, October 6, 2015. https://news.harvard.edu/gazette/story/2015/10/the-spirituality-of-africa/.

Ortelli, Sara. "Las reformas borbónicas vistas desde la frontera. La élite neovizcaína frente a la injerencia estatal en la segunda mitad del siglo XVIII." *Boletín del Instituto de Historia Argentina y Americana "Dr. Emilio Ravignani"* 3, no. 28 (2005): 7–36.

Palmer, Colin A. *Slaves of the White God: Blacks in Mexico, 1570–1650.* Cambridge, MA: Harvard University Press, 1976.

Palomo Infante, María Dolores. *Juntos y congregados: historia de las cofradías en los pueblos de indios tzotziles y tzeltales de Chiapas (siglos XVI al XIX).* México, D.F.: Centro de Investigaciones y Estudios Superiores de Antropología Social, 2009.

Paredes, Alfonso, and Fructuoso Irigoyen-Rascón, eds. "Jikuri, the Tarahumara Peyote Cult: An Interpretation." In *The Mosaic of Contemporary Psychiatry in Perspective*, edited by Anthony Kales and Chester M. Pierce, 121–29. New York: Springer, 1992.

Pastor, Marialba. *Cuerpos sociales, cuerpos sacrificiales.* México, D.F.: Universidad Autónoma de México, 2004.

Pérez Munguía, Juana Patricia. "Derecho indiano para esclavos, negros y castas. Integración, control y estructura estamental." *Memoria y Sociedad* 7, no. 15 (2003): 193–205.

Piñera Ramírez, David, and Catalina Velázquez Morales. "Consideraciones generales." In *Visión histórica de la frontera norte de México Tomo II*, edited by David Piñera Ramírez, 255–63. Baja California: Universidad Autónoma de Baja California-Instituto de Investigaciones Históricas: Editorial Kino/El Mexicano, 1994.

Plumb, J. H. *The Death of the Past*. Boston: Houghton Mifflin Company, 1971.

Prieto Quimper, Salvador. *El Parral de mis recuerdos: datos para la biografía de una noble ciudad de provincia*. México, D.F.: Editorial Jus, 1948.

Proctor, Frank T., III. "African Diasporic Ethnicity in Mexico City to 1650." In *Africans to Spanish America: Expanding the Diaspora*, edited by Sherwin K. Bryan, Rachel Sara O'Toole, and Ben Vinson III, 50–72. Urbana: University of Illinois Press: 2012.

———. *Damned Notions of Liberty: Slavery, Culture, and Power in Colonial Mexico, 1640–1749*. Albuquerque: University of New Mexico Press, 2010.

Rangel, Nicolás. *Historia de toreo en México: época colonial 1529–1821*. Ciudad de México: Imprenta Manuel León Sánchez, 1924.

Rappaport, R. A. *Ritual and Religion in Making a Humanity*. Cambridge: Cambridge University Press, 1999.

Redman, Paul, Cynthia Radding, and Chad Bryant, eds. *Borderlands in World History, 1700–1914*. London: Palgrave Macmillan, 2014.

Restall, Matthew. "Black Conquistadors: Armed Africans in Early Spanish America." *The Americas* 57, no. 2 (2000): 171–205. http://www.jstor.org/stable/1008202.

Richardson, J. "What If? Alternative Histories and Their Future Implications." *Foresight* 9, no. 2: 36–45.

Richter, Daniel K. *Facing East from Indian Country: A Native History of Early America*. Cambridge, MA: Harvard University Press, 2001.

Riley, Carroll L., and Howard D. Winters. "The Prehistoric Tepehuan of Northern Mexico." *Southwestern Journal of Anthropology* 19, no. 2 (1963): 177–85.

Rivera García, Antonio. "Espíritu y poder en el barroco español." In *Barroco*, edited by Pedro Aullón de Haro, 567–96. Madrid: Verbum

Editorial, 2004.

Rojas, Rosa Elena. "Esclavos de Obraje: Consuelo en la Devoción. La cofradía de la Santa Veracruz Nueva fundada por Mulatos, Mestizos y Negros. Coyoacán, siglo XVII." *Nuevo Mundo/ Mundos Nuevos: Debates 2012.* Coord. Rafael Castañeda García, November 18, 2012. https://nuevomundo.revues.org/64339?lang=en.

Ruano de la Haza, José María. "The World as a Stage: Politics, Imperialism and Spain's Seventeenth Century Theatre." In *A History of Theatre in Spain*, edited by María M. Delgado and David T. Gies, 57–78. Cambridge: Cambridge University Press, 2012.

Rubial García, Antonio. *El paraíso de los elegidos: una lectura de la historia cultural de Nueva España (1521–1804).* México, D.F.: Fondo de Cultura Económica, Universidad Nacional Autónoma de México, Facultad de Filosofía y Letras, 2010.

Ruíz, Teófilo. *A King Travels: Festive Traditions in Late Medieval and Early Modern Spain.* Princeton, NJ: Princeton University Press, 2012.

————. *Spanish Society, 1400–1600.* New York: Pearson, 2001.

Sánchez, José. *Hispanic Heroes of Discovery and Conquest of Spanish America in European Drama.* Barcelona: Editorial Castalia, 1978.

Sánchez de Olmo, Sara. "Imagen mariana y construcción de la identidad socio-religiosa en el Michoacán colonial." *Dimensión Antropológica* 55 (2012): 71–92. http://www.dimensionantropolog-ica.inah.gob.mx/?p=8129.

Seed, Patricia. "Colonial and Postcolonial Discourse." *Latin American Research Review* 26, no. 3. (1991): 181–200.

Silva Prada, Natalia. *La política de una rebelión: los indígenas frente al Tumulto de 1692 en la Ciudad de México.* México, D.F.: Colegio de México, 2007.

Soto Posada, Gonzalo. *Filosofía Medieval.* Bogotá: Editorial San Pablo, 2007.

Staley, David J. *Historical Imagination.* New York: Routledge, 2020.

Sutcliffe, Adam, Anna Maerker, and Simon Sleight. "Introduction: Memory, Public Life and the Work of the Historian." In *History, Memory and Public Life: The Past in the Present*, edited by Adam Sutcliffe, Anna Maerker, and Simon Sleight, 1–25. New York: Routledge, 2018.

Sweda, Krystle Farman. "'Of All Type of *Calidad* or Color': Black

Confraternities in a Multiethnic Mexican Parish, 1640–1750." In *Indigenous and Black Confraternities in Colonial Latin America: Negotiating Status Through Religious Practices*, edited by Javiera Jaque Hidalgo and Miguel Valerio, 91–116. Bronx: Amsterdam University Press, 2022. ProQuest Ebook Central.

Sweet, James H. *Recreating Africa: Culture, Kinship, and Religion in the African-Portuguese World, 1441–1770*. Chapel Hill: University of North Carolina Press, 2003.

Taylor, William. *Drinking, Homicide and Rebellion in Colonial Mexican Villages*. Stanford: Stanford University Press, 1979.

Terrazas Williams, Danielle. "Capitalizing Subjects: Free African-Descended Women of Means in Xalapa, Veracruz during the Long Seventeenth Century." PhD diss., Duke University, 2013.

Terry, Philip. *Terry's Guide to Mexico*. Boston: Houghton Mifflin Co., 1935.

Thornton, John K. *Africa and Africans in the Making of the Atlantic World, 1400–1800*. Cambridge: Cambridge University Press, 1998.

———. "Central Africa in the Era of the Slave Trade." In *Slaves, Subjects, and Subversives: Blacks in Colonial Latin America*, edited by Jane G. Landers and Barry M. Robinson, 83–110. Albuquerque: University of New Mexico Press, 2006.

Townsend, Camila. *Malintzin's Choices: An Indian Woman in the Conquest of Mexico*. Albuquerque: University of New Mexico Press, 2006.

Turner, V. *The Ritual Process: Structure and Antistructure*. Chicago: Aldine, 1969.

Valerio, Miguel A. "Cultura afrobarroca mexicana: soberanía negra en las calles de la Ciudad de México, 1610." *Latin American Research Review* (2023): 1–18. doi:10.1017/lar.2023.13.

Villanueva Mayer, Vincent. "The Black Slave on New Spain's Northern Frontier: San Jose de Parral 1632–1676." PhD diss., University of Utah, 1975.

Villegas, Juan. *Historia multicultural del teatro y las teatralidades en América Latina*. Buenos Aires: Galerna, 2005.

Viqueira Albán, Juan Pedro. ¿Relajados o Reprimidos?:Diversiones públicas y vida social en la Ciudad de México durante el Siglo de las Luces. México, D.F: Fondo de Cultura Económica, 1987.

Voekel, Pamela. *Alone Before God: The Religious Origins of Modernity in*

Mexico. Durham, NC: Duke University Press, 2002.

Voigt, Lisa. *Spectacular Wealth: The Festivals of Colonial South American Mining Towns*. Austin: University of Texas Press, 2016. ProQuest Ebook Central.

Von Mentz, Brígida. "Esclavitud y semiesclavitud en el México antiguo y en la Nueva España (con énfasis en el siglo XVI)." *Studia Historica: Historia Antigua* [en línea] 25 (2009): 543–58. http://revistas.usal. es/index.php/0213-2052/article/view/1203.

Von Wobeser, Gisela. *El crédito eclesiástico en la Nueva España, Siglo XVIII*. México, D.F.: Universidad Autónoma de México, 1994.

———. "El uso del censo consignativo para realizar transacciones crediticias en la Nueva España. Siglos XVI al XVIII." In *Memoria del IV congreso de historia del derecho en México*, edited by Beatriz Bernal, 1163–81. México, D.F.: Instituto de Investigaciones Jurídicas, Universidad Autónoma de México, 1988.

———. *Vida eterna y preocupaciones terrenales: las capellanías de misas en la Nueva España, 1600–1821*. México, D.F.: Universidad Autónoma de México, 2005.

Yannakakis, Yanna. *The Art of Being In-between: Native Intermediaries, Indian Identity, and Local Rule in Colonial Oaxaca*. Durham, NC: Duke University Press, 2008.

Walch, T., and M. Harding. "American Mysteries, Riddles, and Controversies!" *Prologue* 39, no. 2 (Summer 2007): 6–10.

Weber, David J. *La frontera española en América del norte*. México, D.F.: Fondo de Cultura Económica, 2000.

West, Robert C. *La comunidad minera en el norte de la Nueva España: El distrito minero de Parral*. Translated by Ricardo Cabrera Figueroa. Chihuahua: Talleres Gráficos del Gobierno del Estado, 2002.

Wolfskill, George, and Stanley Palmer, eds. *Essays on Frontiers in World History*. College Station: Texas A&M University Press, 1983.

INDEX

ABOUT THE AUTHOR

Juana Moriel-Payne is a historian of Colonial Latin America and a novelist. Among her titles are *Trigueña*, historical novel winner of the BRLA-Southwest Book Award. She teaches Afro/Latinx and Latin American Studies, memoir, and novella at Mount Saint Mary's University–Los Angeles. Other pursuits include cultural and intellectual history and cultural theory.

AUTHOR PHOTO BY AMANDA ORTIZ

www.ingramcontent.com/pod-product-compliance
Lightning Source LLC
Chambersburg PA
CBHW020444100426

42812CB00036B/3449/J